# THE
# RIVER SEA

# THE RIVER SEA

## THE AMAZON
### in history, myth, and legend

A Story of Discovery, Exploration, and Exploitation

## Marshall De Bruhl

COUNTERPOINT

BERKELEY

*Library of Congress Cataloging-in-Publication Data*
De Bruhl, Marshall.
The river sea : the Amazon in history, myth, and legend /
by Marshall De Bruhl.
p. cm.
ISBN-13: 978-1-58243-490-2
ISBN-10: 1-58243-490-5
1. Amazon River—History. 2. Amazon River—Discovery and
exploration—European. 3. Amazon River—Legends. 4. Amazon
River Region—History. 5. Amazon River Region—Discovery and
exploration—European. 6. Amazon River Region—Description and
travel. 7. Amazon River Region—Biography. 8. Explorers—Amazon
River Region—Biography. 9. Travelers—Amazon River Region—
Biography. 10. Scientists—Amazon River Region—Biography.
I. Title.
F2546.D39 2010
981'.1—dc22       2010017802

Interior design by David Bullen
Cover design by Gopa and Ted2, Inc.

Printed in the United States of America

COUNTERPOINT
1919 Fifth Street
Berkeley, CA 94710

www.counterpointpress.com

Distributed by Publishers Group West

10  9  8  7  6  5  4  3  2  1

*For my eldest brother, Everett Hines De Bruhl*

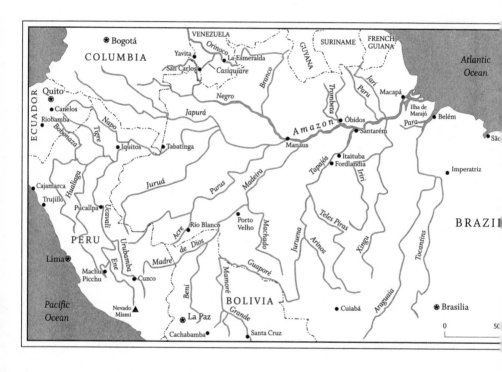

# CONTENTS

# THE
# RIVER SEA

ALTHOUGH THE GREAT AGE of exploration and discovery did not begin in earnest until the end of the Middle Ages, when Europe began seriously to look outward—first to the east, to Asia, and then to the west, to the New World—for hundreds of years Europeans had traveled to the Orient, Africa, and even across the Atlantic to Greenland and what is now Nova Scotia.

The riches of the East—silks, spices, gold, and precious stones—had beguiled the leaders of Europe for centuries, but the Ottoman Empire lay athwart the trade routes, where Muslim officials and middlemen exacted onerous taxes and tributes from the Christian traders.

What if a sea route to the East could be found that would open up direct trade, bypassing the Muslim extortionists? Could not this also have the effect of Christianizing the East and thus bring in allies against the Islamic world?

The most famous of those who dreamed of such a route was Christopher Columbus, who as early as 1484 was advocating his belief that by sailing west he could reach the East.

Rebuffed by the king of Portugal, Columbus went to the rulers of Spain, who were amenable, and in 1492 he realized his dream, although it was not Japan he found but a New World.

Eight years later, one of Columbus's captains returned to this New World and made his own momentous discovery, one that has never ceased to engage the imagination—the Amazon River.

Throughout the five centuries since its discovery, explorers, visionaries, soldiers of fortune, men of God, slavers and the enslaved, scientists, men of good will and men of ill will, and men of appalling cruelty and rapacity have been drawn to the river and its vast basin.

Whether searching for El Dorado, the fabled land of gold and riches, seeking to spread God's word, hoping to exploit or develop the region's natural resources, or traveling out of wanderlust or idle curiosity, many thousands of the brave, the adventurous, and not a few of the foolhardy have come to the Amazon.

Some of them emerged from their journeys along the great river and its thousands of miles of tributaries with amazing, even inspiring, tales. Others set off into the rain forest never to be seen again.

Whether they were charlatans, mountebanks, saints or sinners, good men doing evil things, or evil men doing good things, the Amazon drew them in, and they have become part of the rich history of one of the world's most intriguing and fabled places. Many of their stories are exemplars of triumph over adversity, but just as many also reflect unfulfilled promise and broken dreams.

The broad time frame, the diverse characters, and the many themes present a daunting task to any writer attempting to tell the story. But the narrative is united by the great river, the mightiest in the world.

As outsized as some of the players are in the vast cast of characters that play out their parts in the drama, they are all dwarfed by one of the most exotic and remarkable backdrops in the world, the Amazon Rain Forest and the high Andes, where the river is born and begins its journey to the sea.

# The River Sea

## From the Andes to the Atlantic

THE GREAT RIVER THAT ENDS IN A 250-MILE-WIDE ESTUARY AT THE Atlantic Ocean begins life modestly as a trickle of glacial melt water high in the Peruvian Andes, a continent away and less than a hundred miles from the Pacific Ocean.

During an almost four-thousand-mile journey to the sea, countless small streams, rivulets, and not a few very large rivers—four tributaries are more than a thousand miles in length—add their waters to form a mighty stream, which at some points is as wide as fifty miles.

Ocean-going ships can reach as far as Iquitos, Peru, twenty-three hundred miles upriver from the Atlantic, and smaller vessels even farther, plying the Ucayali and Marañón, the two rivers that come together near Iquitos to form the Amazon proper.

That the source of the Amazon River was in the high Andes had been postulated as early as 1641 by the Jesuit missionary and explorer Cristóbal de Acuña. But which of the river's hundreds of contributing tributaries in the Andes began farthest from the delta and thus could be considered the source of the river?

Through the years many possibilities were put forward, but not until 1971 was a serious scientific survey undertaken. In that year, the National Geographic Society dispatched a team led by Loren McIntyre to the Apurímac region in Peru.

Here, on the eastern slope of the continental divide of South America, McIntyre would find the birthplace of the Amazon. All the moisture from this side of the continental divide eventually finds its way to the Atlantic, from which 90 percent of it originates. The Andean cordillera blocks almost all moisture-laden air from the Pacific, just a few miles away.

McIntyre's party concentrated on the Quebrada Carhuasanta, a small brook that cartographers deemed the longest of the streams that eventually join to form the headwaters of the Amazon. After traveling for days, mostly on foot, they reached the base of a cliff on the Nevado Mismi, from which flowed water that fed into a small lake some thousand feet below.

This lake, which McIntyre said was little more than a pond—it is just a hundred feet across—he designated the true source of the river since he reckoned that there would always be some water in it, unlike the stream that fed it from the mountain above, which could, depending on the season, be dry.

The issue of the birthplace of the Amazon would not be definitively settled until almost thirty years after the McIntyre expedition. And the explanation that accompanied the placing of this final piece in the puzzle was simplicity itself, at least as presented by Andrew Pietowski, the man who led another National Geographic team that returned to the spot at the foot of that cliff on the Nevado Mismi in 2000 to decisively identify the source of the Amazon.

Pietowski, who became obsessed by the Amazon after emigrating from Poland to Peru in 1979, is another in that long line of adventurous, often laconic men and women who for millennia have dared to venture outward. They have always just wanted to see what lies out there, and with few exceptions, Pietowski being one of them, they have left the prose and the poetry to others.

"You have to have it in your genes," Pietowski says of exploration. "You have to want to know what is beyond the horizon line." As for the Amazon, he said forthrightly, "if there is a mouth of the river, there must be a beginning. I wanted to know where it was."[1]

The five-nation National Geographic expedition that Pietowski led in 2000 was the culmination of several years of explorations in which all of the candidates for the exact source of the river were explored—the uppermost reaches of the Apurímac, the Huallaga, the Mantaro, the Marañón, and the Urubamba-Vilcanota.

Using satellite imagery and global positioning instruments that were accurate within a range of three to six feet, the Pietowski party finally settled the issue of the exact birthplace of the river—just where, in 1971, Loren McIntyre said it was. Appropriately, the small pond or lake from which the Amazon originates is now called Laguna McIntyre.

But satellite imagery and global positioning did not definitively settle the other contentious and vexing question. Is the Amazon or the Nile the longest river in the world? The honor of being the world's longest had always belonged, marginally, to the latter, which was generally accepted as being some 150 miles longer than the Amazon.

Proponents of the Amazon's having pride of place have seen their position bolstered, though not confirmed, by the same advances in technology that settled the issue of the Amazon's birthplace—satellite imagery and global positioning devices. National pride and chauvinism sometimes trump scientific facts, so the argument as to which river is the longer still engages the attention of the partisans of each of the mighty streams. But the Amazon camp would seem to hold the higher cards.

Perhaps the view of the compilers of *The Smithsonian Atlas of the Amazon* is the reasonable one to adopt. Since river lengths constantly change because of their meandering nature, especially the tributaries, "it is absurd to state an exact length." Further, according to the *Atlas*, the Pietowski expedition erred seriously by adding their measurements to the distances measured years before, instead of remeasuring everything from the Nevado Mismi to the Atlantic.[2]

While the controversy about length will probably never be settled and agreed to by all parties—nationalism is sometimes too strong an emotion, even among geographers—there is unanimous agreement that the Amazon easily takes the honors as regards the other yardsticks and parameters that are generally applied to the measurements of rivers—namely the amount of flow and the drainage area.

The stream that begins as a trickle of water on an Andean peak in Peru ends in an estuary on the coast of Brazil so broad that it contains an island the size of Switzerland, the Ilha de Marajó. Here, the Amazon discharges some 4.2 million cubic feet of water per second into the Atlantic Ocean.

In order to lend some perspective to the vast flow, which is almost beyond the scope or comprehension of the layman, the compilers of *The Smithsonian Atlas of the Amazon* relate it to the yearly water usage of the citizens of New York City. In just two hours the Amazon discharges into the Atlantic Ocean enough water to supply all the needs of New Yorkers for one year.

During the rainy season the flow increases by more than two-thirds, to seven million cubic feet per second. Estimates of the amount of water released here on the coast of Brazil range from a low of 15 percent to a high of 20 percent of all the fresh water entering the world's oceans.

By way of comparison, the Mississippi River discharges, on average, 640,000 cubic feet of water per second into the Gulf of Mexico and the Nile just 124,000 into the Mediterranean Sea.

As for drainage area, the Amazon Basin dwarfs any other river system in the world. Comprising 2.7 million square miles—more than a third of South America—it is equal in size to two-thirds of Europe and three-quarters of the United States.

The basin drains 40 percent of Brazil, 50 percent of Bolivia and Colombia, 66 percent of Peru, 75 percent of Ecuador, and significant percentages of southern Venezuela and Guyana. A natural canal, the Casiquiare, connects the Orinoco River Basin in Venezuela, the third-largest drainage system in the world, with the Amazon Basin.

The Amazon and its many tributaries and branches also afford more than ten thousand miles of navigable waterways into the interior of South America. It has been remarked that set next to the Amazon, "the rivers of Europe are so many guttered trickles of rain water." [3]

This statement is not without justification. The Rhine's widest point is just thirteen hundred feet. The Danube, equally celebrated in song and legend, is an even smaller stream, although in its lower reaches, it may be as wide as twenty-four hundred feet. And what of Old Man River himself, the mighty Mississippi? It might "just keep rollin' along," but not very grandly. At its widest point, just below its confluence with the Missouri, the Father of Waters is just a mile wide.

By contrast, in many places along the Amazon, especially during the wet season, the horizon is not discernible. Even in the dry season in many places the Amazon is an impressive six or seven miles across.

The sheer size of the river, which cannot easily be captured even in aerial photographs, is its most striking characteristic to the first-time visitor, and this impression is not diminished by repeated visits. Setting foot ashore along the river, one recalls the great German scientist Alexander von Humboldt, who wrote that "the uninhabited banks . . . covered in jungle, busied my imagination. . . . The earth is overloaded with vegetation: nothing prevents its development. An immense layer of mould manifests the uninterrupted action of organic forces." [4]

Alas, the river's immense size, vast flow, and seeming ability to rejuvenate itself perversely contribute to the problems facing the entire region. The environmentally obtuse see the Amazon Basin as just too large and fecund to be permanently or seriously damaged ecologically or environmentally.

A JOURNEY DOWN THE AMAZON is best begun by starting where it is born, about 1,000 feet below the summit of 18,465-foot Nevado Mismi, an extinct volcano on the South American continental divide. The water from the eastern side of the divide flows into the Atlantic, thousands of miles away. The water on the westward side flows to the Pacific Ocean, less than a hundred miles away. One of these westward-flowing streams is the Colca River, which has helped carve out one of the deepest canyons in the world.

The little stream that flows from a black cliff, about 130 feet high, on the eastern face of Nevado Mismi and will eventually end up in the Atlantic Ocean first makes its leisurely way across the grasses and mosses of an alpine valley, down to the lake described by Loren McIntyre.

As Pietowski said, "It's a pretty spot, especially in the afternoon when the sun is lighting the snow higher up on the mountain. . . . On top you see the shape of the mountains covered with snow, contrasting with the dark blue sky at this altitude. It is very silent and serene. I felt great standing there, this incredible beauty permeating me. I was part of the landscape, the ice, the rocks, everything." [5]

From the tiny lake, Laguna McIntyre, the Quebrada Carhuasanta flows through a narrow defile and joins with the Quebrada Apacheta to form the Río Loqueta. Eventually the waters from Nevado Mismi join with various other streams near Cailloma to form the Río Apurímac.

The Apurímac, which is known by various names, depending on the region it passes through—the Ene and then the Tambo—flows more or less parallel with the Urubamba, which is as redolent with history and legend as the Amazon itself.

The Upper Urubamba, known for part of its length as the Vilcanota, flows through a sixty-mile-long valley known as the Sacred Valley of the Incas. Cuzco, the capital and spiritual center of the vast Inca Empire, lies just a few miles west of the southern end of the Sacred Valley. At the northern end is one of the most famous archaeological sites in the world, the mountain retreat of the Inca, the legendary Machu Picchu.

In the Sacred Valley, the Urubamba River flows placidly through a landscape of farms and orchards, much of the agriculture still dependent on the hundreds of miles of terraces built on the steep hillsides by the Inca and their predecessors.

Below the town of Urubamba itself, the calm waters begin to give way to rapids. In a twenty-mile stretch, the river falls over three thousand feet, and at Aguas Calientes, the gateway town to Machu Picchu, the flow becomes even more swift, almost violent, as the water pours over giant boulders dislodged from the almost vertical cliffs above the river.

Many of the rapids on this stretch of the Urubamba are classified as 5+ on a scale of 6, and here many kayakers have come to grief, a portent of what lies in store farther downstream in the rapids of the Pongo de Mainique, a forty-five-meter rift through the wall of the Vilcabamba mountain range.

The Pongo, which is the demarcation between the Upper and Lower Urubamba, is not only famous for its dangerous and challenging white-water rapids, but also noted for being perhaps the most biologically diverse place on earth for its size, only six square miles. It is also a place of great beauty.

Michael Palin, former Monty Python member turned travel documentarian, has called it his "favorite place in the world." In the ninth episode of his documentary *Full Circle*, Palin says, "Nothing I have read or fantasized about has prepared me for this place. It looks as though high explosive, rather than a river, has split through this last mile of the Andes. The walls are sharply fractured, with rocky overhangs, sheared off like the stumps of shattered bridges. Lianas hang down to the water, some tipped with orange-red flowers like upturned candelabra. Water, pouring constantly down smooth, black, mossy flanks, has worn the rock into weird and wonderful shapes—symmetrical fluted surfaces, perfectly smoothed bowls, caves, and chambers." [6]

Little wonder that Palin would be so amazed at the canyon and the more than thirty waterfalls that pour down from the cliffs that reach heights of three thousand feet. However, rafters and kayakers have little time to register the wonder of the scene as the current swiftly bears them through the two-mile stretch of white water.

As every traveler has done before him, Palin marveled at the suddenness of the transition from the Andes to the flatness and calmness of the Lower Urubamba, which after traversing the narrow defile through the mountains at the Pongo de Mainique resumes a more leisurely flow across the countryside until it converges with the Apurímac to form the Ucayali, one of the two great streams that will form the Amazon proper. That junction is still a thousand miles away.

The Pongo de Mainique is not just the border between the Lower and Upper Urubamba; it was also the furthest extent of the Inca civilization. Beyond lay the vast rain forest of the Amazon and tribes of indigenous peoples who lived much as they had done for millennia, untouched by the high civilization of their cousins beyond the mountains.

The elevation of the waters of the hundreds of tributaries that coalesce to form the Amazon decrease with great rapidity as they flow down from the Andes and then level out. From Sepahua, the largest town on the Lower Urubamba, elevation 906 feet, to Iquitos, a distance of a thousand miles, there will be only a drop in elevation of an unremarkable 600 feet.

At the proper beginning of the Amazon, at the juncture of the Marañón and the Ucayali rivers, the elevation of the river is about the same as Iquitos, fifty miles farther downstream, which is just 350 feet above sea level.

The river will continue to drop, but only imperceptibly, in the more than two thousand miles that it traverses from Iquitos to the sea. Thus the Amazon is slow-moving, even sluggish, as it wends its way across South America. From the earliest days of exploration, small sailing vessels, often propelled by oarsmen when the winds were light, were able to travel great distances upriver by tacking repeatedly. And for millennia, fishermen in small boats and dugout canoes have easily moved about on the Amazon.

The other important tributary of the Ucayali, the Apurímac, follows a similarly convoluted course from the Andes highlands until it joins with the Urubamba.

While the Apurímac does not flow through an area even approximating the mystique of Cuzco, the Sacred Valley, or Machu Picchu, the river and its valley are not without interest. The slopes overlooking the valley exhibit the agricultural terracing practiced by the Inca and their predecessors for several millennia, but it is the ruins high above the Apurímac at Espíritu Pampa, elevation 11,483 feet, that have fascinated archaeologists, both amateur and professional, since they were rediscovered by the redoubtable Hiram Bingham in 1911.

Espíritu Pampa is now recognized as Vilcabamba, which was built in the 1530s as a new capital and served as the last refuge for the Inca and his followers in the dying days of the Empire. Bingham, however, gave short shrift to the ruins, dismissing them as the possible site of the legendary Vilcabamba. How could such modest buildings—there were no remains of grand palaces or temples—have served as the center of the empire? he reasoned. Machu Picchu, on the other hand, fit the bill admirably, and it was there that Bingham's often overactive imagination filled in the blanks.

During the two-hundred-mile stretch above Atalaya, where the Apurímac joins the Urubamba, the river undergoes two name changes. It becomes Río Ene after its confluence with the Mantaro, and then, after pouring through the Pongo de Paquiochango and the juncture with the Perené, it is the Río Tambo. It is under the latter designation that it mixes its waters with the Urubamba to form the Ucayali.

In any other context or any other continent, the 1,000-mile Río Ucayali, 675 miles of it navigable by sizable vessels, would be celebrated. It is larger and longer than the Rhine, the Seine, the Elbe, and every other major river of Europe except the Danube. The Ucayali's chief distinction, however, is that it is one of the two rivers that join to form the Amazon River proper.

The other major tributary is the Marañón, also about a thousand miles in length, which arises farther north in the Andes cordillera, only about a hundred miles from Lima. It then flows parallel to the Ucayali for hundreds of miles before they join together fifty miles southwest of Iquitos.

The Marañón is marked by treacherous currents and dozens of rapids and cataracts and is navigable only by shallow draft vessels for about five hundred miles. It thus never became an important trade route, although it looms large in the history of the Amazon Basin. Everyone journeying across the Andes from the coastal regions around Lima in order to descend the Amazon has been obliged to negotiate at least parts of the Marañón.

However, it is a vast tract of undisturbed and pristine land lying in the triangle formed by the junction of the Marañón and the Ucayali that is of major interest to tourists, ecologists, and preservationists. The more than five million acres of pristine wetlands, streams, lakes, and jungle—1.5 percent of the land area of Peru—was set aside in 1982 as the Pacaya-Samiria National Reserve.

The vast reserve is home to pink and gray river dolphins; caimans; howler, woolly, and spider monkeys; tree sloths; peccaries, tapirs, and jaguars; dozens of reptiles; rare fish, hundreds of species of birds, and countless botanical species.

Access to Pacaya-Samiria is limited by nature, by design, and by its isolation. Also since 85 percent of the reserve is flooded for much of the year, even during the dry season, the only way to visit the reserve is by boat.

A hundred or so miles below Iquitos, the Amazon skirts the geographical anomaly of the Tres Fronteras, where Brazil, Peru, and Colombia share a very short border that was often disputed until the issue was settled by the League of Nations in 1934 after a brief war.

Colombia was guaranteed a narrow link with the Amazon River. This sixty-mile Latin version of the Polish Corridor has two ports. The larger of these is Leticia, a city of thirty-five thousand, which enjoyed a brief period of notoriety as a center of the international drug trade in the 1970s. After the government moved in and drove out the cartel, the city reverted to its accustomed somnolence.

The other Colombian town on the Amazon, Puerto Nariño, which was founded only in 1961, has been trumpeted as an ecologically correct community and has drawn much praise for its policy of forbidding all motorized transport. The little town is a pedestrian-friendly haven for its six thousand residents.

From the Tres Fronteras to its confluence with the Río Negro, the second largest in terms of discharge into the main river but the most famous of its tributaries, the Amazon is known to Brazilians as the Solimões. But even the Brazilians finally relent. After the famous "Meeting of the Waters" a few miles from Manaus, where the beige waters of the Solimões run side by side and eventually mix with the dark waters of the Río Negro, the great river is known only as the Amazon.

The Negro, which in terms of discharge is the sixth-largest river in the world, has never been subjected to great influxes of settlers due to the vast floodplain and the sandy soil. However, enormous deforestation has taken place because, as elsewhere in Brazil, cattle ranching and agriculture have increasingly taken hold, bringing with them the environmental problems besetting the rest of the region.

However, another economic activity in the Río Negro Basin has also become of concern to environmentalists: the aquarium trade. A great percentage of the tropical fish that find their way to aquariums around the world are captured on the Río Negro and shipped out of Manaus. In the case of one species, the cardinal tetra, which grows only in the Río Negro, the figure is 100 percent.

The Río Negro is unique for something other than its famous dark color. Some of its waters originate in one of the world's great geological anomalies, the Casiquiare Canal, the natural connector between the Orinoco and the Amazon basins. Water that should flow north into the Orinoco is diverted by the canal, which is actually a river, southwest to the upper Río Negro and thence into the Amazon just below Manaus.

Manaus, a river port of 1.7 million people, more than nine hundred miles from the sea, is the largest and arguably the best known of the cities of the Amazon, although it lies not on the Amazon but on the Río Negro. The city's economic importance is obvious from the population statistics. Nearly 11 percent of all the people in Northern Brazil and almost 20 percent of the population of the Amazon region live in Manaus, many of them migrants from the villages of the rain forest, a diaspora that portends enormous social and economic problems. The metropolitan areas of

Manaus, Belém, and the other cities that lie along the river and its tributaries comprise more than 90 percent of the population of the Amazon Basin, which is estimated to be ten million.

The figures also point up the relatively sparse population in the huge Amazon Basin. The cities in the booming south of Brazil dwarf any city in the Amazon. São Paulo, with a population of over eleven million, is not only the largest city in Brazil, it is also the largest city in the Western Hemisphere. São Paulo State, of which it is the capital, has a population of over forty-two million.

Even in the upper reaches of the Amazon, nothing prepares the visitor, whether for the first, second, even the tenth time, for the immensity of the river, the sheer expanse of water. At the confluence of the Ucayali and the Marañón, the true beginning of the Amazon, it resembles a vast lake more than a river.

And after the influx of the waters of the Río Negro, the Tapajós, the Madeira, and numerous other tributaries large and small, particularly during the peak high-water months of April and May, when the river rises as much as fifty feet and spreads out fifty, seventy-five, even a hundred miles, the Amazon is scarcely a river as they are known in the rest of the world. The sobriquet *the river sea* is entirely appropriate.

The largest river in terms of discharge into the Amazon is the Madeira, which enters the main river not too many miles below Manaus, about 560 miles from the Atlantic. The Madeira is not only the largest tributary of the Amazon, it is also the fifth-largest river in the world. Thus the Amazon Basin has three out of the six largest rivers systems on earth—the Amazon, which is first, the Madeira, which is fifth, and the Río Negro, which is sixth.

With the addition of the waters of the Madeira, the Amazon now has some 80 percent of its annual average discharge, but other streams, such as the Xingua, continue to swell the river until it reaches the Ilha de Marajó, which lies in its mouth.

This island, which comprises an area of 15,444 square miles—roughly the size of Switzerland—is the largest island in the world surrounded by fresh water—a geographical phenomenon made possible by the tremendous outflow of the Amazon, which keeps the salt water of the ocean to the east at bay.

The western end of the island has extensive forests and marshes, which are home to large herds of water buffalo, estimated to number in the hundreds of thousands and predictably a threat to the natural environment.

The eastern part of Marajó is more open, with vast grasslands that have become another center of Brazil's ever-burgeoning cattle industry.

The eastern side of Marajó Island has also drawn the attention of archaeologists, who have discovered pottery and other artifacts in the numerous mounds in the area that purportedly show links between the Marajoara culture that developed on the island with the generally more highly regarded, and certainly more intensively studied, pre-Columbian civilizations a continent away in the Andes.

Marajó acts as a natural dam or dike, diverting almost 99 percent of the Amazon's water northward into a maze of channels that weave through an archipelago of dozens of islands before entering the Atlantic, squarely on the equator. One of these channels, the Canal do Norte, is a major outlet to the sea and serves the small port city of Macapá, the capital of Amapá State.

The remaining 1 percent of the Amazon's discharge, still a vast quantity of water by any measure, flows southward around Marajó, into a channel called the Río Pará, which itself is increased by the waters of the Río Tocantins, flowing in from the south.

On this southern arm is the historic city of Belém, which, since its founding in the seventeenth century, has been the major port of the Amazon region. Here, at a city of 1.4 million inhabitants, the Amazon enters the wide Baía de Marajó, an arm of the Atlantic Ocean.

THE AMAZON'S MIGHTY FLOW, draining the largest river basin in the world, sweeps all before it. Its waters spread out over thousands of square miles of the floodplain in the rainy season. The main river and its tributaries carve out new channels. Hundreds of millions of tons of silt are washed down annually from the highlands or from riverbanks as they crumble into the water, creating new islands and sandbars and adding to the vast alluvial plain.

When one leaves a footprint in the delta of the Amazon, one may be treading on dust brought from as far away as the high Andes—perhaps residue from the gold sandals of the Inca Atahualpa or the rough boots of his conqueror and murderer, the conquistador Francisco Pizarro.

The millions of tons of silt and dust that wash down the river replenish the vast alluvial floodplain and the fields and the small farming plots along its banks. Nutrients in the water help sustain the forests and marine life in the wetlands.

However, it is the billions of cubic feet of fresh water from the Andes and the tributaries of the rain forest that the river contributes to the world's oceans that is paramount. At its mouth the Amazon's outflow is so strong that the incoming tides are overwhelmed. The encroaching salt water is pushed back out to sea. Thus the river and its estuary remain ever fresh.

The Amazon's water may be the color of earth, but it is *agua dulce*, fresh water, until well over a hundred miles out to sea, as a Spanish sailor discovered in early February 1500 when he hoisted a bucket aboard a caravel that was part of a small Spanish fleet beating northward along the coast of present-day Brazil.

The sailors aboard the caravels had already noticed that the blue waters of the Atlantic Ocean had taken on a decidedly brownish cast, and when the curious crewman aboard the lead vessel brought up his bucketful of silt-laden water and tasted it, he discovered that it was not salt water, but fresh water. How could this be? the Spaniard wondered. There was no land in sight. Indeed the ship was clearly many miles out to sea.

When the commander of the fleet, Vicente Yáñez Pinzón, was apprised of this remarkable discovery, he ordered the flotilla to turn to port and lookouts posted to scan the western horizon for a landfall.

As the ships sailed westward, flotsam began to appear in the brown water, and shore birds circled overhead. All hands became alert, and soon the cry came from high in the rigging, "*Tierra!*" Sailing on, Pinzón soon found himself in what appeared to be a broad estuary, which he christened Santa Maria de la Mar Dulce—"St. Mary of the Freshwater Sea."

Proceeding some hundred miles further, the captain put ashore on one of the many islands that lie in the mouth of the great river and planted the flag of Spain—claiming the area for the Crown of Spain, for Ferdinand and Isabella, Los Reyes Católicos.

Pinzon and his men also encountered, in scattered villages along the shore of the river, native peoples who were as curious about these strange, bearded white men and their sailing vessels as the Spaniards were about them.

The natives also proved friendly, but their hospitality was repaid in the usual coin of the time. Pinzón seized thirty-six of them and carried them away as slaves.

This momentous discovery alone should have assured Vicente Yáñez Pinzón, a member of a rich and illustrious seafaring family from Palos, a secure place in the annals of discovery and exploration of the New World. He had already earned a certain measure of fame since he and two of his brothers were major figures on the historic 1492 voyage of Christopher Columbus.

The eldest Pinzón brother, Martín Alonzo, not only helped finance Columbus's expedition, he was part owner of two of the three vessels— the *Niña* and the *Pinta*. However, Martín Alonzo was not content to be simply a backer. He had sailed with Columbus as captain of the *Pinta*. A third brother, Francisco, served as first mate on the *Pinta*. Vicente himself commanded the *Niña*.

The relationship between Columbus and two of the Pinzón brothers was not a happy one, and when the flagship, the *Santa María*, was wrecked on a reef, forcing the admiral to transfer to the *Niña*, Martín Alonzo seized the opportunity to claim credit for the discovery of the new lands beyond the sea. He deserted Columbus off the Azores and sped toward Spain, hoping to bring the *Pinta* into port first.

Although he was blown off course, Martín Alonzo managed to arrive ahead of the admiral, but King Ferdinand refused to receive anyone but Columbus, who deservedly was recognized as the true hero of the expedition. An embittered Martín Alonzo Pinzón died soon after, a forgotten man, except in his native city. In Palos, the citizens still celebrate Pinzón Day, not Columbus Day.

Now, seven years later, Vicente Pinzón had returned to the New World, searching once again for a route to the East. On 7 February 1500, just a few days before his discovery of the river that would become known as the Amazon, Pinzón had made landfall near present-day Cape Santo Agostinho, which should have secured his place in history as the discoverer of Brazil. But, as we shall see, Portuguese nationalism would intervene and deprive him of the honor.

Spain was prevented from following up on Pinzón's discoveries by the Treaty of Tordesillas, which itself had grown out of an earlier attempt by Pope Alexander to settle the rival claims in the New World of two powerful Catholic nations that the Pope was ever anxious to placate—Spain and Portugal.

Soon after Columbus's first voyage, the Spanish-born Alexander issued a papal bull that clearly gave his homeland a head start in the quest for domination over the newly discovered regions across the Atlantic.

Alexander's bull decreed that all lands discovered west of a meridian one hundred leagues west of the Cape Verde Islands should belong to Spain while new lands discovered east of that line would belong to Portugal. This bull also specified that all lands already under the control of a "Christian prince" would remain under that same control. The Christian prince the pope had in mind was presumably Ferdinand of Spain.

Since a league was roughly 3 miles, or 4.8 kilometers, the Pope's decree set the line somewhere in the middle of the Atlantic Ocean, which effectively gave Spain all of the New World. Not surprisingly, the Portuguese king, John II, the nephew of Prince Henry the Navigator, was having none of it since even though no one knew the extent of the newly discovered lands, it was clear that Portugal was being given short shrift.

But a more important consideration was the Portuguese recognition that the papal bull would seriously limit their freedom of action in their continued exploration of the African coast and ultimately what they hoped would be their access to the Indies by sailing around that continent.

Bartholomew Diaz had rounded the tip of Africa in 1488, and thus it was known that such voyages necessitated sailing far to the west in order to take advantage of the winds that would take them around the Cape, which Diaz had named the Cape of Storms, and on to the Indies.

Although there is no evidence to support such a claim, some historians have championed the view that the Portuguese had set foot in the New World before Columbus and thus were well aware of the so-called Brazilian bulge of the South American continent. Conveniently there are no documents that might have supported such a claim since they are said to have been destroyed in the great Lisbon earthquake of 1755 or during the subsequent wars that raged across the Iberian Peninsula.

John II immediately began negotiations with Ferdinand and Isabella of Spain to move the line farther to the west, and ambassadors from both courts met at the small Spanish town of Tordesillas, one of the retreats of the Spanish royal family, to hammer out the details. The Portuguese ministers were clearly better negotiators than their Spanish counterparts, although both camps were basically in the dark geographically.

Under the terms of the Treaty of Tordesillas, which was signed on 7 June 1494, it was agreed that the line of demarcation would be moved from 100 leagues to 370 leagues west of the Cape Verde Islands.

John II died in 1495, but his successors were able to lay claim to the coastal areas of Brazil and eventually extend their claims farther into the interior. Thus Brazil today is a Portuguese-speaking country.

The Spanish were equally sure that the lands were theirs, and the Spanish king rewarded Pinzón with the governorship of the areas he had explored and claimed. But the Spaniards did not press the issue, and there the matter rested. The governorship was only titular, in any event. Pinzón was a seafarer, not an administrator.

Until his death, Pinzon's old commander, Columbus, held firm in his belief that he had found India, a view probably shared by Vicente Pinzón, who alone among his family remained loyal to the admiral throughout his life. Their friendship was no doubt cemented aboard Vicente's ship, the *Niña*, on which Columbus returned to Spain from the first voyage.

It is likely that Pinzón also believed that the silt-laden river he had entered was the Ganges itself and that the naked, or near-naked, gaily painted people dwelling along its shores were true Indians.

Pinzón made two more voyages to South America in a futile search for a route to the East, and another governorship was bestowed on him, this time of Puerto Rico. But once again he seems not to have taken up any administrative duties. Indeed, he disappears from history. Nothing is known of him after 1523.

As for Pinzón's rightful place as the discoverer of Brazil, that was denied him by a combination of the aforementioned Portuguese nationalism and historical amnesia. The Portuguese navigator Pedro Álvarez Cabral is celebrated in Brazil as the country's discoverer.

Cabral, even though he was only about thirty years old and had no maritime experience, was placed in command of a fleet of thirteen, some sources say fourteen, trading vessels that had been dispatched by the Portuguese crown to Calicut, on the Malabar coast of India, to initiate regular trade, particularly in spices.

The previous autumn, another Portuguese, Vasco da Gama, had proved that the route around Africa was feasible when he returned to Portugal in triumph from his epic voyage to India.

One of Cabral's subordinate captains was the more senior Bartholomew Diaz. The great navigator might have been expected to be in command of the entire fleet instead of a single ship, but Cabral had the confidence of the king himself, who came with the court to see him off. In addition Cabral had the support of Vasco da Gama, who supplied him with his sailing instructions.

The fleet sailed on 9 March 1500, and all went well until it was past the Cape Verde Islands off the coast of Africa, some two weeks later. Then, instead of the expected winds that would carry the fleet south and southeast to the Cape of Good Hope, and thence around Africa to the East Indies, contrary winds arose. Cabral found himself headed south, southwest across the Atlantic.

On 21 April, signs of land—birds and various flotsam—began to appear, and the next day, Easter Wednesday, a mountain that lies eighteen miles inland was sighted. The following day, Thursday, 23 April, the first Portuguese, led by Captain Nicolau Coelho, landed on the coast of Brazil, at the Río Cahy. Cabral claimed the area, which he was sure was an island—indeed, he christened it Ilha de Vera Cruz—for Portugal.

Cabral dispatched one of his ships back to Lisbon with the news of his discovery and then meandered along the Brazilian coast for another week. Finally, on 2 May, Cabral directed his fleet to recommence its original mission. He sailed south, southeast, where he eventually picked up the original course, which would take the fleet around the Cape of Good Hope and on to the East.

Left behind in South America were the first colonists in South America—if one can call them that. Two Portuguese convicts were abandoned on the coast of Brazil to fend for themselves. It was said that the two unfortunates' cries of supplication and lamentation could be heard for a great distance as the ships sailed away.

In the East, Cabral made contact with various rulers and potentates in attempts to establish trade, and feeble efforts were also made to fulfill another charge—the introduction of Christianity to those heathen lands. By no means, however, could Cabral be judged wholly successful in carrying out the original purpose of his mission.

Of the grand fleet that had sailed from the Tagus in March 1500, six of the ships had been lost at sea, including that of Bartholomew Diaz. Of the seven that limped home in June and July 1501, only five carried anything of value.

The voyage may have been a failure, but a larger, and more important, point had been made. Cabral had proved the viability of large trading fleets plying a sea route to the East. Europe was no longer dependent on long and dangerous overland caravans. And perhaps of more, or at least equal importance, Cabral's discovery of Brazil and claiming of it for Portugal ensured a vast new land for the mother country.

Portugal established its first permanent settlement in Brazil just three decades after Cabral's voyage, but nowhere near the Amazon. São Vicente, founded in 1532, lies more than fifteen hundred miles to the south, and further Portuguese efforts were concentrated well to the south of the Amazon until well into the next century.

At last, however, in 1616, Portugal established an outpost on the Amazon, Forte do Presépio, about sixty miles from the Atlantic, in order to monitor the activities of rival nations that were trading extensively around the mouth of the Amazon and as far as three hundred miles upstream.

The modest wooden-palisaded fort signaled the beginning of Portuguese hegemony in the Amazon Basin. Today it is the site of the metropolis of Belém, the most important port in the Amazon Basin and the gateway to the riches of the rain forest.

# CHAPTER 2

# The Incas

*The Rise and Fall of the Empire of the Sun*

WHEN THE FLEET OF VICENTE YÁÑEZ PINZÓN SAILED INTO THE vast offshore flow of the Amazon in 1500, they could not have imagined that much of the water through which they were sailing had originated a continent away, in a great empire that extended along the spine of the Andes from present-day Colombia to Chile.

Ruling over this land from his capital, Cuzco, high in the Andes, was a direct descendant of the sun itself—the Sapa Inca—attended by a vast court of nobles, attendants, minor officials, and a priestly caste. The city's importance in the empire is reflected in its very name, Cuzco, which derives from the Quechua word *Q'osqo*, meaning "navel of the world." Thus the Incas, the center of whose empire lay along the valleys of the tributaries and headwaters of the Amazon, are an integral part of any history of the river.

Cuzco, now a city of over 300,000, lies in the valley of a smaller stream, the Huatanay, which joins the Vilcanota-Urubamba southeast of the city in the Urubamba Valley. This "Sacred Valley of the Incas," which runs for about sixty miles, is defined by two legendary sites—one at either end—both of which had, and continue to have, great spiritual meaning to the Inca and their descendants and are of equally serious importance to historians and archaeologists.

One of these "bookends" is, of course, Cuzco. The other, at the northern end of the Sacred Valley, is the mythical Machu Picchu, the so-called lost city of the Incas, which, *pace* Hiram Bingham, was never lost, just overlooked. What is lost, however, is the exact role the city played in Incan society.

The most convincing argument is that Machu Picchu was a royal retreat—an Incan Camp David, as it were—built during the reign of Pachacutec Inca Yupanqui (d. 1471). In any event the city lasted less than a hundred years, perhaps because the inhabitants were wiped out by smallpox or one of the other epidemic diseases introduced by the Spanish that swept through the empire.

For more than four centuries Machu Picchu was visited only by local farmers who grazed their animals and raised their crops on the agricultural terraces. Indeed, it was the son of one of those farmers who guided Bingham to the site high up in the cloud forest.

The Sacred Valley also served a more secular purpose. It was the agricultural center of the Inca Empire, and it still provides the major portion of the agricultural products for the Cuzco region today. Farmers continue to work the rich bottomlands along the Urubamba and the miles of agricultural terraces that for at least a millennium have marked the steep slopes on either side of the valley.

Throughout the empire, there were temples to the sun adorned with all manner of ornaments fashioned from gold, silver, and precious stones, but none compared to the Qorikancha, the Temple of the Sun, in Cuzco, where four thousand priests and their attendants presided and where gold was employed in such lavish amounts as to rival the sun itself.

The walls were covered in sheets of gold, and there were life-sized gold statues and gold altars. The centerpiece was a gigantic gold sun disc so placed that it reflected the rays of the sun and illuminated the temple. A particularly sacred niche, which was reserved for the Inca, was flooded with the sun's rays at the summer solstice.

For the Inca—the name is applied to both the ruler and his people—gold and silver were sacred, but neither held any intrinsic value for them. It was said that gold was the sweat of the sun, silver the tears of the moon. As such the metals were used only for decoration of the temples, the palaces, and the person of the Inca. The Inca and his subjects therefore looked with bemusement, if not astonishment, on the lust for gold and silver displayed by the conquistadors.

The Andean rivers were limited in their usefulness to the Incas as a form of long-range communication and transportation because of the numerous cataracts and rapids as they poured out of the high mountains. Thus the Incas confined their conquest and dominion to the lands that abutted the Andean cordillera.

For example, they did not expand the empire any appreciable distance downstream from the Sacred Valley of the Urubamba because of the Pongo de Mainique, a series of white-water rapids and a deep gorge, at the end of which stand two gigantic blocks of granite—a natural gateway into the lower river and the beginning of the Amazon Rain Forest and the vast basin beyond.

Instead the Inca Empire relied on a vast system of paved roads, which connected Cuzco to every town and outpost in the empire. Runners, working in relay teams, could in just a few days carry a message the entire length of the empire. But just as the roads ensured quick communication with the capital, they also served to hasten the advance of the conquerors from Spain and the spread of disease.

Although the Inca have, perhaps rightly, figured most prominently in the chronicles of the so-called Conquest, they were by no means the first of the great civilizations in Peru. There were several robust and highly developed empires in Peru during the two thousand years preceding the

Inca, who can be said to have truly built on the shoulders of giants. This fact is made abundantly clear at the National Museum of Archaeology, Anthropology, and History in Lima, with its great collection of artifacts dating from as early as 2800 BC.

In addition to highly sophisticated ceramics, jewelry, and statuary, these earlier civilizations also created vast ceremonial centers dominated by pyramids and other stone structures, the ruins of which show that they rivaled those of the much later, and better known, Inca civilization.

According to one of the creation myths of the Inca, the first Inca, Manco Capac, and his sister-wife, Mama Ocllo, both of whom were children of the sun god Inti and his sister-wife, Mama Quilla, goddess of the moon, emerged from the waters of Lake Titicaca around 1200 AD.

They were given a golden staff, which, when they were able to plunge it into the ground with one blow, would show them where they were to found a city and build a temple to the sun. In a high valley in the Andes south of Lake Titicaca, the prophecy was fulfilled and they founded Cuzco.

Cuzco remained a relatively small enclave for two hundred years. The Inca Empire may be said to have truly begun only about 1438, when the ninth Inca, Pachacutec Inca Yupanqui, set out from Cuzco on a campaign of conquest and assimilation, the end result of which was the sprawling agglomeration known as the Inca Empire. So the great empire that has so beguiled the imagination of the world lasted barely a century. When the first conquistadors arrived in Peru, only the third generation, Huayna Capac, the grandson of the real founder of the empire, was on the throne.

Huayna Capac further extended the empire, in particular the subjugation of the whole of the state of Quito in the north, an area of which he became inordinately fond—so much so in fact that he elevated the city of Quito to a position in power and wealth to rival the traditional capital of Cuzco.

As the Inca Huayna Capac was en route back to Cuzco in 1528, smallpox struck and decimated his army, felling Ninan Cuyochi, Huayna Capac's legal son and heir. Soon after, and most alarming for the stability of the empire, the Inca himself was stricken.

Next in line to the throne was his son Huáscar, but on his deathbed, Huayna Capac ignored precedent and divided the kingdom between Huáscar and his favorite, the illegitimate Atahualpa, who according to Inca law and precedent was barred from the succession because his mother was not of Incan royalty. Huayna Capac gave the northern half of the kingdom, with its capital at Quito, to Atahualpa, and the southern half, centered on Cuzco, to Huáscar.

For five years the half brothers ruled their allotted domains in reasonable amity, but the inevitable frictions arose, and the Inca Empire was confronted by a greater threat than epidemic disease or even foreign invasion—civil war.

Atahualpa had much the advantage in his generals and in military experience, and after turning back the armies of Huáscar that had invaded his kingdom, Atahualpa was ready to move south against Cuzco itself, the possession of which would give him undisputed claim to the empire. Atahualpa was cautious, however, rightly fearing that the war might go against him in the lands of his half brother. He thus dispatched his army, under the two most senior and experienced generals, Quizquiz and Chalicuchima, south to Cuzco and remained behind at Cajamarca.

In a fierce and bloody battle on the plains of Quipaypan near the capital, Huáscar's troops were routed and the Inca Huáscar taken prisoner. Back at Cajamarca, the now sole ruler and arbiter of the empire joyfully received the news of the victory and the homage of his subjects.

But the victory over Huáscar was to be the last celebratory event of Atahualpa's short life. As Huayna Capac lay dying, he had received news of the arrival on the coast of a band of tall, bearded white men. The Inca saw this as perhaps a fulfillment of a prophecy of the oracles who had predicted that the arrival of such strangers presaged the destruction of the Empire of the Sun.

The Inca's nobles dismissed the arrival of the Spaniards as a mere speck on the horizon, and their skepticism seemed justified when word came from the coast that the interlopers had withdrawn.

But as W. H. Prescott so artfully phrased it, "The small speck, which the clear-sighted eye of his father had discerned on the distant verge of the horizon, though little noticed by Atahualpa, intent on the deadly strife with his brother, had now risen high towards the zenith, spreading wider and wider, till it wrapped the skies in darkness, and was ready to burst in thunder on the devoted nation." [1]

The small speck and the accompanying thunder was Francisco Pizarro, who did indeed withdraw, but was now back in Peru with his fellow conquistadors. He had returned to and was preparing to leave his base on the island of Puná and remove to the mainland at Tumbes.

From Tumbes, in early May 1532, the Spaniards began their journey of conquest into the Empire of the Sun and the confiscation of its untold riches. Proceeding southward, Pizarro paused to gather his strength and plan his next moves at a fortified settlement that he built and christened San Miguel de Piura.

Word reached Pizarro at San Miguel of the recent war between the brothers and the victory of Atahualpa, who, he also leaned, was still encamped with his court at Cajamarca, where he was enjoying the nearby mineral springs, the Baños del Inca.

Told that Cajamarca was just twelve days' journey from San Miguel, Pizarro at once decided to cross the forbidding cordillera and meet the Inca there instead of proceeding along the well-maintained, direct route to Cuzco, the capital of the empire.

The cordillera, particularly to those men who were in armor and on horseback, presented what appeared to be an insurmountable obstacle, and it very nearly was so. Pizarro's small force—just 168 altogether, 62 cavalry and 106 infantry—left San Miguel on 24 September 1532. They did not enter Cajamarca until 15 November.

En route, embassies and messages were exchanged between the court of the Inca and the headquarters of the Spaniards, and although their entry into a totally deserted Cajamarca was a foreboding sign, Atahualpa, true to his word, was awaiting them at his nearby encampment.

There has been much speculation in the centuries since the Conquest concerning the true intentions of the Inca Atahualpa toward the Spanish. Did he allow the small force to penetrate his kingdom until he could properly assess them and then annihilate them at will? After all, Atahualpa's army of eighty thousand at Cajamarca could easily have overwhelmed and destroyed Pizarro's tiny force.

Atahualpa had already demonstrated some military skill, combining both bravery and unspeakable brutality, in the recent war. Thousands of Huáscar's soldiers had been slaughtered, and afterward anyone related by blood to his rival—women and children included—had been put to death to ensure that there would be no new claimant to the throne.

Or did superstition, curiosity, or perhaps even fear of these tall, bearded white interlopers and the exotic animals on which they rode stay the hand of the Inca? Whatever the reasons, Atahualpa made a fateful, even fatal, misjudgment, which would lead, in a very short time, not only to his death but to the complete destruction of his empire.

Immediately after his arrival, Pizarro sent a fifteen-man delegation on horseback, headed by Hernando de Soto, to the Inca camp. As reinforcements, if needed, there followed just behind another troop of twenty, commanded by Pizarro's brother, Hernando.

Atahualpa, his forehead covered by the *mascaypacha*, a thick red fringe that was the symbol of his power and divinity, received the Spaniards seated on a low stool. He did not deign to speak or even look up at the Spaniards who towered over him on their strange animals.

De Soto, addressing the Inca through the offices of a black slave who spoke poor Spanish and probably even worse Quechua, attempted to engage the emperor in conversation. Atahualpa did not respond. His gaze remained firmly on the ground in front of him, and he continued to ignore these barbarians who were violating every rule of the Incan court by not only looking at the emperor but actually addressing him.

Only when Hernando Pizarro, leader of the backup horsemen, rode into the camp did the Inca respond. Presumably the brother of the leader of the Spaniards had the requisite clout to rouse an emperor.

But Hernando also made little headway with the Inca. Indeed his boasting to the Inca about the prowess of Christian soldiers occasioned a rebuke in the form of a tight smile from Atahualpa.

But that conquistador of conquistadors, Hernando de Soto, seized the moment. He put on a dazzling display of horsemanship in front of the Inca, which ended with a charge directly at that august figure and de Soto's reining in his mount and having it rear up just a few feet from Atahualpa.

The Inca neither flinched nor moved a muscle, but several of the guards drew back in fear and others fled. This demonstrative lack of the royal sangfroid cost the retainers. Atahualpa ordered all of them put to death.

The mini cavalry charge seemed to have broken the ice, however. Atahualpa ordered refreshments for all, and the Spaniards marveled at the gold cups in which they were served. Clearly the empire that they had invaded might prove as rich as that of the Aztecs, which Cortés had conquered just a few years before. The Spaniards returned to Cajamarca, with the promise from Atahualpa that he would come there the next day to meet with Pizarro himself.

The emperor was as good as his word, and the next day, 16 November 1532, Atahualpa and his court came to Cajamarca to treat with, or more likely to annihilate, the Spaniards.

Pizarro, drawing on the experience of Hernán Cortés in Mexico, had determined to take the Inca prisoner as soon as he entered the square in Cajamarca, killing all of his retinue if necessary. The Spaniards secreted themselves in the buildings surrounding the main square in the town and watched nervously as the royal train approached.

As soon as the Inca and his followers entered the square, Pizarro ordered his men to attack, and in a matter of minutes hundreds, if not thousands, of the Indians lay dead or dying.

The Inca was spirited away and imprisoned in one of the low buildings facing the square. The mascaypacha, symbol of his divinity, lay in the dust.

Early in his short imprisonment, Atahualpa sensed at once that his conquerors and captors had more on their minds than his soul. As Prescott said, "It was not long before Atahualpa discovered, amidst all the show of religious zeal in his Conquerors, a lurking appetite more potent in most of their bosoms than either religion or ambition. This was the love of gold." [2]

Playing upon the Spaniards' greed, Atahualpa, to secure his freedom, told them that as ransom, in two months' time, he could fill a room thirty-five feet by seventeen feet to a height of nine feet with objects made of pure gold.

Growing out of this promised ransom was an action that proved the undoing of Atahualpa. Huáscar, Atahualpa's erstwhile rival for the throne, was in a similar predicament. He, too, was under house arrest, at Andamarca. Now, upon hearing of Atahualpa's offer, he sent word to the Spaniards that he could do even better if he could gain his own freedom.

Atahualpa's spies relayed Huáscar's competing offer, and he at once ordered the execution of Huáscar, which was accomplished by drowning him in the river at Andamarca.

Pizarro, who had probably planned to set up the more malleable Huáscar as a puppet of the Spaniards, was angered by his death and charged Atahualpa with murder and fomenting an insurrection, along with other crimes.

But first there was the ransom—which eventually grew to over five thousand cubic feet of gold objects. When this was secured, Atahualpa was brought to trial. He was convicted and sentenced to death. However, there was more to the sad story of the Inca Atahualpa. He was inveigled into accepting Christianity and baptism and taking the Christian name of Juan de Atahualpa. The Inca was then garroted.

The death of Atahualpa effectively ended the custom and tradition of an all-powerful and omniscient Inca. There were successors, but all were installed by the Spanish and all were expected to toe the line.

The first of these puppet Incas was Túpac Huallpa, the younger brother of Atahualpa, but his reign was brief. He died of smallpox a few months after being installed by Pizarro. The second, Manco Inca, another half brother of Atahualpa, was then installed by Pizarro, this time in the recently captured capital, Cuzco. Manco Inca proved not to be as malleable as the Spanish expected, but it took many outrages by the Spanish before he openly moved against them.

He stood silently by as the Spanish stripped the temples and palaces of their gold and silver treasures and melted them down into ingots to be shipped to Spain. He even submitted to the seduction of his wife by another of Pizarro's brothers, Gonzalo. Finally, during Holy Week, 1536, Manco fled Cuzco for the Sacred Valley, where he organized a full-scale revolt against the Spanish oppressors, which ebbed and flowed until 1572, with atrocities and betrayals committed by both sides, often against their own confederates.

In 1538, Pizarro executed his long-time ally and friend Diego de Almagro, who had turned traitor, and in turn in 1541 Pizarro was assassinated by Almagro partisans.

Manco Inca died a violent death in 1544 at the hands of some Spaniards who had insinuated themselves into his confidence, at Vilcabamba, the new Inca capital that had been built in the isolated mountains west of Cuzco. His immediate successor, five-year-old Sayri Túpac, was Inca of only a rump state, centered in Vilcabamba. Finally in 1560, he was suborned by the Spanish and enticed to move to Cuzco, where he died, it was said, of natural causes, but was widely believed to have been murdered by the Spanish.

His successor, Titu Cusi, became a formidable opponent of the Spanish, once again leading the revolt from the fastness of Vilcabamba until his own death, again from supposedly natural causes, in 1571.

For the next year, the Inca were led by a formidable opponent of Spanish rule, Túpac Amaru. But the Indians were now both outmanned and outgunned. Thousands of new Spanish settlers had arrived in the viceroy-alty, and they were in no mood to countenance violence against their new settlements. Vilcabamba was soon sacked, and Túpac Amaru was taken prisoner. The last Inca was then taken to Cuzco, where he and members of his family were put to death in the main plaza.

In the eighteenth century, José Gabriel Condorcanqui, a mestizo who was a direct descendant of Túpac Amaru, became one of the great folk heroes of Peru. Styling himself Túpac Amaru II, this Jesuit-educated rebel led a short-lived revolt against the Spaniards.

But like his famous ancestor, Túpac Amaru II met a grisly death in the main plaza of Cuzco, along with many members of his family. After being subjected to the most terrible of tortures, his arms and legs were tied to horses and he was pulled apart while still alive. Thus ended the Empire of the Sun.

# The Search for El Dorado

Gold, Spices, and Blood

EXPLORATION OF THE CONTIGUOUS TERRITORIES OF THE INCA Empire was a secondary occupation of the Spaniards until they had secured their hold on that vast territory, confiscated the enormous treasure of gold and silver already extant, and then put the captive tribes to work extracting more. And there was, as well, a new capital, Lima, to be constructed.

Finally, in 1540 Francisco Pizarro turned his attention outward. He made his brother Gonzalo governor of the northern province of Quito, and charged him with exploring the regions to the east, where it was rumored there were vast forests of the cinnamon tree.

Gonzalo was quick to organize an expedition, and with a force of 350 Spaniards and 4,000 Indians he set out from Quito. Along with the usual provisions for such an expedition, immense numbers of swine, to be slaughtered for food, were herded along in the rear of the caravan.

For months, these adventurers were subjected to the freezing temperatures of the high cordillera, the heat and fevers of the lowland jungles, and the miasmic swamps of the river basins. And although they found the vast tracts of cinnamon trees, the valuable spice was of little use on a journey marked by privation, starvation, and death. They also, like the explorers before them, were lured on by the local tribes' descriptions of a populous land filled with gold, which was always just ten days' distance. Gonzalo pressed on.

A year later the Spaniards, at least the few who were still alive, found themselves at the juncture of the Napo and Coca rivers (near present-day Puerto Francisco de Orellana).

Faced with starvation—the swine had long since been slaughtered and eaten—the Spaniards allegedly were reduced to boiling their boots for something to eat.

Pizarro ordered the construction of a brigantine and ordered his lieutenant, Francisco de Orellana, to head downstream to search for food. The remainder of the party would wait for him at their camp.

After waiting for weeks for Orellana to return, Gonzalo Pizarro and his band headed downstream themselves, on foot, hoping to find Orellana, or food, or both. Two months later they were at the confluence of the Napo and the Amazon.

There was no sign of Orellana, but they discovered a white man wandering in the jungle and recognized him as one of their own, Hernán Sánchez de Vargas, who apprised them of the actions, some would say deception, of Orellana and his crew.

It had taken just three days, said Sánchez de Vargas, for the little brigantine to reach this spot, just a few miles downstream from present-day Iquitos, Peru.

It became clear, said Sánchez de Vargas, that it would not be possible to sail the boat back upstream, so Orellana was faced with two choices—marching overland to rejoin his companions or surrendering to a wildly improbable and romantic scheme.

As the historian W. H. Prescott said, "An idea flashed across [Orellana's] mind. It was to launch his bark at once on the bosom of the Amazon and descend its waters to its mouth. He would then visit the rich and populous nations that, as report said, lined its borders, sail out on the great ocean, cross to the neighboring isles, and return to Spain to claim the glory and guerdon of discovery." [1]

His men eagerly agreed, for to quote Prescott again, "the love of adventure was the last feeling to become extinct in the bosom of the Castilian cavalier." [2] The little boat was steered into the mainstream of the great river and at once became caught in the current.

Sánchez de Vargas, who had objected to the projected expedition down the river as "repugnant both to humanity and honor," [3] had paid the price for his qualms of conscience by being abandoned by Orellana and his shipmates.

In late August 1542, after six months on the river and eighteen months after leaving Quito, Orellana and the few survivors sailed their small boat into the Atlantic Ocean. They thus became the first white men to traverse the river that Orellana later christened the Amazon, after a band of fierce Indian warrior women whom he said he had encountered on his journey and whom he likened to the Amazons of Greek myth.

Orellana did make his way to Spain, and his tales of the river and his assurances that El Dorado did exist somewhere in the environs he had transited beguiled the credulous. He was outfitted with an expedition comprising ships, settlers, and infantrymen to colonize the Amazon area, which was to be called Nueva Andalucía.

After many delays, Orellana finally sailed in May 1545. Two of his four ships were lost in transit. The remaining two ships became separated, but the ship carrying Orellana arrived in Brazil in December and proceeded about three hundred miles upstream on the Amazon.

Disaster was immediate. The ship was driven ashore and wrecked.

Orellana, however, was not to be deterred from his quest. He built a river-going vessel and began his explorations. The men left behind at the camp eventually became concerned when the commander did not return and built a second boat to go in search of him.

They were unsuccessful, and abandoning the enterprise, they sailed down and out of the river, landing at the island of Margarita, where they found the missing ship that had set out with them from Spain. Among those on board was Orellana's young wife, Ana de Ayala.

Meanwhile, Orellana had returned to find the campsite deserted, but, ever hopeful, he set out again to explore the river. His party was attacked by Indians, and most of his people were killed, but Orellana, who survived the attack, pressed on with his explorations.

Francisco Orellana died in the Amazon Rain Forest in November 1546, probably of illness or, as some have written, rather romantically, of grief that his dreams of founding an empire were shattered.

And what of Gonzalo Pizarro? After receiving the depressing intelligence that Orellana had sailed away down the river, Gonzalo attempted to lead the remnants of his pitiful band downriver himself; but after some few days he realized that the way was hopeless, and he decided to return to Quito.

His men accepted the news with grim resignation, fully aware that the way back could be no easier than the outward journey, which had taken more than a year. Thus they set out and in another year's time reached the capital.

But his travails were, it seems, not behind him. The conquerors of the Inca had, for years, been squabbling over the division of the spoils, and their disagreements finally erupted into a civil war, led by a particularly disaffected Diego de Almagro, whom Pizarro had made governor of Chile. That land to the south turned out not to be the prize that Almagro envisioned, the Otro Peru. On the contrary, it was a land of backward and hostile Indian tribes, and there was no gold or silver.

Almagro's disappointment soon turned to outright hostility toward his patron and rival Pizarro, and he and his troops marched on Cuzco in 1538 in an attempt to seize control of Peru. He was defeated and executed by Pizarro, but the resentment festered and his followers bided their time, and while Gonzalo was on his ill-fated expedition across the Andes they rose up under Almagro's son and assassinated Pizarro.

Madrid, ever anxious to extend firmer control over the colonies, which were now crucial to the financial health of the kingdom, dispatched Blasco Núñez Vela to restore order and enforce the Leyes Nuevas, which were promulgated in 1542.

These "New Laws" were aimed directly at the *encomienda* system, which the Crown feared, rightly, would lead to a powerful hereditary caste system in the colonies, which could, if left unchecked, threaten the control of Madrid.

Under the system, Pizarro had awarded his cohorts vast tracts of land and many thousands of Indians, who were little more than slaves of their Spanish masters. The conquerors were naturally loath to see the system that was enriching them abolished, and Gonzalo Pizarro became their natural leader in the ensuing revolt against the Crown. He and his followers rose up, murdered the viceroy, and took over Peru.

Gonzalo's governorship was short-lived, however. Pedro de la Gasca, the new viceroy, put down the revolt by 1548, and Gonzalo Pizarro was beheaded. There was intermittent resistance to the reforms of the Crown for another ten years, but Gonzalo's death effectively ended the era of the Conquistadors and signaled the beginning of the decline of the *enco-menderos*.

Francisco de Orellana's reputation depends on the teller. Was he a scoundrel who left his comrades to survive as best they could while he sailed merrily downstream? Or was he himself the hapless victim of the current, a man who took advantage of a bad situation and sailed into history?

As for another adventurer, Lope de Aguirre, the second European to descend the length of the Amazon, there is no doubt whatsoever as to his true nature. The only debate is whether he was a psychopath at the outset of his adventure or was driven mad by it.

In 1560, just twelve years after the end of the civil war and the execution of Gonzalo Pizarro, Aguirre also crossed the Andes in Peru as a member of an expedition led by Pedro de Ursúa to explore new lands and search for El Dorado in the headwaters of the Amazon.

Ursúa was born in Navarre about 1525, into a family that was among the local gentry. He was handsome, intelligent, and engaging and might have made a name for himself in his native Spain but instead chose to ship out to the New World to seek his fame and fortune.

He arrived in the viceroyalty of New Granada, now Colombia, in 1545, to join his uncle, Miguel Díaz de Armendariz, a judge who had been sent out by the Council of the Indies to try to put an end to the seemingly endless strife in the viceroyalty. Land disputes between various conquistadors, who were forever striving for primacy in the region, kept the area in turmoil. The nephew's charge was to quiet the restive area around Bogotá.

Young Pedro—he was barely twenty years old—carried out this assignment with great success and not long after was given a more difficult task—pacifying the rebellious Musos Indians. He brought peace of a sort by enticing the leaders of the tribe to meet with him and then murdering them all. Other pacification campaigns ensued—employing similarly brutal tactics—but, not surprisingly, any peace thus gained was always a temporary one.

As elsewhere in the New World, smallpox turned out to be the Spaniards' most effective weapon against the warring indigenous populations of New Granada. Through its insidious agency the warlike tribes were eventually subdued. The few survivors lacked neither the numbers nor the will to resist further.

But meanwhile Ursúa tired of administrative tasks and fighting Indians in New Granada and looked southward, toward Peru, where he hoped to find some undertaking more suitable to his manifold talents and ambitions.

There would be one more war, however. While in Panama, the handsome, charming, and more than capable hidalgo met Andrés Hurtado de

Mendoza, the Marquis de Cuñete, who was on his way to Peru to take up his post as viceroy.

Cuñete enlisted Ursúa to put down a slave rebellion, the so-called Bayano War, named after its leader, a runaway. Two years later, with the slaves either dead or returned to their masters, Ursúa left Panama and set out for Peru.

In Lima, he further ingratiated himself with Cuñete, who made him commander of a cross-Andes expedition to search for the much-talked-of land of gold and spices—El Dorado. Ursúa was thirty-three years old.

Nearly every Spaniard who came out to the New World did so in the hope of becoming not just prosperous but fabulously rich. Hernán Cortés, the conqueror of the Aztec Empire in Mexico, had become not just a legend but an exemplar. Rumors abounded of even greater empires, golden cities, and fabulous wealth in the trackless jungles and the high mountains of South America.

Of the several quests for gold, one of the more unusual is that of an expedition sent out under the auspices of the great German banking house of Welser, based in Augsburg. In exchange for a large loan, the Hapsburg Holy Roman Emperor Charles V—King Carlos I of Spain—gave them a large swathe of Venezuela, extending without limit to the south, as a hereditary fief.

In return the Welsers were obliged to subjugate the natives and colonize the country. Subjugate, or enslave, the natives they did. Colonization was not in their plans. Instead, in 1528 they sent out a rapacious band of Spaniards and Germans whose main occupation was searching for gold.

A particularly nasty member of an expedition that left the coast in 1530, which comprised some two hundred Germans and Spaniards and hundreds of Indian slaves, was Ambrosius Ehinger, or Ambrosio de Alfinger in Spanish. The German became notorious for chaining the slaves together by rings around their necks. When one of these unfortunates died, Alfinger ordered his head cut off rather than bothering with cutting through the iron ring.

For three years, Alfinger wandered around what is now Colombia and

Venezuela, watching his men succumb to fever and the spears and arrows of hostile Indians and the slaves either to overwork or starvation. He found no gold. In May 1533 he was struck in the throat by an arrow. He died an agonizing death four days later.

After further adventures and depredations by the Germans, the Welser grant was rescinded or canceled, and it was to reestablish order and control that Armendariz had been sent out to the colony by the Spanish crown.

Strictly speaking, Alfinger was not looking for El Dorado. That story had not begun to be bruited about among the Spanish until sometime in the later 1530s, after his adventures. According to the legend, El Dorado, or "the golden one," was the name given to the newly appointed ruler or heir to the crown of the Muisca tribe in present-day Colombia. The name derived from the ceremony celebrating the anointed one's ascension to the throne. First the chief's entire body was coated with a sticky substance and then gold dust was applied until he was completely covered. He thus became, literally, El Dorado, the "Golden One" or the "Golden Man."

The new chief was then rowed out into the middle of Lake Guatavita, which is northeast of Bogotá, to the accompaniment of music and chants. Gold ornaments and emeralds were thrown into the lake as offerings, and then the new chief bathed in the lake to offer up the gold dust that covered his body as further tribute.

In fairly short order, the credulous Spaniards had transmogrified the golden man first, into a city; then, into a kingdom; and finally, into an empire of fabulous wealth. An extensive literature grew up around the legend, and there were even maps of the purported El Dorado.

No one was immune, it seems. Kings, poets, philosophers, priests, buccaneers, conquistadors, missionaries all fell under the sway of the legend. And so the search was soon on—a search that has continued for centuries.

Even today, there exist true believers. Somewhere in the Amazon, they say, there exist the remains of El Dorado. They buttress their belief, if not their case, by pointing to the thousands of gold objects, often of great beauty, that were produced by the Indians and that have survived. Many, tellingly, are of a golden man.

Unlike the almost benign voyage of Francisco de Orellana, the first man to descend the Amazon, that of the second, Lope de Aguirre, was marked by unspeakable crimes. And it was a journey that remains unrivaled in the turbulent history of the Amazon region.

Lope de Aguirre was a fifty-year-old of Basque extraction who had come out to the colonies in 1534 and in the succeeding twenty-five years had variously been a tomb robber, mutineer, horse breeder, and hired gun.

For one of his crimes, he was sentenced to a hundred lashes, and salt was then rubbed into the wounds. Three years after this punishment, which left him disabled, he exacted his own judgment on the magistrate who had meted it out. Aguirre followed him to Cuzco and stabbed him to death.

Friends helped him to flee Cuzco for Tucumán, where he joined a rebellion against the new laws forbidding ownership of Indians. When the rebellion was put down, Aguirre was sentenced to death and once more became a fugitive, hiding out in Bolivia.

Taking advantage of an amnesty granted the rebels, Aguirre returned from his exile and joined up with the government forces to fight the rebellious Indians, which included the vestiges of the Inca who were still holding out against the Spaniards. Already a near cripple from the earlier sentence of a hundred lashes, he was further disabled by two bullets in the leg and a hand injury in these Indian wars.

But Aguirre's manifest rage against society and an uncanny instinct for survival kept him going. And now there lay ahead an adventure that would ensure his posterity—or infamy. A marginally less questionable friend and confederate, Martín de Guzmán, found Aguirre in Cuzco, where he had retreated, and told him of the expedition that Viceroy Cuñete was outfitting for the search for El Dorado. Aguirre, realizing that here at last was the main chance that he had been awaiting for twenty-five years, set out with Guzmán for the capital. Accompanying them was Aguirre's young daughter, Elvira, the result of a liaison with an Indian woman.

Cuñete, who was clearly a better judge of men than the man he had appointed commander of the expedition, was appalled by the quality of some of the volunteers who had been recruited by Ursúa, in particular Guzmán, who was a particularly unsavory sort. Guzmán was let go, but his younger brother, Fernando, who appeared to be at least somewhat more trustworthy—which, in the event, proved not to be so—was allowed to stay on. The worst of the lot, Lope de Aguirre, remained unchallenged, as did roughly a dozen others of the same ilk.

Even a small group of malcontents and ne'er-do-wells can terrorize the more civil members of society, and Peru in the 1550s, which had been wracked by civil war, had more than its share of the unemployed and the disaffected. Thus our chief source, Friar Pedro Simon, observed, somewhat cynically, that the viceroy knew perfectly well what he was doing in allowing what the historian James Lockhart called this "brigandage" to go forth. He wanted them out of Lima and thus out of his hair.

Although not contemporaneous with the events he recounts—he was born in 1574—Simon's narrative, first published in 1623, is not only the most complete account of the Ursúa-Aguirre expedition but arguably the most accurate. He drew on the account by Francisco Vasquez, who observed firsthand many of the events he described—he was on the expedition and stayed with it until it reached the island of Margarita—as well as other, more fragmentary, contemporary narratives. Vasquez's professed loyalty to the king had made him an object of suspicion and almost certain death when Aguirre took over, so he bided his time until he could make his escape.

Simon is almost certainly right that Viceroy Cuñete thus "hoped to relieve the provinces of Peru of much corrupt blood, by sending forth many idle people, who might otherwise cause some fresh insurrection, like those which had already placed this famous kingdom in danger. . . ."[4]

Simon's assessment is supported by the fact that the entire Spanish population in the viceroyalty of Peru was not more than ten thousand at the time of the Ursúa expedition. Cuñete's dispatch of this "brigandage" saved his tenuous position only temporarily. He was recalled to Spain the following year.

Creole society must have been somewhat taken aback by the appointment of the relatively young Ursúa as commander and perhaps even more so by Cuñete's bestowal on him of the governorship of any areas that he might discover and conquer.

But there was an even more surprising bit of news, which must have shaken the aristocracy to its very soul. Ursúa was taking along one Doña Inez de Atienza—variously described as mistress, wife, lady of unrivaled virtue, or woman of easy virtue. In other words she was a saint to some and a sinner to others—a woman who was better than most or no better than she should be.

Whatever Doña Inez's morals, it was agreed by everyone that she was a great beauty. She had cast a spell on Ursúa when he first arrived in Peru, and accordingly he was determined to bring her along to ameliorate the rigors of the journey. She would be attended on the journey by two Amerindian women.

Suspicions and unease about the expedition abounded, and Ursúa did not lack advice and counsel, whether it was about the dubious character of Aguirre and his cohorts, who it was feared would become mutinous, or the problems that the presence of Doña Inez and her women would almost certainly present among hundreds of ruffians deprived of female company.

While Ursúa was clearly a brave man, able to vanquish any foe in combat, he was severely limited in his experience of a world marked by more subtle methods of action, such as intrigue and deception. He ignored the advice of well-meaning friends and pressed on with his plans.

The Ursúa Expedition—which because of subsequent events is better known to history as the Aguirre Expedition—finally began to depart Lima in February 1559.

The first group to leave the capital was made up of shipbuilders and their helpers who were to cross the cordillera to the Río Marañón, where they were to build vessels large enough to transport men, horses, and supplies for the exploration of the headwaters of the Amazon. The main party, headed by Ursúa himself, would join them later.

Meanwhile, half a world away, more momentous events had been set in motion. In January, Elizabeth I was crowned queen of England. Her soon to be implacable enemy, Philip II, was already on the throne of Spain. By the convoluted dynastic schemes that were characteristic of the ruling houses of Europe, the king of Spain was related by marriage to the queen of England. Philip had been the husband of Mary Tudor, Elizabeth's half sister and immediate predecessor.

None of this news would reach the isolated viceroyalty of Peru for many months. Meanwhile the disparate groups that made up the Ursúa Expedition began to leave Lima for the rendezvous across the cordillera. Intrigue, infighting, murder, assassination, desertion, the often questionable execution of mutineers and miscreants, incessant warfare with hostile Indians, constant hunger, and the consequent relentless search for food all conspired against them as they struggled across the mountains and negotiated the jungles and tributary streams of the upper Amazon Basin.

It was not until the end of September 1560, near where the Marañón and the Ucayali converge to form the Amazon, that the advance scouts, the boat builders, the stragglers, and the main party, led by the titular leader, finally came together in a single group. It was probably already too late to save the expedition. The situation had become too combustible.

And Ursúa did much to undermine his own authority, even his very legitimacy. He shifted his attention from the search for El Dorado and gold to concentrate on exploration of these new lands.

When a dissident group attempted to break away and return to Peru, instead of being punished they were pardoned. And Ursúa seriously alienated the old Indian-fighters in the party, who had spent their lives killing or enslaving Indians, when he took the part of the indigenous tribes when his men attacked and pillaged Indian villages.

And there was the abiding and disturbing presence of Doña Inez de

Atienza. It takes little imagination to conjure up the jealousy and envy that Ursúa stirred up by his frequent and long assignations with his beautiful mistress in the tent that they shared while just a few feet away some two hundred men, who had not seen a white woman in almost two years, smoldered and plotted.

All the while the expedition continued downstream, building new boats when their craft ran aground and broke up on the rocks and submerged trees of the rivers. And there was the constant search for food, which was in dangerously short supply in this inhospitable and forbidding land.

A wily and ruthless captain was called for, and Ursúa was not that man. He had shown the requisite strength, even ruthlessness, in putting down slave rebellions and Indian uprisings in his early career, but he was seemingly constitutionally unable to deal similarly with his increasingly restive, even mutinous countrymen, at least for the long run.

In the short term, when he talked of the glories to come, he was able to tamp down the rebellious soldiers and adventurers under his command. But they soon became impervious to the aristocratic charm of the hidalgo, and they plotted to assassinate him and replace him with the second in command, Fernando de Guzmán, the brother of the cashiered confederate of Lope de Aguirre.

The expedition, which had spent some weeks in an Indian village, had removed to another village a few leagues downstream the day after Christmas 1560. On the morning of New Year's Day it was decided that the plot against Ursúa would be carried out that very evening.

Under cover of darkness, "the cloak of sinners," said Friar Simon, two of the would-be assassins entered Ursúa's hut, where they found him reclining in a hammock talking to his page, a young man named Lorca. The two men lunged toward Ursúa, but their first blows missed their target, and the governor was able to reach for his sword to defend himself. But Ursúa was no match for the rest of the mutineers, who now stormed into the hut to aid their confederates in dispatching him. Under the rain of blows from swords and knives, he fell dead.

The devout chronicler Friar Pedro Simon may be forgiven for attributing some last words to the dying Ursúa. "*Confessio, confessio, miserere mei Deus,*" Simon reports him as saying as he fell dead.[5] He continues the sad story of Ursúa thusly:

> *This was the miserable end of Pedro de Ursúa, after his power had lasted three months and six days; he having embarked at the ship-yard on the 26th September, 1560, and having been killed on the 1st of January, 1561, aged thirty-five years. He was of middle size, slightly formed, but well proportioned, with the manners of a gentleman; light complexion and beard the same, courteous, and affable, fond of his soldiers, and more inclined to mercy than to justice; thus his very enemies could not complain of his having done them wrong: he was too confiding and had but little precaution, and his great goodness was the main cause which brought him to so sad an end.*[6]

No such description could be attached to the men who had carried out the brutal murder of Ursúa. Their crime was the beginning of an Amazonian version of a Jacobean revenge tragedy, in which "blood begets blood."

The first to die was Ursúa's lieutenant, Juan de Vargas, who, when he heard the cries from the governor's hut, ran from his nearby lodging to the aid of the commander. Vargas met the assassins in the road and was run through with such force that the sword impaled the soldier who was trying to disarm him from behind. Vargas's body was dragged into the hut of the dead Ursúa, and the two corpses were buried together in a hastily dug grave.

Fernando de Guzmán was now commander of the expedition, and Lope de Aguirre was *maestro del campo*, second in command, but the bloodletting was only beginning. Anyone deemed a friend of the dead Ursúa and who might possibly seek revenge was sought out and strangled or hacked to death.

Guzmán soon realized that the carnage must cease and order be restored or the expedition would devolve into total anarchy and blood-lust. He therefore convened a meeting, and a document was drawn up setting forth the reasons for deposing Ursúa, which mainly centered on his failure to look for gold and El Dorado.

Aguirre, who from the beginning had shown contempt for the expedition's stated purposes and had secretly plotted to return to Peru and foment a rebellion there, now seized the initiative. He boldly signed the document, "Lope de Aguirre, the traitor."

What was the use to pretend that they were other than traitors? he said. Had they not mutinied and killed the king's governor? Was this not treason? So why not now return to Peru, a known land and one richer than anything they would discover if they continued on, where they would be met as liberators by their fellow revolutionaries?

Others, who were loyal to the king and the viceroy, objected and argued that they should press on with exploration and the search for new lands. Their arguments met with fierce resistance from Aguirre and his cohorts, and Guzmán was hard pressed to keep the two opposing forces from taking up arms against each other.

Order was restored, and five days later the expedition proceeded downstream, but the dark cloud of mutiny was not dispelled, and Aguirre by no means abandoned his plan to return to Peru as a conqueror. On the contrary, his fevered imagination now hatched a scheme that can only be described as hallucinatory. He would continue down the rivers to the Atlantic, thence north and west along the coast to Panama, where they would cross the isthmus to the Pacific, and then sail south to Peru.

The credulous and easily swayed ordinary soldiery, who were well aware of the riches in the land that they had left behind, were quick to embrace and sign on to Aguirre's scheme to invade and overthrow the government in the viceroyalty of Peru.

Most of the senior members of the expedition also signed on to the scheme, most notably Don Fernando de Guzmán himself, who was a willing party to the most extraordinary occurrence during this tumultuous time—his elevation to the title of prince of Peru and the announcement that when their revolution was accomplished he would be raised even higher. He would be crowned king. None of them would henceforth be subservient to his majesty Philip II.

The gullible Guzmán went along with this farce, dining alone, receiving the obeisance of his subjects, holding audiences, and in general aping the ceremonies of a royal court in the miserable Indian village where they rested while brigantines were being built so they could continue their journey down the Amazon to the sea.

All the while, in order to consolidate his growing power, Aguirre plotted the demise of his rivals, either real or imagined. Thus the expedition was constantly rent by plots and counterplots, subterfuge, dissembling, and murderous machinations, all orchestrated by Lope de Aguirre. One by one his rivals came to a grisly end—hacked to death, beheaded, drowned, or strangled.

When it became obvious that no one was safe from Aguirre's bloodlust and machinations, a plot was set in motion by an opposition group to eliminate him before he eliminated them. The "prince of Peru" was let in on the plan and readily acceded. Since Aguirre was ever on guard and always surrounded by the faithful, it would be no easy task to assassinate him. Thus it was decided to wait until the expedition was aboard the brigantines and en route down the river.

But what of Doña Inez de Atienza, the mistress of the murdered Ursúa? As Friar Pedro said rather indelicately, that lady "had not left the evil ways she had continued in since she left Peru."[7] When her lover and protector was murdered, she transferred her services if not her affections to Lorenzo Salduendo, the captain of the guard of Fernando de Guzmán.

Her new patron was rebuffed by Aguirre when he asked that special arrangements be made aboard one of the brigantines for Doña Inez and her attendant. There were more important items, said Aguirre, than the ladies' baggage and the special mattresses that they required.

Salduendo's angry outburst at this rejection and the equally harsh words of his mistress soon were relayed to Aguirre. Fearing for his life, the captain appealed to Guzmán for protection and took refuge in the prince's house. But Guzmán was now faced with the reality of his position and lack of power when Aguirre invaded his house in pursuit of Salduendo. Ignoring Guzmán's appeal to spare Salduendo's life, Aguirre struck him down as the prince looked helplessly on.

Aguirre then turned his attention to Doña Inez. He dispatched a sergeant and a servant to her house, where they murdered her in the most brutal manner. As the chronicler, Friar Pedro Simon, said, "even the most hardened men in the camp, at sight of the mangled victim, were broken hearted, for this was the most cruel act that had been perpetrated." [8]

It was now clear to even the most obtuse members of the expedition that Don Fernando was only nominally their leader. Lope de Aguirre was now the de facto commander and even the erstwhile plotters now joined his retinue, revealing to Aguirre the details of his planned assassination.

Aguirre was quick to act. The two senior members of the council were put to the sword that very night. Since they were encamped at some remove from Guzmán he was unaware of their deaths when the next day Aguirre and an armed band entered his dwelling, where they "found him on his couch, quite unprepared to be hurried out of this world," as our guide Friar Simon put it.[9]

But hurry him out of this world they did, first firing two harquebuses at him and then falling on him with their swords. Friar Simon writes, "He was scarcely twenty-six years of age, of good stature, well formed and strong of limb, with the manners of a gentleman, fine face and beard, slow to action, more kind than otherwise, and born in the city of Seville." [10]

Whether such an encomium was warranted is questionable. After all, was not Fernando complicit in the murder of Ursúa, and was he not the brother of Martín Guzmán, the shady confederate of Aguirre who was sacked even before the expedition got under way?

In any event, Lope de Aguirre had long since hardened his heart to any virtues that others might have. He was now the sole leader of the expedition, and he moved at once to solidify his power. Calling all the men together, he explained that the bloodletting was necessary to ensure the viability of their mission, which would now proceed in a more orderly and systematic fashion and end, as he had long advocated, in their return to Peru as conquerors.

He now dispensed honors and favors to the loyalists. As for the disloyal, and there were still some under suspicion, they were summarily dealt with. Indeed, eight more men were executed in the next week alone, most of them in the most cruel fashion—they were garroted, hacked to death with a rusted and broken sword, or had curare rubbed into open wounds. But the expedition was now aboard the two brigantines and proceeding apace down the Amazon.

On 1 July 1561, almost two and a half years after leaving Lima, Lope de Aguirre entered the Atlantic Ocean. However, there has long been conjecture that Lope de Aguirre did not enter the Atlantic via the Amazon—that he actually ascended the Río Negro and via the Casiquiare Canal gained the Orinoco and entered the Atlantic near Trinidad.

Some of the descriptions of the landscape through which the party passed add some credence to the idea, as well as the fact that Aguirre established himself seventeen days after entering the Atlantic on the island of Margarita, off the coast of Venezuela. But since it is possible to sail from the Amazon to Margarita in less than three weeks, Aguirre on the Orinoco remains only a conjecture.

Another legend has it that the Río Marañón was named after the members of the expedition who referred to themselves as Marañones, supposedly from the Spanish word *marañas*, for the plots or entanglements that were endemic on the expedition. This was the view of our chief source, Friar Simon.

But according to the eighteenth-century priest and historian Juan de Velasco, in his *Historia del reino de Quito*, the river's name comes from that of a man named Marañon, who was the first Spaniard to see it.

For the next four months, until the end of October 1561, Lope de Aguirre pursued his dream of the conquest of Peru, but instead of doing so by sea, he resolved to do so overland, traversing the unknown and unexplored mountains and jungles of what is now Venezuela and Colombia.

Crossing over to the mainland from Margarita, he began to put his grandiose and mad scheme into effect, terrorizing the local towns and settlers to force them to give him arms and food. Any resistance was met with the usual gruesome deaths, which were notable even for that violent time.

As we have seen, even those close to Aguirre were not immune to his murderous and sadistic whims. On the contrary, they were often singled out for torture or execution. Typical was the maiming of Alonso Rodrígues, who had been promoted to admiral.

When this officer and confidant held out his hand to assist his commander as he was boarding the ship to leave Isla Margarita, Aguirre drew his sword and severed the offending hand. But Rodrígues didn't have to live much longer without a hand. When he further annoyed Aguirre by objecting to two horses and a mule being loaded aboard, he was put to death.

But forces loyal to the king were now massing to confront the rebels and traitors as they marched along the coast of Venezuela and then turned toward the southwest. The army might very well have been something of a ragtag assemblage, but they were seasoned fighters who presented a serious threat to established authority, and they had advanced as far as Barquisimeto, hundreds of miles from where they had landed on the coast. The governor, hoping to avoid a direct confrontation, wisely declared a general amnesty.

Aguirre's troops had everything to gain by accepting a pardon and everything to lose, most notably their heads, if their movement failed. They thus deserted his standard and declared their loyalty to Philip II. Their desertion assured that Aguirre's comeuppance was at hand, and he soon found himself attended by just one soldier.

Toward the end of the march there occurred what was perhaps the oddest, if not the most perverse, action of this most odd and perverse of men—the dictation of a letter to the king of Spain. Alternately fawning and insulting, at one point calling Philip "O Christian king and Lord" and then telling him that he is "worse than Lucifer," the letter is both an apologia and a catalogue of the murders and atrocities committed by Aguirre in his trek down the Amazon and then back across the northern coast of South America.

By his lights, this psychopath's crimes were committed only to further the mission or to save his own threatened life. Even the grisly murder of a Fleming named Monteverde was justified because he was a Lutheran and Aguirre was a defender of the faith.

After further damning the king's corrupt ministers and clergy in the viceroyalty whose actions made his rebellion necessary, Aguirre ends his letter with a prayer that the king will be victorious against the French and the Turks. As for himself, says Aguirre, "I am a rebel against thee until death." [11]

The old conspirator was not quite ready to abandon his illusions, however. And besides, he had one more despicable act to perform from his seemingly inexhaustible repertory of atrocities. His daughter Elvira was still with him. Somehow she had managed to survive the horrors and privations of the past two and half years, as did another young woman from Spain named Torralva.

Now, in a travesty of paternal piety, Aguirre determined to kill his child to spare her the disgrace of being his survivor. He cried out to Elvira, "Commend thyself to God, my daughter, for I am about to kill thee; that thou mayest not be pointed at with scorn, nor be in the power of any one who may call thee the daughter of a traitor." [12]

As he raised his harquebus to carry out this vile act, the gun was wrested from him by Torralva. Aguirre was not to be denied, however. He drew a dagger and stabbed his daughter to death.

Immediately following Elvira's murder, the royalists, headed by two of Aguirre's erstwhile companions, stormed into the house and shot him dead. They then cut off his head, which was taken in an iron cage to Tucuyo, where it was exhibited as a warning to other rebels and traitors.

Friar Pedro Simon wrote that the skull was still in Tucuyo in the early 1620s. So ended the career of Lope de Aguirre, on 27 October 1561.

The pre-Conquest history of the Amazon of course witnessed scenes of appalling barbarity as the indigenous peoples engaged in their endless wars, of which invasion, enslavement, and even cannibalism were an integral part, a brutal fact of life.

However, with the arrival of white Europeans new elements were introduced—avarice, blind ambition, greed, and an insatiable thirst for gold.

# Conquistadors for Christ

*The Holy Fathers and the Indigenous Peoples*

SIDE BY SIDE WITH THE CONQUISTADORS MARCHED THE HOLY fathers of the Catholic Church, whose task it was to lead the aborigines in the New World to the way of the True Cross—by force if necessary. And countless numbers of Indians died rather than submit to the proselytizers or were put to death for having run afoul of the dictates of Christianity as laid out by the Dominican, Jesuit, Franciscan, and Capuchin friars.

Although it is customary to credit Christopher Columbus with introducing slavery to the New World during his second voyage, the tradition or custom of involuntary servitude was long established there. The Indian tribes of the Caribbean often raided tribes on neighboring islands and carried off the inhabitants. And it was commonplace in the vast empires in Mexico and South America to enslave conquered peoples as the rulers expanded their domains.

But Columbus and his successors added a new dimension, the institutionalization of slavery in the New World, which began as early as his second voyage (1493–1496). It was a logical outgrowth of the Spanish system called the encomienda, which evolved during the Reconquista, the five-hundred-year struggle by the Christians of Spain to reclaim their land from the Moors, who had crossed over from North Africa and conquered the Iberian Peninsula in 711.

The Christians began almost immediately to attempt to take back the Iberian Peninsula from the Moors, but it was not until the mid-thirteenth century that most of the territory had been wrested from Muslim control. By then, only a handful of cities remained under Muslim control, but even those were in reality fiefs of the king of Castile.

Indeed, by 1492, the only truly Muslim city remaining in Spain was Granada, but in January of that year it fell to the forces of Ferdinand and Isabella, and Boabdil, the last of the city's Muslim rulers, was driven into exile. Legend has it that on looking back at Granada, Sultan Boabdil began to weep, which brought upon him one of history's greatest reproaches. "Weep like a woman for what you could not defend as a man," the mother of Boabdil allegedly said to her grieving son.

Under the encomienda system, deserving individuals, that is, men who had fought for the Crown or who had otherwise supported it, were given control over conquered populations, who were expected to pay tribute to their new masters in the form of taxes and labor. In return the encomendero was obliged to provide protection to his subjects and, most important, instruct them in the Christian faith.

In the New World, these subjects were not Spanish peasants or conversos, Jews or Muslims who had been forced to convert to Christianity, but the Native Americans. As the saying went, the Spaniards "first fell upon their knees and then fell upon the Indians." The system, from its inception, was subject to abuses and willful disregard for the welfare of the wards of the encomendero.

On his second voyage, Christopher Columbus captured some 1,600 Taíno Indians who had revolted on Hispaniola and shipped 560 of them back to Ferdinand and Isabella. Although they were termed prisoners of war and candidates for conversion, they were in reality slaves. Two hundred of the poor wretches died on the voyage, and eventually the survivors were freed and returned to Hispaniola. The thousand captured Taínos who had remained behind on Hispaniola had been given as slaves to the settlers who had come out with Columbus.

As Spanish settlements grew on the Caribbean islands, the encomienda system was introduced, and the local people were assigned to a conquistador-encomendero. In a fine distinction, these native populations were called "vassals," a term that was introduced to satisfy Queen Isabella, who professedly was concerned about the indigenous people.

The system worked for a few years, providing labor for the nascent Spanish colonies in the New World, but overwork and the diseases brought by the Spanish, against which the indigenous populations had no defenses, soon wiped out the native peoples or reduced them to just a remnant.

Of all the diseases introduced by the Spanish, smallpox was especially virulent. Introduced perhaps as early as Columbus's first voyage in 1492, the disease spread rapidly through the islands of the Caribbean and then jumped to Central and South America, wiping out most of the indigenous population.

Hernán Cortés's victory over the Aztecs was in no small part due to a smallpox pandemic that began in Mexico in 1520. In August 1521, when the capital, Tenochtitlan, fell to the Spaniards, the victors were horrified by the thousands of Aztec corpses lying in the streets.

Some historians dispute the role of smallpox in the conquest of the empires of the Aztecs and the Incas and the number of dead. Robert McCaa, writing in the *Journal of Interdisciplinary History*, takes a moderate and middle-ground position, although he clearly has little patience with those who maintain that smallpox played a small role.

In short order smallpox began to spread rapidly down the west coast into the Inca Empire, doubtless aided by the efficient Inca road system. Within months, the disease had killed the Sapa Inca, Huayna Capac, his successor, Ninan Cuyochi, and most of the other leaders.

As in Mexico, it is impossible to quantify the disaster in South America in terms of actual numbers or percentages, but it is clear that it was comparable, perhaps even worse, than what occurred in Mexico.

Smallpox, however, was only the first of many epidemics to strike the Incas. Typhus struck around 1546, influenza and more smallpox in 1558, smallpox again in 1589, diphtheria in 1614, and measles in 1618. Each of the subsequent epidemics further decimated the Incas and their culture.

With the death of so many Indians, a new source of labor was essential if the newly established plantations were to thrive. The solution, of course, was already at hand. As early as 1502, the first slaves from Africa were toiling in the settlements in the Caribbean, brought there by Portuguese traders.

Until the end of the slave trade in the nineteenth century, some ten million Africans were transported to the Americas—90 percent of them to the Caribbean and to the Spanish and Portuguese colonies of South America. The remainder were sold in North America. The institution would not be abolished in the United States until 1863, during the American Civil War, and in Brazil not until 1888.

Only the fittest could have survived the appalling conditions on the slave ships crossing the Atlantic, so this new stock of workers was almost by definition the fittest of the fit. And, too, they had immunity to most of the devastating diseases of the Europeans, who had been trading with Africa for years.

But this influx of Africans by no means ensured that the surviving Indians of South America were free from bondage or the lash. Whole tribes were still hunted down and sold to work the fields and the mines. The story of slavery in the South American colonies is replete with uprisings and rebellions of the enslaved against their Spanish and Portuguese masters, upheavals characterized by the most appalling barbarities committed by both sides in the struggles—slaves and masters alike.

Many men of the Church, Cristóbal de Acuña, Bartolomé de Las Casas, and Antonio Vieira, among others, were compassionate humanists as well as missionaries, and they raised objections to the treatment of the Indians—it took many years before they would espouse the cause of Africans—often directly to the kings of Spain and Portugal and even to the Vatican. But their voices were drowned out by the rapacious plantation owners and their more venal colleagues in the Catholic Church.

Even the conquistadors allegedly believed that their major task was spreading the gospel and converting the heathen. According to that great chronicler of the Conquest, William H. Prescott, the typical conquistador "felt that he was battling for the Cross, and under this conviction, exalted as it was . . . in the predominant impulse, he was blind to the baser motives which mingled with the enterprise." [1]

In our secular age, it might be hard to credit the great historian's rather benign view that the saving of souls for Christ was the primary mission of the conquistadors rather than the amassing of gold and silver. But it was, arguably, the primary motivation of the mendicant friars, or at least most of them, who accompanied them to the New World.

The old religious orders were well established in the Americas when a newcomer on the religious scene, the Society of Jesus, the Jesuits, arrived there in 1549. Founded in 1540 by Ignatius Loyola, a Spanish priest, the order sent its first missionaries to South America just nine years later.

Just as in Europe, where their exponential growth and subsequent power were fed by their militant defense of the Catholic Church against the inroads of Protestantism, which had found a ready audience, the Jesuits were soon a power in South America.

Their combination of preaching and teaching, particularly among the indigenous peoples, made the Jesuits a force to be reckoned with in the Amazon region for over two hundred years. But this power and its by-product, the accumulation of great wealth, engendered envy in other orders and outright fear in kings and popes.

The missionaries threw themselves into their work, establishing missions and building churches in even the most remote areas of the Amazon Basin. In their imposition of Christianity on the Indians of the Americas, the friars simply emulated the campaign against the Moors and the Jews of Iberia of just a few years before: submit or run the risk of execution.

But conversion was not enough. All vestiges of paganism had to be excised. Temples, altars, and palaces were razed wholesale by the Spanish, erasing centuries of pre-Contact civilization, and churches and cathedrals were erected on the sites. The ancient Inca capital of Cuzco particularly suffered from the vandalism of the Spanish.

Above the ruins of the Qorikancha, the Temple of the Sun, the most sacred site in the Inca Empire, the Dominicans erected the church and convent of Santo Domingo.

The Convent of Santa Catalina was erected on the ruins of the destroyed Acllawasi, the dwelling of the Virgins of the Sun, who figured prominently in the worship of Inti, the Sun God.

The Cathedral of Cuzco, also dedicated to Santo Domingo, was built on the foundation of the palace of the Inca Viracocha, the father of Pachacutec Inca Yupanqui. And on the ruins of the palace of the great Inca Pachacutec himself, the Franciscans built the immense Iglesia San Francisco.

The Jesuits, however, were not to be outdone. Across the square from the Cathedral, on the site of the destroyed palace of the Inca Huayna Capac, they built their grandiose Templo de la Compañia de Jesús. This church was destroyed in 1650 by an earthquake, but it was replaced by an even more elaborate edifice, which, with its famous gilded altar, exacerbated even further the ill feelings toward the order.

The Jesuits may very well have been guilty of architectural pomp and decorative excess, but their defense of the natives and advocacy for their rights as human beings created even more serious problems for the order. Their task was made more difficult by economic realities.

The American colonies of Spain and Portugal were the chief source of wealth for the mother countries. Therefore a steady supply of labor was essential to keep the mines and plantations operating, and the major source of this labor was the indigenous population.

The task of the defense of the Indians was complicated for the friars in that many of their superiors and not a few of their colleagues aided and abetted the enslavement and exploitation of the Indians even though Pope Paul III, in the papal bull Sublimus Dei in 1537, forbade the enslavement of the indigenous peoples of the Americas. Charles V, who was both holy Roman emperor and king of Spain, shared the moral qualms of his grandmother, Queen Isabella, in regard to the Indians, and he followed the pontiff's lead, as did the devout John III of Portugal.

Charles was not so morally punctilious when it came to the blacks from Africa who were toiling in his possessions. Twenty years before, in 1518, he had made black slavery legal.

But the Spanish and Portuguese colonies were a vast distance from the courts in Lisbon and Madrid and the Holy See in Rome. There in the mines and on the plantations life proceeded as before, especially in Brazil, where a group with no rights and no protection from popes or monarchs had been introduced in 1539—African slaves from Guinea.

The Jesuits, under the aegis of both Charles V and John III, advocated resettling the Indians in settlements, called reductions, which were a form of commune not unlike the missions that were set up later in the American Southwest. Here they would lead a more settled life, supporting themselves by agriculture, hunting, and fishing. Also, and this was of overriding importance, in reductions the Indians could be more easily indoctrinated with Christianity.

The reductions also had the advantage of isolating the natives from their more worldly European neighbors and their immoral blandishments. But besides conversion of the natives to the Christian faith and the supervision of their souls, the Jesuits had another, equally important argument for such settlements. In these reductions, the natives would be safe from the depredations of the slave traders, particularly the Portuguese, who ignored papal bulls and royal decrees.

Such an arrangement assumed, as a matter of course, that the natives needed such protection because of their childlike ways and their innate inferiority to Europeans. Bartolomé de Las Casas, a Dominican preacher and fiery advocate of native rights, rejected such thinking.

Las Casas was born in Seville in 1484, and little is known of his life until 1502, when at age eighteen he went out to the recently established colony on Hispaniola in the Caribbean. Apparently the family had land there that had been given to his father, one of the colonists who had accompanied Columbus on his second voyage in 1493.

The young Las Casas was repelled by the rapacity and cruelty of the Spaniards toward the natives on Hispaniola and later on Cuba, which he witnessed firsthand and would write about with ferocious clarity years later in his *A Short Account of the Destruction of the Indies*.

As a settler in the Spanish possessions in the Americas, Las Casas was himself a beneficiary of the encomienda system, which entitled him to land and Indians. However, revolted by the treatment of the Indians, he became an acolyte of a Dominican friar, Antonio de Montesinos, who preached against the mistreatment of the natives.

Montesinos shocked the congregants at the mass on the first Sunday of Advent in 1511 when he told them that their treatment of the Indians was a mortal sin and their very souls were thus in danger.

Soon after Montesinos left for Spain to plead the cause of the Indians directly to the authorities, and at a conference at Burgos he was able to present his arguments for humane treatment of the Indians directly to King Ferdinand himself.

Others argued, using Aristotle as their source, that if certain people were born to be slaves, as Aristotle contended, the barbarians of the New World certainly qualified.

Montesinos and the others who argued for the humane treatment of these new subjects of the crown carried the day, and in December 1512, the Laws of Burgos were adopted, with the full endorsement of Ferdinand. The laws set out the rules for Christianizing the natives, instructing them in the ways of the Church, and ensuring their physical and spiritual well-being.

As the historian Hugh Thomas observed, "These laws began an intellectual revolution." He also added, "The practical consequences were more uncertain." [2] As indeed, they were. If the Indians were made good Christians, they could not be exploited or abused or enslaved. Opposition was widespread and immediate.

Meanwhile, Las Casas, who was now an ordained priest, and as such forfeited any claim to either property or slaves, returned to Spain, where he immediately took up the cause of the indigenous peoples.

Las Casas had one meeting with Ferdinand, who was as sympathetic as he had been with Montesinos, but the king's sudden death seemed to be a serious blow to further reform.

However, Las Casas soon found perhaps an even more powerful and sympathetic patron at court, Cardinal Francisco Jiménez de Cisneros, primate of Spain, head of the Inquisition, and, with the death of Ferdinand, regent for the kingdom until the sixteen-year-old prince, the future Charles V, could assume the throne.

Las Casas's compelling accounts of the terrible events he had witnessed on Hispaniola and Cuba resulted in his being sent back to the Antilles by the cardinal as a member of an investigative commission.

It is doubtful that any measures taken by the commission, short of total emancipation and integration into society of the Indians, could have satisfied Las Casas, and he returned to Spain disappointed at what he considered barely adequate reforms recommended by the commission. However, another problem made any reforms moot. There were hardly any Indians left to protect. Most of them had died off, victims of disease or abuse.

Las Casas soon returned to the Americas, this time to Cumaná, in

Venezuela, where he had been given a new land grant, which it was hoped could be administered according to his own enlightened views. The experiment came to naught when the Indians, presumably not his own, revolted and Las Casas was forced to flee to Hispaniola (Santo Domingo), to the Dominican monastery where he had first heard Montesinos preach and where he remained until 1535.

The twelve years at Santo Domingo were not fallow ones, however. Las Casas joined the Dominican Order and began work on the two provocative books that made him famous or infamous, depending upon the reader—*In Defense of the Indians* and *A Short Account of the Destruction of the Indies*.

Neither work was completed until after his final return to Spain in 1547—after further adventures in the New World, which included an aborted journey to Peru. Las Casas was now sixty-three years old.

*A Short Account of the Destruction of the Indies*, which appeared in 1552, has been credited as the basis for the so-called Black Legend—that the Spanish systematically pillaged, raped, murdered, and exterminated wholesale the native populations of the New World—a view that has more or less dominated accounts of the Conquest and settlement of the New World for five centuries. The book, dedicated to Prince Philip, who would succeed his father Charles V, is indeed inflammatory.

In a synopsis that begins the book—the author clearly was taking no chances that the twenty-five-year-old prince's attention would stray—Las Casas gets right to the point:

*Everything that has happened since the marvellous discovery of the Americas—from the short-lived initial attempts of the Spanish to settle there, right down to the present day—has been so extraordinary that the whole story remains quite incredible to anyone has not experienced it at first hand. It seems, indeed, to overshadow all the deeds of famous men of the past, no matter how heroic, and to silence all talk of other wonders of the world. Prominent amid the aspects of this story which have caught the*

*imagination are the massacres of innocent peoples, the atrocities committed
against them and, among other horrific excess, the ways in which towns,
provinces, and whole kingdoms have been entirely cleared of their native
inhabitants.*[3]

Las Casas is clearly condemning the conquest and destruction of Mexico and the Aztecs by Hernán Cortés and the subjugation and decimation of the Inca Empire by Francisco Pizarro.

The subtitle of the second of Las Casa's famous treatises, *In Defense of the Indians*, lays out perfectly Las Casas's views and what he hoped to achieve—*The Defense of the Most Reverend Lord, Don Fray Bartolomé de Las Casas, of the Order of Preachers, Late Bishop of Chiapa, Against the Persecutors and Slanderers of the Peoples of the New World Discovered Across the Seas.*

In the book Las Casas argues forcefully that the Indians are entitled to the respect and dignity that we should accord any of our fellow human beings and that we would expect for ourselves. Such advocacy could only anger the encomenderos and plantation owners in the New World as well as their confederates in Spain.

Chief among them was Juan Ginés de Sepúlveda, a fellow Dominican, who in a famous debate with Las Casas at Valladolid in 1550–1551 argued that the Indians were innately inferior to Europeans and should be subdued and converted to Christianity by force if necessary.

Neither side can be said to have won what has been called the Valladolid Controversy, although Las Casas's arguments brought attention to the plight of the Indians, not always for the better as it turned out.

In South America, there was immediate backlash, and Las Casas was vilified. A civil war broke out between the encomenderos and the viceroyal government over the New Laws abolishing the encomienda system.

The fight was bitter, but the government forces prevailed, and the political system remained intact. The Indians, however, were still subjected to harsh treatment and little protection, and slavery would continue until well into the nineteenth century in South America.

Bartolomé de Las Casas's ideas had lit the flame of abolition, even though his reputation was tarnished by his endorsement of the enslavement of black Africans to replace the Indian laborers. Indeed, Las Casas had taken seven black slaves with him on his abortive mission to found a settlement in Venezuela.

To his credit, "The Defender and Apostle to the Indians" did reverse his view of blacks, and he strongly, even vehemently, later came to defend them as well. They were, he said, equally deserving of the rights and privileges that he had long expounded for the Native Americans.

Not until the twentieth century was Las Casas widely recognized as the seminal figure that he was, not just for his role as defender and apostle to the Indians, but as a precursor of the movement known today as liberation theology, which redefined politics in South America in the twentieth century.

In its simplest form liberation theology held that it is incumbent upon Christians to advance the cause of the poor and oppressed and not shy away from political activism to achieve this goal. Its often overt socialism, even Marxism, ran counter to the authorities at the Vatican, which was sharply critical of the movement. But popes have not been able to stamp it out, and at least the ideals of liberation theology remain a potent force in politics in the Amazon region.

Theologian Martin Marty wrote that Bartolomé de Las Casas was "a profound and impassioned soul who helps make some issues of the 500-year-old events seem current, still demanding, still urgent."[4]

Bartolomé de Las Casas does indeed still speak to us across the ages. Article 1 of the United Nations Universal Declaration of Human Rights could have been lifted from either of the two works that continue to inspire after five centuries: "All human beings are born free and equal in dignity and rights. They are endowed with reason and conscience and should act towards one another in a spirit of brotherhood."

# The Great Powers
# in the Amazon Basin

*The Struggle for Control*

AMERIGO VESPUCCI, WHO FOR OVER FIVE HUNDRED YEARS HAS BEEN indelibly linked with both the northern and southern halves of the New World—the very name *America* was derived from the Italian navigator's Christian name—has also been a complex and puzzling figure to historians for all of that time as well.

Amerigo's biographer Felipe Fernández-Armesto, in his cheeky and entertaining life of Vespucci, forthrightly says on the very first page that the man "who gave his name to America was a pimp in his youth and a magus in his maturity." [1]

Vespucci was the younger son of a poor but respectable family of

Florence with ties to the ruling Medici, which later would be of great use to Amerigo, who, because of the family's relative poverty, was ever on the lookout for the main chance.

After stumbling along for years in various capacities with the Medici, opportunity seemed finally to have knocked with his employment by Lorenzo di Pierfrancesco de' Medici, a boyhood friend and a cousin of Lorenzo the Magnificent.

Vespucci, who nominally was in charge of collecting debts and selling wine for Lorenzo di Pierfrancesco, was charged by that worthy to sound out replacements to head the Medici establishment in Seville, a city that was increasingly attracting the interest of European investors and businessmen.

Vespucci recommended a fellow Florentine, Gianotto Berardi, who was already established in Seville, and his endorsement of Berardi for the post soon bore fruit for himself as well. By the of end of 1491 or early in 1492, Vespucci had removed to Seville to work for Berardi. He would never return to Italy.

Berardi had already ingratiated himself with the Spanish court, and he had become an ardent advocate and friend of another Italian expatriate, Cristoforo Colombo (Christopher Columbus) of Genoa. Convinced that Columbus's dreams of a westward route to the East would result in untold profits and riches, Berardi ensured that some Medici financing was forthcoming to help in outfitting the ships for the first voyage.

As Berardi's associate, Amerigo too became well acquainted with Columbus and as besotted as he with the idea that the East could be reached by sailing to the west.

From this point, Vespucci's story becomes vastly more complicated because of his genius for self-promotion and reinvention, which sometimes involved not just exaggeration but outright lies. It is a story that has vexed historians for centuries. In letters and documents that appeared between 1500 and 1504, Vespucci wrote of four voyages that he had made to what he would call the New World.

His first voyage left Cádiz on 10 May 1497 and reached the American mainland on 16 June. A second voyage, which sailed from Cádiz on 14 May 1499, supposedly reached the coast of Brazil in late June 1499.

If one were to credit these accounts, Amerigo Vespucci was the first European to set foot in North America and also on the coast of Brazil— giving him priority over John Cabot for North America and both Vicente Yáñez Pinzón and Pedro Álvarez Cabral for Brazil.

Two other voyages supposedly followed, in 1502 and 1503, but as with the first two, the only proofs that they actually occurred are based on Vespucci's questionable writings and, in at least one case, to an alleged, indeed probably an outright, forgery—the 1504 letter to Pier Soderini, gonfaloniere of the Republic of Florence.[2]

Vespucci's claims are particularly hard to credit since in his narratives he passed himself off, variously, as a pilot, as a navigator, or even as a captain—although in 1497 he was forty-three years old and had had no maritime experience.

He may, of course, as his biographers have pointed out, have gone on at least two voyages, but as a passenger, not as an integral or important member of the crew. Later, in the honorable tradition of travel writing, he exaggerated his role, and his adventures, refracting them through the lens of the works of Dante, Homer, Virgil, Petrarch, and Marco Polo, whose works he would have known.

Vespucci's fame or notoriety spring from two documents. The first was a 1503 letter to his old patron Lorenzo di Pierfrancesco de' Medici, which survives in a Latin translation and bears the title *Mundus Novus* or *Epistola Albericii de Novo Mundo*. The second is the famous but question- able Soderini letter, the Latin version of which was widely disseminated. Both of these documents contained Vespucci's startling hypothesis, soon accepted by geographers and scholars, that the new lands across the sea were not the East but a Mundus Novus (a "New World").

A third document, called the Ridolfi fragment after its discoverer, came to light in 1937. Most scholars agree that the fragment, or letter, is authentic, although it is probably a copy of Vespucci's original—a view buttressed by the fact that it is a spirited first-person defense against accusations of his critics that he had not made the voyages in question or, even if he had, he certainly inflated his role in them.

However, some scholars maintain that Vespucci undermined his case in the "fragment" by misstating the number of voyages he alleged that he had made. Others excuse this as simple mistakes or errors in transcription.

Fabulist, liar, mythologizer, or confidence man, or perhaps an honest writer, it matters little. Amerigo Vespucci's name and fame were assured forever when the cartographer Martin Waldseemüller published his famous map, *Universalis Cosmographia*, in 1507, which showed the New World as two continents joined by a narrow isthmus. In an accompanying book, *Cosmographiae Introductio*, Waldseemüller acknowledged using Vespucci's letters and notes.

However, Waldseemüller didn't limit his gratitude to a simple statement praising Vespucci's contributions to geography. In what turned out to be one of the more resonantly unfair actions in history, he named the southern continent depicted on his map not Columbia, or perhaps some other variant of Christopher Columbus's name, but America, a Latinized version of Amerigo. And as if to compound the injury to the great admiral, Waldseemüller's map is emblazoned with a portrait engraving of the usurper Vespucci, alongside a matching portrait of Ptolemy, the great geographer of antiquity, whose work was still the gold standard in 1507.

Waldseemüller's cartographical descendants and heirs continued to apply the name *America* to the New World, and by 1538, with the publication of a map by Gerardus Mercator, on which both the northern and southern continents of the western hemisphere were designated America, "The tradition was secure, the decision irreversible," says Fernández-Armesto.[3]

Poor Columbus was spared the injustice. He died in 1506, still thinking he had found the East and that it would be just a matter of time before Europeans made contact with the imperial courts of China and Japan.

As Columbus biographer Samuel Eliot Morison wryly observed, America was discovered by "a man who was looking for something else" and named for someone who discovered nothing. Such are the vagaries of fortune—according to Morison history is "chancy"—especially if fortune is manipulated by a Renaissance conman aided by a credulous public.

The naming of the New World is an interesting digression, but little more than that—a sidebar to the larger issue of imperial expansion and wealth, the most obvious symbol of which was gold.

The search for gold consumed Columbus's successors, the conquistadors, two of whom, while they did not find the mythical El Dorado, did find gold and silver in such vast quantities that it enabled Spain to rise to a position of unrivaled power in the world.

The first, Hernán Cortés, conquered, subdued, and then destroyed the fabled but very real Aztec Empire in Mexico. Cortés's achievements, while impressive, were just the preamble to an equally celebrated feat of arms by his distant cousin, Francisco Pizarro, who with an even smaller force toppled the Inca's Empire of the Sun in South America.

The Inca Empire was born high in the Andes, along the valleys of the streams that make up the headwaters of the Amazon. Throughout the sixteenth century, the attention of the European powers centered on this area, with its enormous deposits of gold, silver, and emeralds. Indeed, it was not until the early seventeenth century that any serious attempts were made to found settlements along the lower reaches of the river.

The English, Irish, Dutch, and French began to look at the vast coastal floodplain of the Amazon as possible places of expansion, and they established several small settlements there.

Farther north, on the Orinoco, which had been known to Europeans since Columbus discovered it on 1 August 1498, on his third voyage, settlement had come earlier. The area now known as Venezuela saw the first Spanish colonization on the mainland of South America, beginning in the early 1500s. Later in the century, the English, led by Sir Walter Raleigh, attempted to set up a rival colony in Guiana, and to that end Raleigh himself came to South America in 1596.

Raleigh's South American colonial dream came to naught although it was not as disastrous as his North American enterprise of a dozen years earlier. All the inhabitants of that ill-fated settlement in Virginia, on the coast of what is now North Carolina, disappeared without a trace, and it became famous as the Lost Colony.

Raleigh came through the North Carolina fiasco relatively undamaged, and even though the expedition to the Orinoco did not establish any serious English presence in South America, it did result in the *Discoverie of Guiana*, a book that not only burnished Raleigh's literary reputation but firmly planted in the minds of its many readers the legend of El Dorado, to which, it seems, no one was immune, not even the king himself, the scholarly and intelligent James I.

The king who acceded to the throne in 1603 was naturally predisposed to look unfavorably on Raleigh, the erstwhile favorite of his predecessor Elizabeth, and his suspicions were fanned by the host of Raleigh's enemies at court. Raleigh was accused of treason, tried, and sentenced to death.

The sentence was commuted to life in prison, but in 1616, after thirteen years in the Tower, in one of those reversals of fortune that were characteristic of the age and particularly of the life of Sir Walter Raleigh, he was released by the king and charged to go again to Guiana to search for gold and El Dorado.

James had recently made peace with England's traditional enemy Spain—the memory of the Armada was still fresh in English minds—and he was anxious that no actions be taken that might endanger the shaky truce between the two former bitter enemies and still great rivals. Raleigh, whose life was still forfeit to the whims of the king, readily agreed to do nothing to arouse the Spanish, on whose overseas possessions he would indeed be trespassing.

The expedition arrived off the coast of Venezuela in 1617, but Raleigh was too ill with fever to travel up the Orinoco and stayed behind aboard his ship at Trinidad. Leadership passed to Laurence Keymis, his lieutenant.

The party, which included Raleigh's son Wat, crossed over the narrow strait between Trinidad and the mainland and began the ascent of the Orinoco to look for gold. The situation soon disintegrated.

The English, for vague and ill-defined reasons—anger at not finding any gold or just visceral hatred of the Spanish?—attacked the Spanish settlement at San Tomé. The outpost was sacked and burned, and the Spanish governor was killed. In the assault, Wat Raleigh was killed by a musket ball.

When he heard the news from San Tomé, Raleigh realized that not only had the mission failed but his very life was in danger. As he wrote to his wife, about the duplicitous Keymis, "I told him that he had undone me and my credit was lost forever." [4]

Raleigh's dressing down of his old friend and confederate left Keymis bereft. He went to his own cabin aboard the ill-named *Destiny* and committed suicide. Raleigh was left alone to face the wrath of the king, who wrote to him that his actions had "maliciously broken and infringed the Peace and Amity" between England and Spain. [5]

James, it was said, was in thrall to the Spanish ambassador, the count of Gondomar, who demanded, on behalf of his master Phillip III, that Raleigh be put to death for the outrages against the Spanish settlement on the Orinoco. The English king obliged. Raleigh was arrested and taken to the Tower, from which he was taken on 28 October 1618 to Westminster, where he spent the night in a gatehouse. The next day he climbed the scaffold that had been erected in the Old Palace Yard and was beheaded.

Raleigh's body was buried in St. Margaret's, Westminster. As for his head, the Spanish demand for it was presumably metaphorical, even for that violent age. In any event they were denied that grisly object. It was given to Raleigh's wife, who purportedly kept her husband's embalmed head—and later, after the flesh decomposed, the skull—until she died in 1647, when it passed to her son Carew. Raleigh's head, or at least the skull, was reunited with his body when Carew was entombed near his father at St. Margaret's in 1666.

While Raleigh was going his foolhardy way in Guiana, an attempt was made to found a British colony on the Amazon. Almost immediately it was sacked and burned by the Portuguese. Two other attempts, in 1620 and 1630, suffered similar fates, with the latter coming to a particularly grisly end. No one was allowed to just pack up and leave. Everyone, men, women, and children, was slaughtered.

British interest in the area lying between Brazil and Venezuela waned until the mid-1600s, when Lord Willoughby of Parham took over Paramaribo from the Dutch under the terms of the first of that bewildering series of treaties that awarded the various areas making up Guyana to first one country and then another, mirroring the unrest on the Continent.

The Dutch resumed control within a few years, but the various areas changed hands regularly between the British, the Dutch, and the French until the end of the Napoleonic Wars and the Treaties of Paris (1814, 1815), which brought some order to the chaos.

Britain was given possession of the northwestern area, which in 1966 became the independent Republic of Guyana. The Dutch retained the central section, which in 1975 became the independent Republic of Suriname. As for the French, who were given, or allowed to retain, the southeastern section of historical Guyana, they have been more reluctant to surrender control. French Guyana remains an overseas department of France.

The Guyana Highlands, which lie across Venezuela, Guyana, Suriname, and French Guyana, are an important source of water for the Amazon Basin. Two vital tributaries—the Branco and the Trombetas—originate in the Highlands, as well as the water in the Casiquiare, the connector between the Orinoco and the Amazon basins.

During the centuries that these great power rivalries were playing out on the northern border of the Amazon region, the adversaries, particularly the Dutch, were also attentive to the areas lying to the south.

The Dutch Republic, through the offices of the Dutch West India Company, was a major presence along the coastal areas of Brazil from 1630 until 1654. Indeed, the area was known as Nederlands-Brazilië or Nieuw-Holland or New Holland.

The French who were not bound by the Treaty of Tordesillas had no compunctions about colonizing areas of Brazil and as early as 1555 established a short-lived colony on an island in the bay at present-day Rio de Janeiro. They were driven out by the Portuguese in 1567.

Although the Portuguese for the most part continued to concentrate on the southern and middle sections of their Brazilian colony, in 1616 they established an outpost on the Amazon, Fort Presépio, about sixty miles from the Atlantic, in order to monitor the activities of rival nations that were trading extensively around the mouth of the Amazon and as far as three hundred miles upstream.

In 1612, the French also returned to the game, founding a settlement that they called France Équinoxiale on the site of present-day São Luís. But the Portuguese were quick to react and in 1614 expelled the French settlers. France had now only their colony in Guyana in South America, but in an irony of history, it is today the only European power with a presence on the continent.

And in yet another of those confusing and complicated geographical exchanges of the seventeenth and eighteenth centuries—either by treaty or conquest—São Luís was controlled by the Dutch from 1641 to 1644.

The Portuguese were by tradition as well as by treaty the rulers of Brazil and the Amazon, and they zealously guarded their territorial rights. They also by temperament were scornful of the marginally more enlightened views of the northern Europeans who were trying to encroach upon their territories.

The Dutch, for example, extended protection to Jews and allowed those who had been forced to convert to Christianity not only to return to their faith but to build a synagogue in Recife.

The Portuguese also were disturbed by the view of the Dutch toward the native population, which the Portuguese planters and miners saw only as an inexhaustible supply of slave labor. The Dutch, of course, were infamous slavers themselves, but their consciences seemed to be unbothered if the slaves were African.

The friction between the opposing forces, fueled in part by religion—

one was devoutly Catholic and the other resolutely Protestant—finally led to open warfare, with the Portuguese triumphant. They permanently expelled the Dutch from Brazil in 1654.

Although Portugal controlled the gateway to the Amazon—Fort Presépio had now grown into a proper port, Pará, which in turn would become known as Belém—the Amazon remained something of a stepchild. This changed in 1637 when Spain, the fifth of the great European powers with a presence in South America, and arguably the most important and most powerful, made its presence known.

Further complicating the situation in South America and on the Iberian Peninsula was the fact that since 1580, during the reign of Philip II, Portugal and Spain had been united under a single ruler. The union had from the outset been an uneasy one, although Philip had managed to allay Portuguese fears by granting almost total autonomy to his Portuguese subjects. His successors, Philip III and Philip IV, were not so punctilious, and by 1634 the resentment of the Portuguese had grown into outright rebellion.

Spain's emergence on the Lower Amazon was in the person of two Franciscan priests, who arrived in Belém in a small canoe in 1637. The two padres, Domingo de Brieba and Andres de Toledo, had traveled all the way from their mission in Quito in the viceroyalty of Peru. The Portuguese were not only astonished by the tales that the Franciscans told but also alarmed at the possibility that Spain was already in control of the lands to the west.

Portugal had since the Treaty of Tordesillas assumed that it controlled much more land than the treaty actually allowed, so it was clear that someone needed to be sent upriver to investigate and report on what inroads the Spanish might have made into Portuguese territory.

That someone was Pedro Teixeira, a former governor of Belém who was an old hand at ridding the area of interlopers. He had led the expedition against France Équinoxiale and also had a hand in ridding the Amazon of the English and the Dutch. He was also a notorious slaver and slave trader.

Teixeira left Belém on 28 October 1637 in a flotilla of forty-seven canoes, carrying seventy soldiers and twelve hundred Indians and their families—a total of some two thousand people—and the two Franciscans who had made the arduous journey from Quito and were desirous of returning to their brethren in Peru.

Within a year, Teixeira was in Quito, where he was received guardedly by the viceregal representatives, who were as suspicious of the Portuguese as the Portuguese were of them, in spite of their alleged shared fealty to the crown.

Finally, after much delay, the viceroy at Lima gave his permission for Teixeira and his party to begin their return journey, back across the mountains and down the river to Belém, which they did on 16 February 1639. There was one stipulation: they were to be accompanied by the Jesuit Cristóbal de Acuña, who was charged with producing what in modern times would become known as a "white paper," a detailed description of the river and its environs for the court in Madrid and the Council of the Indies.

In spite of the fact that it had been 139 years since the Spanish had first set foot in the Amazon, almost nothing was known of the river. Acuña was charged to "take particular care to describe, with clearness, the distance in leagues, the provinces, tribes of Indians, rivers, and districts which exist from the first embarkation, to the said city and port of Pará. . . ." [6]

On 12 December 1639, Teixeira and his party arrived back in Pará (Belém), and while awaiting transport to Spain, Acuña whiled away the time by drafting his report on the journey down the Amazon. His *A New Discovery of the Great River of the Amazons* remains one of the richest sources of material on the river and its basin. Nothing it seems escaped the attention of the brilliant and perceptive Jesuit. Animals, birds, insects, fish, river currents, vegetation, minerals, the food, drink, rituals, dress, and religious customs of the Indian tribes, as well as the legends and myths of the region—all were observed, recorded, and commented on. Clearly for Acuña control of the Amazon was vital if Spain was to remain a world power.

Alas for Acuña and Spain when he arrived back in the mother country, the fragile union of Spain and Portugal had passed the point of reconciliation, and Philip IV and the Council of the Indies were in no position to follow through on his call for Spanish hegemony in the Amazon. Indeed the friction between Spain and Portugal enabled the Dutch to reestablish themselves in Brazil, although as we have seen their renewed presence was temporary.

In 1640, the union was dissolved in a bloodless revolution, and the Portuguese monarchy was restored. Even though Portugal was by far the lesser half of the aborted Iberian union, it was now ascendant in a large part of South America.

But Cristóbal de Acuña continued to press his case, and with the publication of his *New Discovery of the Great River of the Amazons* in 1641 he reached a wider audience. He called on the king of Spain to exercise his clear right to the Amazon and wrest the entire river, from the Andes to the Atlantic, from the usurpers—"to put a bridle on the insolence of the Portuguese, and they will be driven from the mouth of this river," as the good father rather indelicately put it.[7]

Acuña listed many reasons for Spain to establish hegemony over the Amazon from Peru to the Atlantic, not least of which was that it would be the fulfillment of a dream, indeed an obligation of all Spanish monarchs, which dated back to the time of Charles V.

The Jesuit was also concerned with the souls of the indigenous peoples, which was only a minor concern of the Portuguese with "their small amount of Christianity," as Acuña sneeringly wrote.[8] His fellow Iberians were more interested in enslaving the Indians.

But Acuña's suggestions also had a more practical end than dynastic sentiment or the protection of the indigenous peoples. The wealth from the viceroyalty of Peru, which was continuing to pour into Spain, had to be taken up the west coast of South America, then across the Isthmus of Panama before being loaded onto ships, where it was always subject to the depredations of the pirates who lay in wait along the Spanish Main.

Would it not be better, Acuña argued, for this treasure to be transported across the mountains and then transported down the Amazon to Belém, from whence it would be taken across the Atlantic to Spain? There would be still some danger involved, but there would be an immense saving in time.

It was not to be. The political situation in Europe had foreclosed any extension of Spanish power beyond what Madrid already controlled in South America, which was a vast swath of territory indeed. But Pedro Teixeira's expedition resulted in the extension of Portuguese territory more than a thousand miles beyond the limits, however ill-defined they were, of the Treaty of Tordesillas.

Portugal now had de facto, if not de jure control of the Amazon from its mouth to the Tres Fronteras, where the borders of Peru, Colombia, and Brazil meet near Tabatinga. The situation was codified in 1750 by the Treaty of Madrid, which recognized, according to Roman law, *Uti possidetis, ita possideatis,* "who owns by fact owns by right," Portugal's right to the entire area. The 1494 Treaty of Tordesillas—"More honor'd in the breach than the observance"—was finally laid to rest.

The Portuguese colony of Brazil thus came to comprise 43 percent of the land area of the continent of South America. The great river was now firmly under Portuguese control and would remain so until 1822, when Brazil declared its independence from Portugal.

Unlike its neighbors, whose independence grew out of the revolutionary fervor that had begun with Bonaparte and spread to the New World, Brazil's break with Portugal resulted from the prince regent and the Portuguese court fleeing Lisbon in 1807 after Napoleon's invasion and taking refuge at Rio de Janeiro.

With the presence of the prince regent and the court—the queen, who was insane, remained behind in Portugal—Brazil was the seat of the Portuguese government and remained so until 24 April 1821, when John, who was now King John VI, set sail for Lisbon. His return was deemed essential to prevent Portugal from sliding into complete anarchy after the collapse of Bonapartism and a flirtation with dictatorship.

The new Portuguese king left behind his son, Dom Pedro, as regent, but the Brazilians themselves had become infected with independence fever, and bowing to popular sentiment on 7 September 1822, Dom Pedro proclaimed that the colony henceforth was an independent country.

The monarchical traditions were not so easily dispensed with, however. Brazil did not become just a country but an empire, and on 1 December Dom Pedro was crowned emperor. His rule lasted a scant nine years. In 1831, he abdicated in favor of his five-year-old son, and Brazil was ruled by a quasi-regency until fourteen-year-old Dom Pedro II acceded to the throne in 1840. He ruled until his own forced abdication in 1889, when Brazil became, at least in name, a republic.

The political and sociological changes wrought during this time, while of great moment along the seacoasts, at first were barely discernible along the Amazon, where life continued much as before. However, beginning in the 1850s, with the introduction of the steamboat and the beginning of the rubber boom, change swift and incalculable came to the region.

But a third movement was sweeping the region, and its effect was, indeed, of vast import, particularly in the hitherto insulated and isolated regions of the Amazon Basin—the abolition of slavery. The great landowners, planters, and rubber barons naturally fought against freeing the slaves, but Amazonas was one of the first regions to do so, in 1884. The rest of the country followed suit, and by 1888 abolition was total.

As we shall see, there was a great gap between abolition and true freedom for the almost one million enslaved Brazilians and their descendants. The "peculiar institution" was never completely eliminated. Vestiges remain even in the twenty-first century.

While the revolutions of the nineteenth century marked an end to outright great power rivalry in South America and the Amazon, the struggle was by no means at an end. Instead it just became more subtle, cloaked in the arcana of economics, trade, and that most shifting of late twentieth-century shibboleths, globalization. Brazil and the Amazon Basin were thrust into the forefront because of the vast natural resources of the region and its new role as a leading producer of food for an ever-increasing world population.

# CHAPTER 6

# Nature's Grand Laboratory

*European Science Discovers the Amazon*

THE MERE MENTION OF THE WORD *Amazon* CONJURES UP IMAGES OF an impenetrable jungle populated by giant snakes and jaguars, streams teeming with small fish that can reduce large animals to skeletons in a matter of minutes, and Indians padding softly through the dense undergrowth carrying curare-tipped arrows and spears. Or the Amazon is defined by conquistadors, explorers, adventurers, and not a few mad men.

However, the story is also filled with the exploits of a generally, but not always, more self-effacing group of men. Indeed, some of them were every bit as brave as the more colorful archetypes of Amazonian history. And many of them became towering figures in the history of science.

The first practicing scientist who saw in the Amazon a fertile natural laboratory was the Frenchman Charles-Marie de La Condamine, who traversed the river from the Andes to the Atlantic in 1743. The trip was a long-planned pendant, a dénouement, to a larger scientific expedition that set out from France in 1735.

La Condamine was a member of the minor nobility, and like many young men of his class he had tried for a success in the military, where he distinguished himself for his bravery. But he soon abandoned the army for a career in the sciences and became an adjunct to the French Academy.

On the strength of a report to the Academy on his travels throughout the Middle East, La Condamine was appointed to a commission that it was hoped would settle the great scientific question of the day: what was the shape of the earth?

Was the planet a spheroid that was flattened at the poles, as Isaac Newton had postulated? Or was it, as Jacques Cassini and his followers held, a prolate spheroid, elongated at the poles and cinched at its waist—the equator?

Two expeditions were being dispatched—one to South America to measure an arc of several degrees of meridian at the equator and another to Lapland to make similar observations. When their measurements were compared, it was hoped the question would be answered definitively.

The expedition to Lapland was just that, a scientific expedition with no political overtones. The expedition to South America was very different from any other that had embarked for that continent. It had no interest in gold, silver, or the saving of souls. Its purpose was only to observe and record.

And particularly of note, the expedition was made up of non-Iberians. With the exception of pirates and freebooters, few people who were not Spanish or Portuguese had set foot in the areas of South America controlled by these two nations—which included all of the continent except the sparsely populated and largely ignored Guianas—since the Treaty of Tordesillas in 1494.

La Condamine and his group of fellow measurer-surveyors, which included Pierre Bouguer, Louis Godin, and Joseph de Jussieu, sailed from La Rochelle for South America in May 1735. After many delays and bureaucratic fumblings, the commission, which had traveled across the Isthmus of Panama and then sailed south along the Pacific Coast, arrived in Quito, in the viceroyalty of Peru, in June 1736.

The expedition throughout its long stay in Peru was rent by infighting, feuds, and at least one murder—a Peruvian mob stabbed to death one of the Frenchmen who was having a very public affair with a local woman—and by the time their work was finished, their professional relationships were effectively wrecked. But their work, which took seven years to complete and another two years before it was published, helped vanquish the Cartesians and Cassinians. The expedition to Lapland had already established the correct shape of the earth, but the expedition to Peru provided additional and final proof. Newton's view was triumphant.

With their work in Peru finished, the commissioners went their decidedly different ways, although Louis Godin, who had run up enormous debts during his time in Peru, was refused permission to leave until he had satisfied his creditors. He was obliged to stay on at Lima, where he taught mathematics at the University of San Marcos. He did not leave for Europe until 1751. He had been away for sixteen years.

Bouguer left Peru in 1743 and returned to France by going overland to Bogotá, a more difficult journey than the more expeditious coastal route, and then down the Río Magdalena to Cartagena. He arrived back in Paris in 1744.

Jussieu, because of his medical expertise, was obliged to stay on because of a smallpox epidemic. Also, as he was incapable of not answering the call of the wild, he wanted to explore further the rain forest with its flora and fauna, the mountain ranges, the mining industry, and anything else that took his fancy. He did not return to France until 1771, after an absence of thirty-six years.

Long before the commission's work was finished in Peru, La Condamine had begun to plan his own return to Europe by a more dramatic route. He would strike out across the Andes and travel down the Amazon to the Atlantic, where he would take ship for France. He began his great adventure in May 1743.

La Condamine crossed the cordillera, heading southeast for the mission at Borja on the Río Marañón. Just above the mission, the party had to negotiate the dangerous rapids in the Pongo de Manseriche, the two-thousand-feet-deep gorge that cuts through the cordillera, before settling into a more leisurely course as it wends its way to its junction with the Ucayali to form the Amazon proper. The Frenchman was now in the vast Amazon Rain Forest.

At the mission of Lagunas, La Condamine was joined by a kindred spirit. Don Pedro Maldonado, the governor of the province of Esmeraldas, had welcomed La Condamine when he first arrived in Peru in 1736, and the two had become fast friends. The governor was himself an amateur scientist of wide-ranging interests, and it had been arranged that he would join La Condamine on his journey down the Amazon. He had been awaiting La Condamine at Lagunas for six weeks.

The two men set forth in a large canoe, and for mile after mile everything was new and interesting. But even the most dedicated of scientists and observers can sometimes nod off, and this true son of the Enlightenment was no exception. As he said, much of his work was busy work, designed to counter "the tiresomeness of a weary, though tranquil, voyage through a country in which the continued sameness of objects, however novel in themselves, tended to fatigue rather than please the eye." [1]

In his baggage, La Condamine was carrying two products, which while he had not been the first European to encounter he was the first practicing scientist to study—*quinquina* (quinine) and *caoutchouc* (rubber).

In Peru, he had been apprised of the medicinal qualities of quinine, which had been known for centuries by the Indians and used for a hundred years by the Creoles in Peru. He also saw the practical uses for caoutchouc, that it was not just a novelty for making balls that bounced. It was useful for making waterproof cloth and carrying sacks for his equipment.

La Condamine also observed the Indian tribes and their use of curare to stun or kill fish or animals or even each other, and his many astronomical observations were also remarkably accurate given the instruments and the knowledge of the time.

But it is as proselytizer that La Condamine is most important in any study of the Amazon. His firsthand account of his travels and observations in the Amazon further fed the European fascination for the still New World.

And for sheer exoticism and mystery, the Amazon easily trumped all other areas of the Western Hemisphere. Its birds and flowers were more numerous and brighter. Rubber and quinine were perhaps just the beginning of the discovery of valuable products. Strange tribes dwelled along the riverbanks, using rare poisons on the tips of their arrows to kill or stun prey. Massive snakes did indeed hang from the trees and glide through the waters. Large tigerlike cats patrolled the forest, along with giant rodents, sloths, monkeys, and anteaters. And if they existed anywhere, could not the eponymous Amazons be at home there as well?

The French mission to measure several degrees of an arc of the meridian in Peru had a more romantic dimension than most scientific enterprises, and the story captivated Europe in the late eighteenth century.

# CHAPTER 7

# The Peruvian Evangeline

*The Journey of María Isabel de Jesus Gramesón y Godin*

IN EARLY JANUARY 1770, AS TWO INDIANS PREPARED TO LAUNCH their canoe from their campsite on the Río Bobonaza in Peru, they were startled to see a small figure—barefoot, clothes shredded, hair matted, features swollen and distorted from sunburn and insect bites, the skin a mass of scratches and bruises—stagger out of the dense forest bordering the river.

As the apparition came closer, they were astonished to see that it was a woman, and not one of their own but a middle-aged white woman. They were further amazed when she spoke to them in Quechua.

Who was she and how had she come to this desolate spot on the banks of the Bobonaza?

THE WOMAN WHO HAD SO IMPROBABLY emerged from the rain forest bordering the Bobonaza was María Isabel de Jesus Gramesón y Godin, the sheltered daughter of an aristocratic family in the viceroyalty of Peru. Her maternal ancestors were descended from Alfonso XI of Spain and were among the first permanent settlers in the viceroyalty. Her father, Don Pedro Gramesón y Bruno, was a military officer who had come out to Peru in the 1720s with the new Spanish viceroy.

Soon after his arrival he married into the family descended from Spanish royalty, and their connections and his own to the viceroy assured his success in both business and colonial society. He not only advanced in the military but was appointed governor of Otavalo, near Quito. His position was thus secure both financially and socially.

It was expected that his daughter Isabel would marry well, and every effort was made to ensure this would be so. As with all females of the upper class, Isabel knew only a protective and closed society and at age six was sent to a convent school, where she would remain for the next six years.

But this sheltered child early on exhibited an independent streak, which became even more pronounced when she left the care of the nuns and returned to her family. The Gramesóns immediately set about to marry her off to one of the scions of the local gentry or, better yet, to a young man from Spain, which was considered a step up the social ladder by the Creoles of South America.

Isabel, however, demurred. From an early age she had become much interested in French language and culture. Her paternal grandfather was French—the original name was Grandmaison—and the family had maintained their connections in that country. She was fluent in French and often expressed a desire to travel to France, perhaps even live there someday. Besides her native language, Spanish, and French, Isabel knew Portuguese and Quechua, the language of the indigenous people of Peru.

When she was thirteen, an age when most Peruvian girls of her class were either affianced or already married, her dreams seemed within reach, in the person of a young Frenchman, Jean Godin des Odonais, who had come to Peru in 1736 as part of the French expedition to measure the arc of the meridian. One of the three leaders of the expedition was Louis Godin, Jean's cousin.

Along with his countrymen, Jean was welcomed into Peruvian society, and he had been entertained many times at the Casa Gramesón well before Isabel returned from the convent.

When the twenty-seven-year-old Jean met the thirteen-year-old Isabel, he was immediately captivated. She was not only charming, she could talk to him in his native language. The Gramesóns no doubt disapproved of such an alliance. Godin was only an assistant on the grand scientific expedition and clearly was penniless or nearly so. But Isabel was determined, her father was won over, and the courtship proceeded according to the rules and customs and strictures of colonial Spanish society.

Jean and Isabel were married the following year, on 29 December 1741, at the Dominican College of San Fernando in Quito. Within less than a year, she had given birth to their first child, a girl. She was fourteen.

The arrival of the Godins' child coincided with Jean's final work for the French expedition, and he began to bid farewell to his colleagues, in particular to Charles-Marie de La Condamine, who had become something of mentor to the young assistant.

La Condamine planned to return to France by a rather unusual route. Not for him the journey by ship up the west coast of South America, then the traversal of the Isthmus of Panama to a port on the Atlantic. He would first cross the Andean cordillera and thence down the smaller rivers to the Amazon and on to the Atlantic.

Jean Godin planned to follow the same route when he returned to France with his wife and child, which he hoped would be in the very near future. It was not to be.

The Godins' infant daughter lived just four months, and after a devastating plague hit Quito and the surrounding area in 1744, the entire Gramesón ménage, with Isabel again pregnant, departed for what was hoped was the more salubrious atmosphere of the town of Riobamba some one hundred miles south of Quito.

The Gramesóns and Godins might have felt safer fleeing the epidemic that killed some eight thousand people, but the climate and air of Riobamba can have been only marginally different from that of Quito, which actually lies some hundred meters higher than Riobamba.

Jean and Isabel still planned to remove to France, but their dream was deferred year after year, with more pregnancies, more infant deaths, and increasing indebtedness. Finally, after years of delay, the decision to begin the move to France could no longer be delayed. Late in 1748, Jean received news of the death of his father. He therefore had to return to France in order to settle his estate. He immediately set about preparing for the journey.

He first would cross the Andes cordillera, travel down the Amazon to the Atlantic, thence to Cayenne, in the French colony of Guiana, marking his path and suitable stopping places as he went. He would then travel back up the river, recross the Andes to Riobamba, collect his relatives, and then return the way he had come. If all went well, the three Andes–Amazon journeys, which totaled some ten thousand miles, would take at least two years, followed by the final stage—the transatlantic voyage from Guiana to France.

If Godin's plans for the move seem the ultimate folly now—indeed they bordered on madness—they must have seemed even more so in the mid-eighteenth century, at least in European circles. But as he observed years later in a letter to La Condamine, "Any one but you, Sir, might be surprised at my undertaking thus lightly a voyage of fifteen hundred leagues, for the mere purpose of preparing accommodations for a second; but you will know that travels in that part of the world are undertaken with much less concern than in Europe. . . ." Besides, he added, he had spent twelve years working for the commission to measure the arc of the meridian in more extreme situations, which had him "perfectly a veteran."[1]

On 10 March 1749, Jean Godin bade good-bye to Isabel, who was again pregnant, and began the trek across the South American continent. His optimism seemed justified. The first half of his two-year plan unfolded without a major incident or setback. He arrived in Cayenne in April the following year, 1750.

His return was immediately beset with problems. As a French citizen he was, he discovered, forbidden to reenter Portuguese territory. Thus began the laborious process of obtaining documents from three countries—France, Portugal, and Spain—that would allow him to begin the return journey from Cayenne to the viceroyalty of Peru in order retrieve his wife and family and bring them to Guiana to embark for France.

Godin had throughout his life made himself useful to the rich and powerful, and this talent was now to be fully employed, at least as much as it was possible to be in the turbulent 1750s and 1760s. He not only cultivated La Condamine but also sent along a grammar of the Incas to the great naturalist the Comte de Buffon as well as seeds for the French king's garden. The king reciprocated by directing the governor and intendant at Cayenne to assist Godin with the authorities at Belém in Brazil.

La Condamine now inserted himself into the process, and Godin was assured that the passports had been forwarded to the governor of Pará. However, when Godin wrote to the governor at Belém, that estimable gentleman replied that he knew nothing of the affair. There thus began years of correspondence with various authorities, with the exiled Godin becoming increasingly desperate.

His personal problems were of no concern to the authorities, however. The Seven Years' War—which has rightly been called the first world war—had begun in 1756. Personal events and concerns were now subsumed by conflict that involved all of Europe and the possessions in the New World. France was at war with England, and the other two countries—Spain and Portugal—with which Godin had to deal were soon drawn into the conflict on opposing sides.

With the end of hostilities in 1763, Godin was able to renew his suit to return to Peru, and his efforts were rewarded in 1765. In the autumn of that year, a galliot, a small vessel powered by thirty oars, arrived at Cayenne. The vessel had been ordered dispatched by no less a personage than Jose I, the King of Portugal, to deliver Godin to Belém and thence up the river as far as the first Spanish settlement. From there he would continue overland to Riobamba.

Godin left Cayenne on board the galliot in November 1765, but at a stopover down the coast of Guiana at the fort at Oyapock, he was stricken ill. After six weeks, it was clear that he would not be able to continue on, and fearful that the mission would be canceled, he prevailed upon the captain to accept a deputy in his stead and to proceed down the coast and up the Amazon.

Godin entrusted Tristan D'Oreasaval, an old and trusted confidant, to act as his surrogate. D'Oreasaval agreed to deliver a packet containing letters and orders from the father-general of the Jesuits, directing the provincial of Quito and the Jesuit superiors of the missions en route to notify his wife in Riobamba that a galliot was waiting for her at Tabatinga in order to carry her to Cayenne and a reunion with her husband. The priests and missionaries were to provide all necessary canoes and equipment for the journey.

The galliot left Oyapock 24 January 1766 and arrived at Loreto on the Amazon some six months later, where D'Oreasaval disembarked. The captain then turned the galliot back downriver to Tabatinga, as ordered, to await Mme. Godin and her party.

D'Oreasaval's charge was to proceed to Laguna and there contact the Jesuit superior who was to set the plan in motion for Mme. Godin to cross the mountains to the waiting vessel. Instead, D'Oreasaval turned the travel documents and letters over to a Jesuit missionary who was traveling to Quito and remained at Loreto, where he set up a trading facility.

Eventually, word percolated through the religious community in Peru that a Portuguese vessel sent to fetch Isabel Godin was tied up in the Amazon on the other side of the cordillera and that a missionary had brought documents and letters addressed to her.

Isabel's brother, an Augustinian friar, set about determining the truth of the matter and was able to locate the Jesuit missionary, who relayed the sad news that the documents, alas, had been passed on to yet another messenger and probably even a third or fourth for delivery. There was clearly no hope of locating the packet, and therefore her family was loath to allow Isabel to set out to meet the supposed galliot.

A faithful black slave named Joachim and two Indians were sent across the mountains to Loreto to try to found out the truth of the matter. Their mission ended in failure—they were unable to cross the cordillera and descend the river—and the three returned to Riobamba.

Mme. Godin was not to be deterred. She again dispatched the family retainer across the Andes, and this time he succeeded in reaching Loreto and finding the duplicitous D'Oreasaval, who assured him that what they had heard was true. There was, indeed, a galliot waiting at Tabatinga.

When the servant returned with the joyful news that after twenty years Isabel and Jean might be reunited, arrangements began at once to dispose of possessions, sell property, pack up what was necessary for the journey, and leave Peru.

Isabel would be accompanied by her two brothers, the aforementioned Augustinian friar, and the other, a businessman, who would bring along his young son to be educated in France. Isabel also would have three Indian women to attend her en route.

In addition there were thirty-one others in the party, whose duties included setting up the campsites, collecting wood, cooking, and perhaps most important of all, taking turns carrying Isabel across the mountains.

A French physician, at least that is how he presented himself, and two companions who were anxious to return to Europe also asked to travel with them, and after much discussion it was agreed that it might be a good idea to have a medical man along on such a difficult journey. The three Frenchmen were allowed to come along.

Much as Jean Godin had done so many years ago, Isabel's father, Pedro Gramesón, had left Riobamba a month earlier to scout out the route and ensure that his daughter would be well looked after on her own journey.

The proposed route led across the Andean cordillera to the embarkation point at Canelos on the Río Bobonaza. From this mission station and Indian village, they would travel by canoe and raft down the Bobonaza to its confluence with the Pastaza, then on to the Marañón, which joins with the Ucayali to form the Amazon proper.

If all went according to plan, Señor Gramesón would await his daughter, his two sons, and his grandson at Tabatinga, the rendezvous on the Amazon, where the captain and crew of the Portuguese galliot had been waiting for over three years.

At last, all was in order. On 1 October 1769, more than twenty years after she had bade farewell to her husband, a caravan transporting the now forty-two-year-old Isabel Godin left Riobamba for the longed-for reunion with Jean.

Some of the men in the party traveled on horseback. The heavy baggage, personal possessions, and foodstuffs were loaded onto mules.

Women of Isabel's class would have ordinarily traveled by carriage or sedan chair in colonial Peru. She therefore may have left Riobamba in the relative comfort of one of these conveyances, most probably a sedan chair, but such conveyances were not just impractical but impossible on the narrow and rugged paths that her party must eventually negotiate across the cordillera.

For such routes a less grand means of transport but one much used for travel on rough terrain by the upper classes in colonial South America was employed—the *silla*. As the name implies, the silla was a simple, but often padded, wooden chair, which was attached, facing to the rear, to the back of a porter. The carrier then leaned forward and a tumpline was wrapped across the top of his head.

Carrying the petite Isabel across even the lower reaches of the Andes required that a porter be spelled every few hours or miles. And as the terrain became rougher, the task became commensurately so. Therefore, even the men on horseback had to accommodate the slower pace of the porters.

As the crow flies, the distance is only about sixty miles. But the heavily forested lower reaches of the cordillera are laced with countless streams, rivulets, and gullies, and the party often had to ascend further up the slopes to find places narrow or shallow enough to ford or build rough bridges across. Thus the trip from Riobamba to Canelos took a week's time.

When Don Pedro had passed through Canelos in early September, he had found a thriving mission and community. When Isabel's party arrived there around 8 October, they found nothing but desolation.

Smallpox, the scourge of the indigenous peoples of the Americas, had ravaged the settlement. The survivors, believing that fire would eliminate the pestilence, had burned the village to the ground and fled into the forest. Worse, the promised canoes and raft that had been hired by Don Pedro to transport them downriver were nowhere to be found.

After spending the night in the ruins, the party awoke to discover that their hired porters and attendants had also fled, fearing that they themselves would become victims of the plague. Isabel, her two brothers, her nephew, the three Frenchmen, and four loyal servants were alone.

The next day, four Indians, who had survived the epidemic but had not fled, were found nearby. They were also able to locate a raft and a canoe. Isabel at once hired the Indians as guides and pilots, and the remaining goods and food were loaded aboard the two vessels. The party, now comprising fifteen people, prepared to embark the next morning.

When day broke, however, the party had again been reduced to eleven. The Indians, whom the trusting Isabel had paid in advance for their services, had disappeared into the forest.

There was some discussion as to whether they should terminate the journey and retrace their path and return to Riobamba, but Isabel dismissed this out of hand. They would proceed.

There was some reason for her optimistic outlook. The river facing them, although fast flowing, was broad and appeared relatively benign. And did they not now have transport enough to carry them along to the mission of Andoas, five days' travel downstream?

Not be discounted was her overriding desire—indeed, the very reason for the journey—to be reunited with her husband, for whom she had waited twenty years. Nothing would dissuade her from pressing on. Thus, on or about 10 October 1769, the canoe and raft, which presumably carried the majority of the party, were launched on the Río Bobonaza, with one of the Frenchmen acting as pilot in the canoe.

Disaster was not long in coming. As the canoe sped along, a gust of wind tore off the French pilot's hat. As he reached out to retrieve it, he fell overboard and was drowned. His replacement as pilot did not manage the canoe as well, and the craft overturned after hitting a log. Everyone was thrown into the water.

All were saved, but much of the equipment and food was lost. The canoe was salvaged, however, which prompted the physician to propose that he and the faithful Joachim proceed aboard it to Andoas, which was now only four days distant, to seek help. It was reckoned that a rescue party could be back to the campsite on the river in ten days or so.

With their departure, Isabel, her brothers, her nephew, her three women servants, and the young servant of the French physician, who had left him behind, were now effectively stranded on a sandspit on the Bobonaza. And there they would remain for more than three weeks, until Isabel, realizing that help was not forthcoming, again took charge.

At her direction, the party began to assemble another raft, on which it was planned to resume the journey. Nothing in any of the builders' backgrounds or inclinations suited them for such a task, and almost immediately after they boarded their flimsy, makeshift craft and headed downstream, they came to grief. The raft hit a submerged tree and broke up, spilling all of them into the river.

Everyone managed to make it ashore and back to the original campsite, but they had lost everything. Their situation had turned from desperate to life-threatening. The choices had now been reduced to one—set out on foot along the riverbank to Andoas.

As it makes its way toward its confluence with the Postaza, the serpentine Bobonaza makes countless turns and switchbacks, which would extend such a journey on foot along its banks by many days. Adding to the difficulty of such an undertaking is the dense undergrowth and swampy land along the riverbanks.

Isabel's party soon realized the futility of following such a route and struck out across the countryside, yet another disastrous decision. For weeks they wandered aimlessly in the rain forest. Finally, around the third week in December, for lack of food, water, shelter, and hope, the party collapsed. No one could go on. One by one they began to expire from fatigue, hunger, fever, and despair. For four days, Isabel lay on the ground and watched helplessly as her brothers, her nephew, and her faithful women servants died by her side.

For two more days, she stood watch over the corpses of her relatives and companions, unable to move. Finally, on the third day, summoning again the strength that had sustained her through the deaths of her four children, the long years separated from her beloved husband, and the trials she had overcome since she left Riobamba, Isabel roused herself again—determined to escape this place of death.

But first she needed shoes. Her own delicate ones had long since been torn to pieces. She took a knife and cut the soles off the boots of a dead brother and fastened them to her feet. She made what modest obsequies for the dead were possible to her and then, leaving the bodies of her loved ones where they lay, set off once again.

For over a week, Isabel Godin wandered alone through the darkness and vastness of the South American rain forest, home of the jaguar, poisonous snakes, and hostile Indian tribes.

The second day, she found water, but her throat was so parched that she had difficulty swallowing. On the days following, she managed to forage wild fruit and birds' eggs, which sustained her as she pressed on through the jungle. At night she shivered in the damp and cold, recoiling from the sounds that echoed around her until she fell into an exhausted sleep.

But each day, at first light, she set out again, pushing her way through the dense foliage of the trackless forest. On the eighth or ninth day after she had left the dreadful clearing, the final resting place of her companions, she heard voices ahead of her.

Fearful that she may have encountered some of the Indians who still roamed the region, she stopped and retreated back into the forest. Then, reasoning that whoever was there or whatever might befall her at their hands could hardly be worse than what she had endured already, she moved on. Soon, through the trees, she could see light reflected from water. She had reached a river.

As Isabel emerged from the forest she saw that the voices she had heard were from two Indians, who stood on the riverbank, preparing to launch a canoe. She made her way slowly toward them, calling out to them in Quechua as she drew near.

The two Indians and their wives had fled the smallpox epidemic at Canelos and were living in a hut nearby. After so many weeks of travail, misery, and death, it was devastating to Isabel to hear that she had traveled such a short distance from where she and her companions had started out.

Her saviors, for that is how she viewed them, were themselves headed to the mission at Andoas, and they obligingly agreed to let her come with them and took her on board.

In a few days' time they delivered her to Andoas, but to her dismay, the Jesuits, who had run the mission at Andoas for more than a century, had been expelled during the great suppression of their order, and the mission was now controlled by a venal member of the secular clergy.

When Isabel rewarded the two Indians who had saved her life by giving each of them one of the two gold chains that she was still wearing, the missionary in charge of Andoas confiscated the chains. In their stead, he gave the two Indians two or three yards of coarse cotton cloth. An outraged Isabel determined to quit Andoas at once and demanded a canoe and some men to carry her on to Lagunas, which even though it was not on the direct route to the Amazon—the mission lay some miles up the Huallaga—was the nearest and largest stopping place.

Before departing Andoas, she was given a cotton petticoat made for her by an Indian woman, and she converted the soles that she had cut off the boots of her brother into a pair of sandals. For the rest of her life, she kept both the petticoat and the sandals as "mournful tokens."

While Isabel and her companions waited in vain for the rescue that was to be organized by the French physician, that scoundrel did not linger at Andoas but went on to Omaguas.

The ever faithful Joachim, however, did return upriver with some companions to search for his mistress. They found the deserted hut on the Bobonaza and after many days of tracking the lost party found the spot where lay the decomposing corpses. Convinced that all had died, they returned to the hut, collected the belongings that remained, which turned out to be considerable, and returned to Andoas. Isabel meanwhile was wandering alone in the forest.

Joachim went on to Omaguas, where he turned over the belongings that he had collected at the hut to the French physician, who kept the property and sent Joachim back to Quito. It was later charged that he did so to prevent Joachim's ever telling anyone what he had delivered to Omaguas. The Frenchman maintained he had dispatched him back across the Andes because he was afraid that Joachim might murder him.

Meanwhile, Isabel had arrived in the canoe at the mission at Lagunas, where, because of her precarious health, she remained for the next six weeks.

The director of the mission, a Señor Romero, passed the word to the governor of Omaguas that Mme. Godin had not perished, as was believed, but was alive and residing with him at Lagunas. Thus the Frenchman, who was in possession of her property, had no choice but to hasten to her side.

He carried with him four silver dishes, a silver saucepan, some clothing, and various small items of little worth that had belonged to her brothers. As for the many missing items, he explained that they had rotted away. As Jean Godin wrote years later, the wretch seemed to have forgotten that bracelets, golden rosaries, and earrings set with emeralds do not easily disintegrate.

Isabel, who had learned the hard way of the treachery of the man she was dealing with, turned on him in a fury, telling him, "Go your ways, Sir; it is impossible that I can ever forget that, to you, I owe all my misfortunes and all my losses; manage henceforward as you may, I am determined you shall make no part of my company." [2]

The kindly Romero was not so condemning of the Frenchman, however. At least, he was more forgiving. He convinced Mme. Godin that without her protection the Frenchman would be in a very bad state and might very well perish. So with great reluctance, Isabel consented, and the author of her many troubles rejoined her on her journey.

Romero also wrote to Don Pedro Gramesón at Tabatinga, telling him that his daughter was alive and safe at Lagunas and asking him to dispatch Tristan D'Oreasaval to come for her and transport her to the waiting Portuguese vessel.

He also set himself the task of convincing Isabel that it would be best if she abandoned what he saw as a quixotic journey to the other side of the continent and return to Riobamba. He gently pointed out that much the greater part of the journey lay ahead of her. She had covered only a fifth or so of the distance thus far, and the hardships she had already suffered might pale against what she might still have to endure before she reached Cayenne.

Isabel was determined more than ever to continue. She argued that a divine providence had spared her when everyone else had died. Therefore it would be a blasphemy to abandon her quest, as well as dishonoring the memory and sacrifice of all those who had helped her.

The godly Romero relented and when it was clear that D'Oreasaval was not coming for her, readied a canoe and provisions for the journey and bade her farewell, telling the crew to stop nowhere until they reached the Portuguese vessel at Tabatinga.

The governor of Omaguas, who was alerted and told that she would stop nowhere en route, sent a canoe to meet her with additional supplies, and the commander of the galliot dispatched a pirogue loaded with supplies to meet her at Pebas.

The commander also doubled the number of oars on the galliot and worked his vessel up the Amazon as far as the mission at Loreto, where at last Isabel Godin was received on board.

There still remained a journey of almost three thousand miles, but Isabel was now safe and secure. The voyage down the Amazon was blessedly uneventful although there were several anxious days. One of her thumbs, which still had thorns embedded in it from her trials in the jungle, became infected, and it was feared that it might have to be amputated. Isabel refused even to consider such a course of action. Instead, the thorns were extracted, and the injured thumb healed by itself. But she suffered from the injury for the rest of her life.

When the galliot entered the Atlantic, where the currents can be treacherous off the mouth of the Amazon, an anchor was lost, and the captain sent a boat to Oyapock for assistance. Thus did Jean Godin learn that his wife, whom he had not seen in over twenty years, was only some three hundred miles away.

He immediately left Oyapock aboard another galliot, and in four days' time he drew alongside her vessel opposite Maracá. "On board this vessel," he later said, "after twenty years' absence, and a long endurance on either side of alarms and misfortunes, I again met with a cherished wife, whom I had almost given over every hope of seeing again." [3]

The reunion was not a completely joyful one. Jean lamented the loss of "the fruits of our union," but he saw their premature deaths in Peru as almost a blessing, since they would certainly have perished on the journey. The demise of her children in the jungles might have been too much for even the dauntless Isabel, and she might well have perished herself.

The joyous couple landed at Oyapock on 22 July 1770 and from there proceeded to Cayenne, where yet another travail awaited them, in the person of the duplicitous and traitorous Tristan D'Oreasaval, Jean's erstwhile friend and confidant.

D'Oreasaval brought suit against Jean Godin for wages dating back to the time when he had first been engaged by Jean to go and fetch Isabel. Jean offered him eighteen months' salary—1,080 francs—based on the time it should have taken D'Oreasaval to complete the assigned task had he done what he had been charged to do.

The court ruled that D'Oreasaval was entitled to the salary, but he, in turn, was ordered by the court to pay Godin the value of the goods and effects—long since lost or sold off—that had been entrusted to him. D'Oreasaval could not, of course, pay the difference, some 6,000 francs. He was insolvent.

Godin could have had D'Oreasaval imprisoned for debt, although he felt that the miscreant, whose actions had resulted in such misery for his wife and death for eight others, deserved much worse punishment. However, Godin, according to the laws of the time, would have had to pay for D'Oreasaval's maintenance while he languished in prison. Jean, whose own financial situation was precarious, declined to do so, and the matter was dropped.

Isabel's still fragile health and the probable exigencies of a long voyage by sea delayed the Godins' departure for France for almost three years. But, at last, sail they did, accompanied by Isabel's father, who, because of the deaths of his sons and grandson, realized that any hope for a peaceful old age lay not in Peru but with his daughter in France. The family arrived at La Rochelle on 26 June 1773.

At the end of the famous letter to La Condamine of 28 July 1773, which has served as the basis for all accounts of Isabel Godin's harrowing journey across South America, her husband summed up his wife's formidable and admirable character.

He felt that she had kept from him many of the details of her journey in order to spare him further pain. But he never pressed her to do so. He was ever solicitous and loving when she suffered her frequent bouts of melancholy. As he wrote to La Condamine: "I can even readily conceive that from delicacy, she has abstained from entering into many details, the remembrance of which she was anxious to lose, and which, known, could but add to the pain I feel. Nay she was even anxious that I should not prosecute Tristan, compassionating even that wretch. . . ." [4]

Isabel and Jean Godin settled in Jean's birthplace, Saint-Amand-Montrond, in the very house in which Jean was born, at 10 Rue de l'Hôtel-Dieu. Isabel's father, Don Pedro Gramesón, remained with them. In spite of the love and care lavished on the old man by his daughter and son-in-law, he never stopped grieving for the other members of his family until he died in 1780. Jean and Isabel Godin lived on for another twelve years, dying less than seven months apart, Jean in March and Isabel in September of 1792.

Isabel Godin's story made her famous throughout Europe and the Americas, but she was untouched by attention or renown, if she even deigned to notice such. She remained, as her husband had written to La Condamine in 1773, a woman who followed "the gentle impulse of a heart inspired with the purest benevolence, and the genuine principles of religion!" [5]

# CHAPTER 8

# "I Must Find Out About the Unity of Nature."

### The Explorations of Alexander von Humboldt

EUROPE MAY HAVE BEEN ENTHRALLED BY THE LOYALTY AND HERO-
ism of Isabel Godin, but of more interest to a new generation of scientists
and explorers was the work of La Condamine. Most notable among his
immediate successors and disciples was a Prussian aristocrat, full name
and title Baron Friedrich Wilhelm Karl Heinrich Alexander von Humboldt, who was born in Berlin in 1769.

Humboldt, even as a child, was attracted to the natural sciences, and early on determined to devote his life to scientific study and exploration. Studies at Frankfurt an der Oder, Göttingen, and at Freiberg in Saxony, which covered everything from economics, geology, and mining to botany and natural history, prepared Humboldt well for a life devoted to the sciences.

He was familiar with the writings of La Condamine, but he was particularly influenced by the writings of Jean-Jacques Rousseau—who advocated travel to South America as a surefire way to throw off the shackles of European prejudice and bias—and Louis Antoine de Bougainville, who had circumnavigated the globe and returned with a vast collection of exotic plants. The latter's dictum that "one cannot speculate from an armchair without the risk of making mistakes" could well serve as Humboldt's credo.[1]

The young German's first two serious proposed scientific adventures came to naught. As he would write years later, "A determined will and an active perseverance are not always sufficient to overcome every obstacle."[2]

In Paris in 1798, Humboldt learned of the preparations of the grand voyage of circumnavigation of the globe by Thomas Nicolas Baudin. The French expedition planned to explore South America, cross the Pacific, and return via the Cape of Good Hope. It was a voyage that Humboldt could only have dreamed of, and he signed on. However, Revolutionary France, which was faced by enemies from every direction, was in no position to launch such a grand expedition in 1798, and it was postponed.

But another almost equally interesting expedition now presented itself, and Humboldt left Paris in October 1798 for Marseille to take advantage of what promised to be an exciting opportunity. He was accompanied by a new friend and companion, Aimé Bonpland, a twenty-six-year-old French doctor and scientist who was also to have gone on the round-the-world voyage with Baudin.

At Marseille the two young men planned to board a Swedish vessel bound for North Africa, where they hoped to study the geography of the Atlas Mountains and then proceed to Egypt, perhaps to join up with the scientific expedition attached to the military campaign of Napoleon Bonaparte.

But here, too, Humboldt was to be disappointed. The Swedish vessel was damaged in a storm off Portugal and was laid up for repairs in Cádiz. The earliest it could reach Marseille was spring 1799.

Rather at loose ends in Marseille—"the sight of the sea continuously reminded us of the failure of our plans"—Humboldt and Bonpland decided to spend the winter in Spain, which was a fortuitous and life-changing decision. In Spain the young men's hopes to find some outlet for their ambitions were fulfilled. As Humboldt said, "Arriving at Madrid I soon congratulated myself on my decision to visit the peninsula." [3]

In the Spanish capital the Saxon ambassador smoothed the way for his countryman, and he soon was introduced to Don Mariano Luis de Urquijo, the Spanish secretary of state, who suggested that Humboldt and Bonpland redirect their sights. Why not South America? he said. It was still unknown and unexplored. Humboldt, no doubt still under the sway of La Condamine, was easily persuaded, and Bonpland readily agreed as well.

Although the Spanish colonies were not open to anyone but citizens of Spain—indeed, no foreigner, and certainly no scientists, had been there since La Condamine's expedition in 1735—Don Mariano promised to help overcome this obstacle. He was as good as his word. In March 1799, Humboldt was introduced at court and allowed to present his petition to travel to the Spanish colonies directly to the king. In short order he and Bonpland were issued two passports, one from the secretary of state and the other from the Council of the Indies.

Thus, under the protection of no less an authority than the Spanish crown, in July 1799, they found themselves at Cumaná, in the viceroy-alty of New Granada (now Venezuela), on the northeast coast of South America. They spent the next several months in the coastal areas of the viceroyalty, botanizing, studying volcanic activity, and just plain sight-seeing. They also tested the large array of scientific instruments that they had brought from Europe—among which were a telescope, thermometer, sextant, and barometer. Finally, in February 1800, they headed south, to explore the unknown and largely uninhabited regions on the upper Orinoco River.

La Condamine had heard of, and written about, a supposed connection between the Orinoco and the Amazon basins, and Humboldt was seized with the idea of finding and mapping this singular geographical oddity.

Crossing the flat and seemingly endless llano, the coastal plain of Venezuela, the two adventurers longed for anything that would distract them from the desolate landscape, which was unbroken by any tree, rock, or escarpment. And the heat and humidity were unremitting. But they were young, physically up to any task, and they pressed on. After all, hadn't they walked much of the distance from Marseille to Madrid and then from Madrid to La Coruña?

The continent had already offered up some extraordinary sights, a spectacular shower of meteors, for example. But there were to be many more wonders in the next months and years. In the swamps and waters near Calabazo, they encountered *Electrophorus electricus*, the so-called electric eel, which is actually not an eel but a knife fish.

Although ever curious and empirical, Humboldt resisted the impulse to see for himself if the fish's charge was as great as rumored. But his curiosity was accidentally assuaged when he stepped on one of the fish that had been brought ashore. He received a shock that, had it occurred just a short time before, when the fish was still in or had just been removed from the water, could have killed him. Electrophorus electricus is capable of producing as much as six hundred volts of electricity. Humboldt had the good fortune to step on the fish when its "batteries" were depleted.

In any study of these wild regions, one is constantly astounded, even moved, regardless of one's religion or lack of it, by the dedication and bravery of the Spanish friars who established missions in some of the most isolated and inhospitable spots on earth. There was an obverse side to their ministrations, however. They controlled the only viable routes into the interior of South America and for three centuries were able to block exploration.

Humboldt and Bonpland were, for all practical purposes, emissaries of the Spanish court and thus were able to travel where they pleased. All subjects of the Crown were thus, perforce, to give them comfort and aid on their journeys.

The good fathers at the Capuchin mission of San Fernando de Apure sheltered them and provided them with a dugout canoe large enough to carry themselves, their scientific equipment, four paddlers, a servant, and a pilot. There was also the brother-in-law of the provincial governor, who, not unlike Maldonado, the provincial governor who accompanied La Condamine, wanted to go along for the ride.

The nine wayfarers set forth down the Apure for its junction with the Orinoco, from whence they would head upstream to search for the alleged connector with the Amazon.

Humboldt no doubt knew of the adventures and misadventures of his English, Spanish, and Portuguese predecessors on the Orinoco and its tributaries, but that belonged to a distant past—the late Middle Ages, the Renaissance, and the Elizabethan and Jacobean ages. Alexander von Humboldt was the avatar of the Age of Enlightenment, the exemplar of the emerging modern man of science.

Humboldt, in his account of the journey, conjures up an earthly paradise of plant life, animals, and the native Indians living in harmony, but he doesn't ignore the violence of nature. Crocodiles, jaguars, and poisonous snakes were an ever-present danger, and the party was attuned to the possible suddenness of the threats to life and limb if it let down its guard.

However, it was not predatory mammals or reptiles that presented the greatest threat to exploration or settlement. As Humboldt observed, "Those who have not traveled the great rivers of tropical America . . . cannot imagine how all day long, ceaselessly, you are tormented by mosquitoes that float in the air. . . . However used to the pain you may become, without complaining; however much you try to observe the object you are studying the mosquitoes, jejenes and zancudos will tear you away as they cover your head and hands, pricking you with their needle-like suckers through your clothes, and climbing into your nose and mouth, making you cough and sneeze whenever you try to talk." [4]

More common than "Good morning" or "Good day," said Humboldt, was the expression "How were the *zancudos* last night?" or "How are we for mosquitoes today?"

And, as he also observed, contrary to the received view, the native populations were just as susceptible to and suffered just as much from the bites of these insects as any newly arrived European.

Humboldt also remarked on the thousands of crocodiles that infested the banks of the rivers and the great numbers of "tigers," the jaguars. Both the crocodile and jaguar, while of some concern to man, had sufficient prey in the form of vast numbers of capybaras, the world's largest rodent, and peccaries, a wild pig that roamed the area.

But in spite of the threat of dangerous mammals or amphibians or the plague of mosquitoes—which would never abate during the entire journey—Humboldt and Bonpland pressed on, proceeding more or less apace for the six days that the canoe was borne along on the current of the Apure until its convergence with the Orinoco, which presented a vastly different landscape to the travelers.

Here, the confluence of the two streams creates what Humboldt described as less a river and more of a vast lake, which stretches to the horizon. Thus the pilot and crew were able to dispense with the oars and proceed under sail.

Soon, however, this more leisurely form of passage would end. Ahead lay the Great Cataracts, at Atures and Maipures, where they would be obliged to portage until they again reached navigable water and could launch their craft and continue on their way upstream. All of this would be of consequence only to the paddlers. From their relatively comfortable positions, Humboldt and Bonpland continued to observe the passing scene and make their observations.

The looming exigency presented by the cataracts necessitated a transfer at La Urbana to a more maneuverable craft and the recruitment of a crew that would be familiar with the area that lay ahead. The task of acquiring such a boat, which in the event turned out to be a dugout canoe forty feet long and three feet wide, was made easier through the intervention of Friar Bernardo Zea, a missionary who was based at the mission near the Great Cataracts and thus knew the area well.

To further show his appreciation for being allowed to join their party and travel upriver with Humboldt and Bonpland, Friar Bernardo, who was suffering from a tropical fever and was anxious to leave the lower elevations, also took on the task of recruiting the new crew.

The good friar's methods shocked the more fastidious Europeans—the priest tied up and beat into submission any Indian who shirked or was foolish enough to be recalcitrant—but Humboldt and Bonpland did not interfere, and in a few days' time all was in order and they were ready for their journey to resume.

As they approached the Great Cataracts on the Orinoco, the dugouts were beached and the supplies and scientific instruments were offloaded to be carried by porters overland to an embarkation point farther upstream. The crewmen were left in the now empty and lighter canoes to negotiate the rapids as best they could, a task that turned out to be simpler than Humboldt had dared hope. In six hours, the canoes were once again in navigable waters, and the next day Humboldt, Bonpland, and Friar Bernardo reboarded their dugout to continue the journey.

Other cataracts lay ahead, which necessitated repeating the portage process, but in just a few days, sometime "during the night," Humboldt said, "we had left the Orinoco waters almost without realizing it. At sunrise we found ourselves in a new country, on the banks of a river whose name we had hardly heard mentioned. . . ." [5]

They were now on the Atabapo and heading almost due south. Another long portage, some four days or more, would be necessary before they could embark on the Pimichín, which led directly into the Río Negro, a major tributary of the Amazon. The rivers now had an amazing clarity, said Humboldt, and mercifully the mosquitoes, which had tormented them for months along the more turbid Orinoco, were no longer a curse, nor were the fearsome Orinoco crocodiles. However, enormous water snakes, some as long as fourteen feet, now appeared; but their malignant presence was countered by the benign pink river dolphins, which delighted both Humboldt and Bonpland.

After only four hours on the Pimichín, the Humboldt party entered the Río Negro on 6 May 1800. "The morning was fresh and beautiful," he wrote. Forgotten were the privations, the dangers, the discomforts of three months on the rivers and in the jungles, thirty-six days of it in a cramped and narrow canoe. "After all we had endured, it gives me pleasure to speak of the joy we felt in having reached a tributary of the Amazon. . . ."[6] He continued:

> In this interior of a new continent you get used to seeing man as not essential to the natural order. . . . Crocodile and boa are the masters of the river; jaguar, peccary, the dante and monkeys cross the jungle without fear or danger, established there in an ancient heritage. This view of a living nature where man is nothing is both odd and sad. Here, in a fertile land, in an eternal greenness, you search in vain for traces of man; you feel you are carried into a different world from the one you were born into.[7]

Humboldt descended the Río Negro as far as the fort at San Carlos just below where the Casiquiare enters the river. After three days at the fort, on 10 May they retraced their steps to go the short distance back upriver to enter the connector between the Orinoco and the Amazon basins. Once again they were in white waters, which as Humboldt wryly observed, "brought us a clear sky, stars, mosquitoes and crocodiles."[8]

While at San Carlos, Humboldt and Bonpland had given serious consideration to continuing down the Río Negro to the Amazon and returning thence up the coast to Venezuela. The commandant of the fort discouraged such a change in plans because of the always unsettled relations between the Spanish and Portuguese in the region.

His advice was well taken. After his return to Europe, Humboldt learned that the Portuguese in Brazil knew of this presence in the frontier regions and had issued a warrant for his arrest. Their more enlightened superiors in Lisbon had countermanded the order, but the scientist would have had an uneasy several months—and perhaps a trip to Lisbon as a prisoner—until the affair was straightened out.

Although popularly known as a "canal," the Casiquiare is anything but. It is a river in its own right and one of the most, if not the most, unusual in the world in that it is a natural connector between two of the world's great river systems—the Amazon and the Orinoco. At its beginning, the bifurcation with the Orinoco, it is roughly three hundred feet wide, and where it joins the Río Negro it is almost two thousand feet in width. Thus the Casiquiare is far from being a meandering, sluggish canal. The river does, indeed, meander as it makes its way through some of the densest jungle on earth. But it is also an important fast-flowing river, which is navigable for small boats and barges its entire two-hundred-mile length.

The stream first became known in the 1630s through the writings of that indefatigable Jesuit explorer and missionary Cristóbal de Acuña, who had heard rumors of such a connector. However, Acuña's report was met with skepticism even by some of those who believed in El Dorado, the Amazons, and the wild man of the forest.

It was not until a full century later, in 1744, that another Jesuit missionary provided what should have been proof of the existence of such a connector. A priest named Roman wrote of descending the Casiquiare with some Portuguese slave traders, whom he had met on the Orinoco. La Condamine was impressed and reported on Father Roman's trip to the French Academy. However, it took a boundary commission, which surveyed and mapped the route in 1756, to convince the skeptics that the Casiquiare did connect the two great river systems. Almost fifty years later Humboldt arrived to give his scientific imprimatur to the Casiquiare.

As they ascended the river, Humboldt was, as he had been for much of the time, never more than a day or two's journey from one of the missions established throughout South America by the Spanish.

As Humboldt observed and set up his surveying and astronomical instruments to plot more accurately the location of the Casiquiare and correct the existing maps of the region, Bonpland pursued his own interests. As his companion attested, Bonpland found himself in a sort of botanical nirvana, collecting with great abandon new plants, as well as the occasional bird and small animal.

Hundreds of specimens were packed up and shipped to France, but many of the rare species did not survive the great changes in humidity and heat encountered throughout their journey. But Bonpland's and Humboldt's descriptions served to whet the appetites of generations of botanizers who would follow them to the rain forests of South America.

There were no beaches or landing sites along the banks of the Casiquiare, and the vegetation was so dense that the Indians accompanying Humboldt were obliged to hack out with machetes enough space for the group to camp each night.

And the curse of the mosquitoes was more pronounced than at any time on the trip. Even Father Zea, that veteran of years in the tropics, allowed as to how the mosquitoes at his missions were larger, but the Casiquiare ones were more vicious and their bite more painful.

At last, on 21 May 1800, Humboldt, Bonpland, and their small party reentered the Orinoco and headed upstream the few miles to the Esmeralda mission. But their last night on the Casiquiare had not gone without incident, a reminder of how close to nature they really were.

Since they left Caracas, they had had as company a large mastiff. For many months, this "young, tame, and affectionate dog" had evaded crocodiles, snakes, and jaguars. But as they loaded the canoe after this last night in the jungle, they discovered that their faithful companion had disappeared. They had heard a jaguar in the night, and apparently the predator had invaded their camp and carried off the unfortunate animal while the party slept.

At Esmeralda, where they stayed for two days, the mission was overseen by an old soldier who was nominally in charge. A priest showed up from downriver only five or six times a year to say Mass. Again, Humboldt reported without censure on the often extreme treatment of the indigenous people. Referring to the martinet who ran the mission, he said, "Sometimes he used the sacristan's stick in ways that did not amuse the Indians." [9]

Humboldt's journey into the rain forest and the northern tributaries of the Amazon now rapidly drew to a close. He and Bonpland descended the Orinoco in just three more weeks, landing at Angostura, now the city of Ciudad Bolívar, on 13 June 1800.

Humboldt still had hopes of a rendezvous with the Baudin expedition on the west coast of South America, and to that end he traveled to Peru, arriving there in September 1802. Baudin's route, however, took him across the southern Pacific, and Humboldt's dream of a circumnavigation of the globe was not to be.

Disappointments that may have discouraged or even crushed other men never seemed to deter or impede Alexander von Humboldt. He turned his attention to other scientific and political subjects and began to arrange his notes and diaries for publication. Then, after four years in the New World, he began his journey home.

First, however, the ever curious humanist had to observe for himself the world's greatest political experiment. On 10 May 1804, Humboldt landed in America, first visiting Philadelphia and then on to Washington DC, where he was received enthusiastically and feted by a like-minded Thomas Jefferson.

After another stay in Philadelphia, the man who has been called the "scientific discoverer of America" was honored by election to membership in the American Philosophical Society. Soon after he sailed for Europe.

Humboldt's journey to America was the beginning of his great fame and his outsized reputation. Only Napoleon Bonaparte, it was said, was more famous than Alexander von Humboldt in nineteenth-century Europe.

Aimé Bonpland's life turned out to be not as exemplary as Humboldt's, but it was not without a certain interest or excitement. After his return to France, he supervised the gardens at Malmaison for the Empress Josephine and married a widowed friend of the empress.

Something of a radical politically, Bonpland was sympathetic to the revolutionary ideals of Simón Bolívar, whom he met while the future liberator was living in Napoleonic France. All the while, perhaps recalling the less constricted life he had enjoyed with Humboldt in their more halcyon days, and also, it has been speculated, to escape his marriage, Bonpland longed to return to South America. This was accomplished sometime after Josephine's death in 1814.

He settled in Argentina, but in 1821 he was arrested by the rabidly xenophobic dictator José Francia of Paraguay for allegedly trespassing on that nation's territory. Bonpland was not freed for ten years but presumably was allowed to continue his scientific work.

The ever-faithful Humboldt always stood by his old friend and traveling companion. He was able to secure for Bonpland, who never returned to France—he died in Argentina in 1858—the Legion of Honor, election as a corresponding member of the Academy of Sciences, and a lifetime pension.

Although the long scientific exploratory hiatus following the voyage of La Condamine down the Amazon in 1743 ended with the expedition of Humboldt and Bonpland to the Río Negro in 1800, the Spanish and Portuguese suspicion of foreigners in general and the Church's distrust of science in particular were by no means completely laid to rest.

But more powerful forces were now on the move, and those peculiarly Iberian fears were being swept aside or replaced by the powerful impetus of geopolitical concerns—set in motion by the Napoleonic Wars.

Bonaparte's subjugation of Spain and Portugal led directly to the Spanish and Portuguese colonies of South America severing their ties with the mother countries. Although nominally influenced by the revolution in North America, the Spanish and Portuguese in South America were either unable or unwilling to make the compromises necessary to form viable governments, and the continent was rent for decades by bloody civil strife.

But even in the midst of the unrest, a new generation of travelers and scientists began to look southward, often risking their very lives to traverse and study the vast natural laboratory of the rain forest of South America.

In 1817 two intrepid young Germans, the zoologist Johann Baptist von Spix and the botanist Karl Friedrich Philipp von Martius, sailed from Trieste for Brazil as part of a scientific party accompanying the daughter of the Holy Roman Emperor Frances II, the Archduchess Leopoldina, who was the betrothed of the crown prince of Portugal, Dom Pedro.

The Portuguese royal family had been living in Brazil since they were forced to flee their homeland by an invading French army in 1807. With thousands of loyal subjects, they had established the royal court in Rio de Janeiro, which was now the de facto capital of the Portuguese Empire. In another example of the convoluted dynastic genealogy of the time, Leopoldina's sister was none other than Marie Louise, the second wife of Napoleon and the mother of the exiled emperor's son and putative heir, Napoleon II—king of Rome and duke of Reichstadt.

Spix and Martius became the first Europeans since La Condamine to visit the Amazon proper—Humboldt had explored only a major tributary of the river, the Río Negro. Spix and Martius traveled together as far as Tefé, where they separated in early December 1819. Spix then proceeded up the Amazon as far as Tabatinga near the border with Peru.

Martius meanwhile explored and collected on the Río Japurá, but in March 1820 he was back in Manaus, where he rejoined Spix, who had just returned from a journey farther up the Río Negro, as far as Barcelos. The two Germans then journeyed back downriver to Belém, where they took ship for Europe in June 1820.

Together Spix and Martius brought back 6,500 preserved plant species as well as 2,700 insects. In addition they identified 85 mammals, 350 birds, 150 amphibians, and 116 fish. Spix is perhaps best known today for Spix's macaw, which he first identified in 1817. It is now one of the most threatened bird species in the world. There have been no confirmed sightings of a Spix's macaw since 2000.

The expedition of Spix and Martius, which was called "one of the most important scientific expeditions of the nineteenth century," marked the end of the first important stage of European scientific exploration of the Amazon region.[10] Political instability and unrest made such efforts increasingly hazardous, although other less well-known scientists and adventurers continued to ascend or descend the Amazon or slogged their way along jungle trails or explored the hundreds of tributaries.

However, it was not until the midnineteenth century that the scientific study of the vast region took a giant step forward when three young British amateurs of science arrived in the Amazon Basin and began years of collecting, study, and analysis. Their work would not only prove seminal in the history of science, it would permanently open the Amazon to serious scientific inquiry.

# Three Eminent Victorians in the "Garden of the World"

*Wallace, Bates, and Spruce Explore the Amazon*

ON 28 MAY 1848, TWO OF THE THREE ENGLISHMEN WHO WOULD leave an indelible imprint on scientific research in the Amazon in the nineteenth century, Alfred Russel Wallace and Henry Walter Bates, disembarked at Pará. The third of the triumvirate, Richard Spruce, would not join them until the following summer.

Neither the twenty-five-year-old Wallace nor his companion, the twenty-three-year-old Bates, had much formal education beyond the basics afforded to young men of their class and background. Both were solidly lower middle class, if that. But they were autodidacts. They had read widely and voraciously—not only the classics but also, and more important, the treatises of Alexander von Humboldt and the works of Thomas Malthus, Robert Chambers, and Charles Lyell.

And a powerful influence was the work popularly known as *The Voyage of the Beagle*, which had appeared only in 1838. Charles Darwin's journal and notes of his long sojourn aboard *HMS Beagle* had gripped the imagination of the English public, and no one more so than these two impressionable young men.

According to Darwin biographer and historian of science Sir Gavin de Beer, "The five years of the voyage were the most important event in Darwin's intellectual life and in the history of biological science."[1]

Bates and Wallace instantly identified with Darwin, who, like them, had no formal training in science when he began his research. Indeed, who did before the age of specialization? The great man was, like most other practitioners of science, an enthusiastic amateur, in the true meaning of the word, which derives from the Latin *amator*, lover.

Bates and Wallace first met in 1844 and soon after began exchanging notes and specimens, chiefly insects and butterflies, and also making short scientific excursions together in the English countryside.

In 1847, after reading W. H. Edwards's *A Voyage Up the River Amazon*, Wallace was seized with the idea of going to the Amazon himself. Indeed, such an idea probably came to him after reading only a few pages. Edwards's paean to the Amazon occurs early in the preface and easily could have done the trick: "The country of the Amazon is the garden of the world, possessing every requisite for a vast population and an extended commerce. It is, also, one of the healthiest of regions; and thousands who annually die of diseases incident to the climates of the North might here find health and long life."[2] Wallace immediately suggested to Bates that they join forces for their own trip to "the garden of the world."

The eighteenth and nineteenth centuries in the history of science were a golden age for the botanical collectors who roamed the globe on behalf of private clients or such government institutions as the Royal Botanic Gardens at Kew or the Jardin des Plantes in Paris. These botanizers shipped back thousands of specimens of plants to their patrons in Europe and England, and not a few made their way to America.

These patrons, scientific amateurs themselves, amassed large collections of plants and animals, live, stuffed, or dried, and until the institutionalization of science were central to the dissemination of scientific knowledge. It was de rigueur for educated aristocrats to have these collections and so-called cabinets of curiosities. As the biologist and journalist Carol Kaesuk Yoon observes, Charles Darwin, who himself was from a prominent family, would have seen it as a matter of course for "any dinner party conversation to turn taxonomic, after an afternoon of beetle-hunting or wildflower study." [3]

Wallace convinced Bates that they too could collect specimens for sale to these deep-pocketed aristocratic collectors in order to finance their explorations in South America. His optimism carried the day, and they did, indeed, manage to eke out a precarious living from their adventures. But both men suffered real want during their stays in the Amazon. Bates, for example, realized a total profit of only £800 for the years he spent in South America, or about £73 a year.

But collecting and adventure were not the only reasons for their going to the Amazon. Their work in South America might also, Wallace reasoned rather portentously, be a real contribution to the advancement of scientific knowledge and theory, even leading, he said, "towards solving the problem of the origin of species." [4]

This statement was doubtless prompted by his reading of another seminal work, Robert Chambers's *Vestiges of the Natural History of Creation*, which appeared anonymously in 1844. Chambers presented a flawed, even naive view of evolution, but his work nevertheless served a worthwhile purpose by bringing the attention of the public to the question of the origin of species. The book, which eventually sold over twenty thousand copies, also acted as a lightning rod for Charles Darwin by deflecting some of the hostility directed at him in the inevitable battle with doctrinaire religion over the issue of evolution.

In any event, Wallace was an early convert to what would become known as natural selection as opposed to the doctrine of divine origin, which would itself evolve into a belief known as creationism. His friend Bates was not, it seems, so easily swayed. In a letter to him on 28 December 1845, Wallace said, "I have a rather more favourable opinion of the 'Vestiges' than you appear to have." [5]

Bates's initial skepticism—which may have had to do with his Unitarian religious beliefs—was soon swept away, however. He became an enthusiastic supporter of natural selection.

As for the voyage to South America, it was not difficult for Wallace to persuade Bates to sign on. And, once in the Amazon, he became as besotted with it as W. H. Edwards ever was, so much so in fact that he stayed there for eleven years.

Wallace and Bates's first short walk when they arrived in Belém did not disappoint. Vegetation ran riot even along on the streets and byways of the town: "Slender, woody lianas hung in festoons from the branches, or were suspended in the form of cords and ribbons whilst luxuriant creeping plants overran alike tree-trunks, roofs and walls, or toppled over palings in a copious profusion of foliage."

Everything was a revelation, even an epiphany, to the two young men, "whose last country ramble of quite recent date was over the bleak moors of Derbyshire on a sleety morning in April."

Besides the lushness of the vegetation, another aspect of the rain forest began to make itself known as they walked on and night began to descend that first evening in Belém. The forest seemed to come alive:

> As we continued our walk the brief twilight commenced, and the sounds of multifarious life came from the vegetation around. The whirring of cicadas; the shrill stridulation of a vast number and variety of field crickets and grasshoppers, each species sounding its peculiar note; the plaintive

*hooting of tree frogs—all blended together in one continuous ringing sound—the audible expression of the teeming profusion of Nature. As night came on, many species of frogs and toads in the marshy places joined in the chorus—their croaking and drumming, far louder than anything I had before heard in the same line, being added to the other noises, created an almost deafening din. This uproar of life, I afterwards found, never wholly ceased, night or day. In the course of time I became, like other residents, accustomed to it. It is, however, one of the peculiarities of a tropical—at least, a Brazilian—climate which is most likely to surprise a stranger. After my return to England, the deathlike stillness of summer days in the country appeared to me as strange as the ringing uproar did on my first arrival at Pará [Belém].*[6]

Wallace and Bates remained in the area around Belém for three months, becoming acclimated and botanizing and collecting. But at last, on 26 August 1848, they set out on their first serious scientific journey, traveling up the Tocantins River. The list of provisions and equipment for this journey detailed by Wallace in his *A Narrative of Travels on the Amazon and Rio Negro, with an Account of the Native Tribes* provides insight into how two proper Victorians braved the rigors of the Amazon.

They traveled in a canoe, twenty-four feet long and eight feet wide, fitted with sails but designed mainly to be rowed. A palm-thatched hut, called a *tolda*, was erected in the stern, which provided shelter for Wallace and Bates. Another tolda, in the bow, protected their baggage and three months' provisions.

For the native crew there was farina, fish, and the inevitable *cachaça*— a potent, rumlike liquor that at the time was strictly a drink of the lower classes. For the two Englishmen there was tea, coffee, biscuits, sugar, rice, salt, beef, and cheese. They also brought along changes of clothing, crockery, and a sackful of copper coins, the common currency in the settlements along the rivers and tributaries. In addition there were guns, ammunition, and boxes for whatever they collected en route.

This trip, a relatively brief excursion—they returned to Belém on 30

September—was to be Wallace and Bates's only trip together in the Amazon region. Some writers have hinted at a rift, but there is no evidence that there was a rupture in the friendship. They continued to share a rental house near Belém, and in his 1905 autobiography, Wallace acknowledged that the two real turning points in his life were meeting Henry Bates and reading Thomas Malthus.

A more likely explanation is the men realized early on that science would be better served and they could accomplish a great deal more by separating and thus covering a greater amount of territory.

On 7 December 1848, Bates went alone to explore and botanize on the island of Marajó, in the mouth of the Amazon. On that immense island—it is the size of Switzerland—Bates encountered one of those besotted devotees of the Amazon that crop up regularly in the history of the region.

On first landing he ran into two red-haired, blue-eyed boys who spoke perfect English. They were the sons of a German named Petzell, who had come under the spell of tropical life while a soldier in the employ of Brazil.

Petzell later drifted to the United States, where he married, had five children, and tried his hand at farming in Illinois. But the Amazon kept calling, and he packed up his family and embarked on a journey that involved many detours and false starts—including stays in New Orleans, New York, and Guiana.

At last, the Petzells had managed to reach Marajó, where they were ensconced in a small log house and where they were eking out a subsistence on a few acres of tillable land. They were now enlisted by Bates to help in the collection of insects. When he left the island and returned to Belém on 12 February 1849, he brought back twelve hundred species of insects. This was the beginning of a remarkable collection of flora and fauna Bates would amass during his years in South America—some fourteen thousand species, mostly insects, of which eight thousand were new to science.

Four months later, in June, Bates made another trip up the Tocantins to Cameta. Wallace, meanwhile, left to explore the Guama and Capim rivers to the east of Belém.

Enter now the third Englishman, Richard Spruce, who, with the encouragement and, more important, financial aid, of the noted botanist and collector George Bentham, sailed for the Amazon from Liverpool on 7 June 1849. Accompanying Spruce was an assistant, Robert King, and a fellow passenger was none other than twenty-year-old Edward Wallace, who was on his way out to South America to join his brother Alfred Russel. Thus Spruce, who already knew and admired the work of both Wallace and Bates, had an even more immediate introduction to the two naturalists when he arrived at Belém on 12 July.

The personal narratives of those eighteenth- and nineteenth-century scientific pioneers in the South American rain forests do not dispel the myths of privation and ever-present danger that have accrued over the five centuries of Amazon exploration. Indeed, their accounts are filled with tales of danger, discomfort, and foreboding. And to be sure, there were and always have been dangers aplenty, but these intrepid men chose to defy them even as they wrote about them.

Bates's remark on arriving in Belém might serve equally well as a credo for Wallace and Spruce: "Where are the dangers and horrors of the tropics?" he wrote. "I find none of them." [7]

Bates's airy dismissal of "the dangers and horrors of the tropics" would return to haunt him during his almost twelve years there. He would fall victim more than once to the real dangers facing Victorian adventurers as they made their way in the jungles of the Amazon.

Few escaped either malaria or dysentery, and the most dreaded disease of all, yellow fever, would remain the deadliest scourge until it was hypothesized by Carlos Finlay late in the nineteenth century and proved by Walter Reed in the early twentieth that the vector for yellow fever was the mosquito. For centuries it was believed that the epidemics that killed hundreds of thousands around the world were caused by filth, meteorological conditions, or miasmas.

Wallace and Bates both suffered grievously from illnesses while in

South America, but they were not inclined to submit to either disease or the climate, and they remained in South America for years. Wallace was the first to conclude his sojourn in the Amazon, but he stayed until 1852. Bates, who stayed on until 1859, bid a regretful farewell after eleven years of trekking through the jungles and traversing the rivers. And his valedictory was rather the same as his initial impression. Nothing in the intervening years seemed to have altered his view of his "Naturalist's Paradise." Spruce did not leave until 1864.

These adventurous Victorian Englishmen would between them cover vast areas of the rain forest and, in the case of Spruce, beyond the Andes. They collected thousands of specimens, and their work helped immeasurably in building what would be the besieged but indestructible fortress of evolution.

But for months after their arrival in Belém, their dreams of wider exploration were stymied. Initially they had to content themselves with exploring and collecting in the lands adjoining the tributaries and byways of the Lower Amazon—themselves vast bodies of water to be sure. Indeed, many of the streams that flow into the Amazon are by any measures important rivers and large drainage systems themselves. But Wallace and Bates and Spruce did not come to the Amazon to limit themselves to the area around Belém. They were anxious to set off up the Amazon proper.

At last, their plans for ranging farther afield in the rain forest began to be realized. The first to depart was Wallace, who left Belém for Santarém, five hundred miles up the Amazon, at the mouth of the Tapajós, in early August 1849. He was accompanied by his brother Edward. Their transport was a sailing canoe that had been used to carry salt-fish and hides, but the brothers ignored the foul odor. As Wallace said, "voyagers on the Amazon must not be fastidious."

In some twelve days, the small craft entered the Amazon. In the colorful style of Victorian travelers, Wallace recalled the moment. It was "with emotions of admiration and awe that we gazed upon the stream of this mighty and far-famed river," he wrote.

*Our imagination wandered to its sources in the distant Andes, to the Peruvian Incas of old, to the silver mountains of Potosí, and the gold-seeking Spaniards and wild Indians who now inhabit the country about its thousand sources. What a grand idea it was to think that we now saw the accumulated waters of a course of three thousand miles; that all the streams that for a length of twelve hundred miles drained from the snow-clad Andes were here congregated in the wide extent of ochre-colored water spread out before us! Venezuela, Colombia, Ecuador, Peru, Bolivia, and Brazil—six mighty states, spreading over a country far larger than Europe—had each contributed to form the flood which bore us so peacefully on its bosom.*[8]

After a journey of twenty-eight days, the brothers disembarked at Santarém. They lingered there only a few days, however, preferring instead to settle in the village of Monte Alegre, on the northern shore and three days' travel back down the Amazon.

At Monte Alegre, which offered richer opportunities for exploration and observation, and not so incidentally the required solitude for such pursuits, they rented a house and settled in for two months. They returned to Santarém by early November, where they passed another month before heading further upriver to Óbidos.

Bates had left Belém for the long journey to Santarém on 5 September, aboard a schooner engaged in the river trade. Since such a vessel was totally dependent on the tides and wind, it could take as many as forty days to get to Santarém from Belém.

For almost a month the vessel negotiated the myriad streams and channels leading from Belém into the Amazon, but finally, around midnight on 3 October, Bates's dream was realized. He was on the Amazon. While his paean to the river does not quite rise to the level of Wallace's, he was clearly transported by the sight. "I rose long before sunrise to see the great river by moonlight," he wrote. "There was a spanking breeze, and the vessel was bounding gaily over the waters. The channel along which we were sailing was only a narrow arm of the river, about two miles in width: the total breadth at this point is more than twenty miles. . . . The river, notwithstanding this limitation of its breadth had a most majestic appearance." [9]

The vessel carrying Bates docked at Santarém on 9 October 1849, but he did not linger. The schooner sailed again the next morning at sunrise and by midnight of 10 October, Bates was at Óbidos, fifty miles farther up the Amazon.

He remained at Óbidos for over a month, exploring the countryside and the rain forest and observing the flora and fauna. He was particularly struck by the great number and variety of monkeys in the environs of Óbidos, but his account of the hunting of these benign creatures for food is a melancholy pendant to his scientific observations.

Once again finding passage on a trading vessel heading upstream, Bates left Óbidos on 19 November. Sixty-four days later, on 22 January 1850, after what he described as a "tedious voyage," Bates disembarked at Manaus, which at the time was known as Barra, on the Río Negro.

Meanwhile, after their return from Monte Alegre and another short stay in Santarém, Wallace and his brother managed to obtain a canoe and a crew and set out for Óbidos themselves. Spruce had wangled passage a week earlier in a trading canoe, but rough water and wind had delayed his own passage so that he arrived at Óbidos only a day before the Wallaces.

Óbidos was only a temporary way station, and, finally, on 31 December 1849, Wallace arrived at Manaus, that legendary jumping-off point for travelers to the Upper Amazon.

Three weeks later, Bates arrived to find his old traveling companion already settled in at Manaus. Like ships in the night, they had passed each other on the river below Serpa. Bates might have been marginally more comfortable aboard the larger sailing boat, but a sailing canoe, which could also be rowed as necessary, was clearly the faster mode of transportation on the rivers in 1849.

After such a long period of relative isolation, Bates was delighted to find some congenial company at Manaus. In addition to the Wallace brothers, there were other sympathetic types, and "we passed a delightful time; the miseries of our long river voyages were soon forgotten, and in two or three weeks we began to talk of further explorations," he said.[10]

At Manaus, there were long hikes in the rain forest, convivial meals, and good conversation. But soon enough it was time to move on. Much as heads of state might carve up conquered territories, Bates and Wallace now divided up the Amazon Basin. "Mr. Wallace chose the Río Negro for his next trip, and I agreed to take the Solimoens [the Amazon]."[11]

Wallace seems not to have shared Bates's rather benign view of the rainy winter months spent in Manaus. As he said, "I had now a dull time of it in Barra [Manaus]." Although he did allow that the people Bates found "congenial" did contribute "a little amusement."[12]

Bates managed to get away from Manaus on 26 March 1850 to start up the Amazon. Wallace's own escape was not realized so quickly. He was not only at the mercy of the high waters of the Río Negro but also subject to the whims of river traders who only occasionally ascended that rarely traveled river.

Finally, in late summer 1850 the stars were aligned, and on 31 August, Wallace boarded a trading canoe, thirty-five feet long and seven feet wide, and quit Manaus.

His brother Edward did not join him on the long-delayed journey up the Río Negro. The younger Wallace had given up the idea of being a naturalist and wished to return to England. In a letter dated 30 August 1850, to his sister and mother, Edward set out his plans. The £10 that Alfred advanced him was nowhere near enough to finance the trip home, so he was obliged to continue on at Manaus, where he hoped to collect enough birds and insects for sale to cover his passage. This he hoped to accomplish in a few months.[13]

Alfred Wallace's journey up the Río Negro ended at the village of Pimichín, on the small river of the same name, which is connected by a road with the village of Yavita, where he arrived around 13 February 1851. On the last leg of the journey, from the village of San Carlos and the nearby Casiquiare, where he arrived on 4 February, to Yavita, Wallace was, as he pointed out, retracing the steps of his esteemed predecessor, Alexander von Humboldt.

On the road through the forest from Pimichín to Yavita, Wallace had one of the most frightening and at the same time thrilling encounters of his stay in the Amazon. As he put it, he was "rewarded by falling in with one of the lords of the soil, which I had long wished to encounter." The "lord" in question was a black jaguar, "the rarest variety of the most powerful and dangerous animal inhabiting the American continent."

"This encounter pleased me much," said Wallace. "I was too much surprised, and occupied too much with admiration, to feel fear." But, he added, "I was, however, by no means desirous of a second meeting, and, as it was near sunset, thought it most prudent to turn back towards the village." [14]

In this same village, another, probably even more dangerous denizen of the rain forest was not only present but ubiquitously so—the *jararaca*, a genus of fer-de-lance, one of the deadliest snakes in the world. Hundreds if not thousands of people are bitten each year in South America. Wallace returned from his encounter with the jaguar to find the dried head of one such creature hanging in the eaves of his hut.

Since Wallace and his naturalist colleagues often found it more convenient to adopt the ways of the local Indians and go about much of the time barefoot, it is something of a miracle that they did not fall victim to these venomous reptiles. Bates recorded stepping on the tail of a jararaca in Belém, which fortunately buried its fangs in a flapping trouser leg instead of his flesh.

Wallace remained at Yavita for forty days. It was not a happy experience. It was the height of the wet season—the rain was incessant—which meant very few chances for scientific exploration. And in the third week of his enforced isolation, he suffered a serious setback. He awoke one morning and instead of finding a fire lit and coffee brewing, he found himself alone. His Indians had deserted him and fled in the night to return downriver. It took two weeks, during which time he had to shift for himself, to arrange for a replacement canoe and crew.

At last, on 31 March 1851, Wallace began the return journey down the Río Negro to the planned rendezvous at Guia with a guide who had promised to take him up the Río Uaupés.

There were the usual maddening delays, and Wallace did not set out for the Uaupés until 3 June, but the Uaupés turned out to be one of the defining experiences of Wallace's life and his scientific career. Far up the river, he entered a hut in a village and stepped back into the Stone Age. "On entering this house," he wrote, "I was delighted to find myself at length in the presence of the true denizens of the forest." [15]

Here, indeed, were indigenous peoples who were still untouched by the trappings of civilization. All were naked or nearly so, their bodies were pierced and painted, and they were adorned with the jewellike feathers of the birds of the jungle.

He learned that the Indians scattered whenever traders arrived. Sometimes their freedom if not their lives was forfeit if they did not do so. Too many had been impressed and enslaved by the unscrupulous Portuguese, and sometimes they were murdered if they did not go willingly. But slowly, the inhabitants of the village returned to stare at Wallace as much as he at them.

During this voyage Wallace also came down with a severe case of dysentery, which, coupled with various fevers, bothered him for the remainder of his time in the Amazon. In true British fashion, however, he soldiered on.

Wallace remained on the Uaupés until 1 September, and although he wanted to continue on up the river, he realized it was wiser to return to Manaus until the dry season, when it would be easier to continue his explorations. Also, of more importance, his extensive collections of insects, live and mounted small animals and birds, as well as hundreds of plants needed to be looked to and prepared for shipment to England.

As large and unique as his collections were, Wallace realized, as did everyone who has worked in the rain forests, that he had barely scratched the surface of the area with the greatest biodiversity on earth. This was particularly true of the insects.

Wallace collected hundreds of new species, but he did not know, nor could he have known at that time, that there are an estimated thirty million species in the Amazon Basin. There are seven thousand species of butterflies alone. He did speculate and lament that vast numbers no doubt lived in the canopy of the forest, which was inaccessible to him and would remain so to researchers until late into the twentieth century.

Now, in the summer of 1851, Alfred Wallace was, quite simply, homesick for his native land, and he now hoped to return there by July or August 1852. How he missed "the green fields, the pleasant woods, the flowery paths, the neat gardens—all so unknown here!" He also waxed poetic about "the social tea-table, with familiar faces around it!" [16]

But flowery paths, tea tables, and society would have to wait. Wallace first wanted another go at the Uaupés. To prepare, he would rest up at Manaus and gather the necessary supplies for a four-month expedition.

On 15 September 1851, Wallace arrived at Manaus, where he received news of the yellow fever epidemic that had raged in the spring and summer at Belém and the serious illness of his brother. Ominously, there was no other news of Edward from his friends at Belém or from Edward himself.

Wallace was pleased to be back in an at least marginally civilized town, and he was even more pleased that his old friend and confederate, Richard Spruce, was there. But he was anxious to return to the Uaupés, and within two weeks he was en route back up the Río Negro. The trip was perhaps the most arduous of the many that Wallace had taken. He was stricken twice with malaria, and it was mid-February before he actually entered the Uaupés.

During the enforced idleness occasioned by his bouts of malaria, Wallace dreamed of perhaps remaining in his tropical paradise and combining the lushness of the rain forest with that English penchant to control nature. "In the whole Amazon," he said, "no such thing as neatness or cultivation has ever been tried." Perhaps he could have pulled off such orderly fancies, but Wallace came to his senses, and these feverish dreams subsided. [17]

This second trip was marred by more illness and the difficulties of engaging Indians to help with the transport of the canoe up and over the dozens of waterfalls and rapids on the Uaupés. In addition, there were fewer insects, birds, and animals to collect. Instead, Wallace was obliged to pay more attention to the various groups of Indians he encountered. Although he was not an anthropologist, his observations are still of keen interest to that discipline since he was the first European to set foot in many of the villages and settlements along the Uaupés.

At last, Wallace decided that there was little point in proceeding further up the Uaupés and on 25 March 1852 he began the journey back down the river. Jammed aboard the canoe were fifty-two live animals, which included monkeys and parrots and a huge number of dried insects. He also had accumulated a large collection of Indian arms, implements, and ornaments, for which he had traded mirrors, fishhooks, and other small goods.

Again, on the voyage back to Manaus and on to Belém, Wallace fell ill from a recurrence of malaria. And he was laid up as well with an infected foot caused by an insect that bores into the skin and lays its eggs. There was also the problem of the wildlife. Many of them had died or were lost on the voyage down the Uaupés and the Negro, but he arrived at Manaus with thirty-four live animals, which had to be accommodated and fed.

Wallace arrived at Belém on 2 July 1852 and almost immediately received the grim news about his brother Edward. The younger Wallace had not returned to Belém until the middle of May 1851, but he had been able to book passage to England at once and was scheduled to sail for Liverpool on 6 June. In the meantime, he stayed at the same house where he had lived with his brother earlier, and everything seemed in order.

The young man who had survived the rigors of thousands of miles of travel on the rivers and in the rain forest of the Amazon Basin was now confronted by that scourge of the tropics—indeed of much of the civilized world of the time. Edward had arrived in Belém in the midst of a yellow fever epidemic.

In just a few days, he began to exhibit the early symptoms characteristic of the disease, a mild fever and a headache. But within hours he entered the so-called "toxic phase"—chills and fever, bleeding into the skin, slow heartbeat, headache, back pains, and fatigue. In another day or so, he also exhibited the nausea, vomiting, constipation, and jaundice that are characteristic of the disease.

As is usual with yellow fever, Edward began to feel somewhat better after the third day, an illusion of hope that is soon dashed. Within hours, he entered the final stage—internal bleeding and bloody, coffee ground vomit. There followed delirium and coma, and on 8 June 1851 Edward Wallace died.

Henry Bates, who had returned to Belém in April, apparently nursed Edward and then wrote to the Wallace family informing them of the young man's death. He also, for whatever reason (perhaps science trumped human feelings), felt compelled to supply the family with the rather gruesome details of Herbert Edward Wallace's last days.

At first, said Bates, they thought it was just constipation, but the doctor knew otherwise and began the treatment for yellow fever, which according to Bates seemed to be effective, and Edward was progressing. But the next day, "the fever immediately struck inwards and black vomit declared itself . . . he died . . . after suffering fearfully."

Bates also felt obliged to recount his own bout with the disease. "I was rather alarmed," he wrote, "by being suddenly seized with similar symptoms myself, shivering fever and vomit in rapid succession. . . ." He, however, had made a full recovery.[18]

Wallace was bereft at the death of his brother, but he had no time to mourn. A brig, the *Helen*, was preparing to sail for England and could take him and his collections. He boarded the ship on 12 July, and the *Helen* headed down the Amazon Estuary for the sea and England.

Early in the voyage, he suffered another attack of fever, but it turned out to be his old nemesis, malaria, and not the plague that had carried off so many thousands back in Brazil. But on 6 August an even worse calamity struck. While reading in his cabin, Wallace was rousted out. The ship was afire, and the crew was unable to contain it. The command was given to abandon ship, and everyone was ordered into small boats, from which Wallace watched as his animals and his collections were destroyed.

After being adrift for ten days, the passengers and crew were picked up some two hundred miles from Bermuda by a vessel en route to England. They landed at Deal on 10 October 1852. Wallace's Amazon sojourn had ended in great sadness. His brother lay in a grave in Belém, and his vast collections were lost in the disaster at sea. He wrote:

> With what pleasure had I looked upon every rare and curious insect I had added to my collection! How many times, when almost overcome by the ague, had I crawled into the forest and been rewarded by some unknown and beautiful species! How many places, which no European foot but my own had trodden, would have been recalled to my memory by the rare birds and insects they had furnished to my collection! How many weary days and weeks had I passed, upheld only by the fond hope of bringing home many new and beautiful forms from those wild regions. . . . And now everything was gone, and I had not one specimen to illustrate the unknown lands I had trod, or to call back the recollection of the wild scenes I had beheld! [19]

The material loss of his collections was, of course, a calamity of the first order, but the observations made in the wilds of Brazil were not and could not be erased. Alfred Russel Wallace had already begun to formulate the principle of natural selection, the foundation of one of the most revolutionary theories in the history of science—evolution.

WHILE WALLACE WAS HEADING HOME, Bates and Spruce were still cultivating their own large patches of the Amazon Rain Forest. These two intrepid Victorians would spend, collectively, some twenty-five years in the Amazon region before returning to the damps and fogs of England.

Indeed, while Wallace was suffering his misadventures on the Atlantic, Henry Bates was far up the Tapajós. Wallace had hoped to see Bates when he passed through Santarém on his return journey to Pará in June 1852, but Bates had left just a few days before.

They had last seen each other on 26 March 1850, when Bates left for Ega (now Tefé), four hundred miles up the Solimões or Amazon. He traveled in a vessel called a *cuberta*, which was "manned by ten stout Cucama Indians."

On this journey, Bates first encountered what has become the almost mystical view of the Amazon Rain Forest. Unlike the lower reaches of the river, which are marked by hills, savannas, sandy soil, and relatively thin forests, the Upper Amazon, some 600,000 square miles, "is covered with one uniform, lofty, impervious, and humid forest. . . . The climate is healthy, although one lives here as in a permanent vapour bath. . . . The country . . . is a magnificent wilderness where civilised man, as yet, has scarcely obtained a footing; the cultivated ground from the Río Negro to the Andes amounting only to a few score acres. Man, indeed, in any condition, from his small numbers, makes but an insignificant figure in these vast solitudes." [20]

On the evening of 30 April, the cuberta entered the calm waters at the mouth of the Río Tefé. Since it was late, the Indians shipped their oars and went to sleep to await the dawn. The twenty-five-year-old Bates was in a more contemplative mood:

> I sat up for two or three hours after my companions had gone to rest, enjoying the solemn calm of the night. Not a breath of air stirred; the sky was of a deep blue, and the stars seemed to stand forth in sharp relief; there was no sound of life in the woods, except the occasional melancholy note of some nocturnal bird. I reflected on my own wandering life; I had now reached the end of the third stage of my journey, and was now more than half way across the continent. It was necessary for me, on many accounts, to find a rich locality for Natural History explorations, and settle myself in for some months or years. Would the neighbourhood of Ega turn out to be suitable, and should I, a solitary stranger on a strange errand, find a welcome amongst its people? [21]

At sunrise, the journey recommenced, and the cuberta entered the so-called Lago de Tefé, the five-mile-wide sheet of water formed by the convergence of the Tefé and the Amazon. Across the lake, on the south shore, could be seen their destination, Ega, a settlement of a hundred or so palm-thatched cottages and white-washed houses with red tile roofs. It was 1 May 1850, and the third stage of his journey had, indeed, begun.

As for the longed-for "welcome amongst its people," Bates seemed to have succeeded there. Throughout his two stays in Ega, which together totaled four and a half years, his relations with the local people were never less than cordial, and he mingled with them as much as was necessary but apparently no more than that. For as he said, "Refined society, of course, there was none." [22]

And there was always the problem of thievery. Bates's money was stolen, and from time to time objects would disappear from his house, but he was generally left to his own devices, rising with the sun and bathing in the river each day, about which he mordantly observed that one had to be rather careful since "alligators were rather troublesome in the dry season. During these months there was almost always one or two lying in wait near the bathing place for anything that might turn up at the edge of the water—dog, sheep, pig, child, or drunken Indian." [23]

After his bath and breakfast he spent five or six hours collecting and then passed the rest of the day drying and preserving his specimens and making copious drawings and even more copious notes.

Bates's first sojourn at Ega lasted until the spring of 1851, when he was obliged to return to Belém, fourteen hundred miles downriver. Any reading material had long since been exhausted, his clothes were in rags, and no remittances had arrived from London. He then botanized and explored on the Lower Amazon and the Tapajós until 1855, when he returned to Ega, a trip that was now made much easier with the introduction, in 1853, of the steamboat, which cut the journey from Belém to Santarém to just eight days.

During his second, longer stay at Ega, Bates fell into much the same routine that he had established earlier, but this time he ranged much farther afield, sometimes on trips three hundred or four hundred miles farther into the interior.

On 7 November 1856, he boarded the *Tabatinga* for a journey to Tonantins. Not only was he more comfortable traveling by steamboat, now he carried a new device that increased his comfort many-fold—a mosquito tent, which further transformed travel in those mosquito-laden areas.

He returned to Ega on 25 January 1857, again marveling at the speed at which he was now able to navigate the rivers. The trip downstream took just sixteen hours, more proof that life on the river was changing rapidly, or so it seemed.

In September 1857, again aboard the *Tabatinga*, Bates arrived at São Paulo de Olivença, some four hundred miles upstream. Soon after his arrival he heard a chilling story, which brought home the fact that the inroads of civilization had still not completely penetrated the Upper Amazon.

Four months earlier two young men had left the village to trade with the Majeronas Indians on the Jauari. The Majeronas' reputation for ferocity toward their enemies was overshadowed by an even more terrifying trait. They were cannibals. Anyone falling into their hands was likely to be eaten, and that is what happened to the unfortunate traders from Paulo de Olivença. They were killed by arrows, then roasted and eaten.

Throughout these journeys Bates was particularly struck by the vast numbers of turtles in the Upper Amazon. Indeed, turtle meat and eggs were a chief source of sustenance for everyone, whites and Indians, on the river.

He also was fascinated, but at a greater distance, by the almost equal numbers of what he alternately referred to as alligators and caimans. The farther up the Amazon he went, the more of them there were.

Bates remained at São Paulo for five months, during which time he collected thousands of additional specimens. Plans to travel farther west to the foot of the Andes had to be canceled because of an attack of what he called the "ague of the country."

The ague responded somewhat to quinine, which probably meant that it was malaria, but in any event Bates did not give in to it other than canceling the long journey to the Andes.

Instead he went out every day to botanize and collect specimens even though he was often overcome by violent attacks while in the forest. When such an attack came on, he said, "I then used to stand still and brave it out." To do otherwise, that is "if the feeling of lassitude is too much indulged," terrible damage can be done to the liver and spleen. Rudyard Kipling could not have said it better.

Unlike Wallace, who had left after four years, Henry Walter Bates had stayed on even though he shared the ambivalence of all expatriates, longing for home while extolling the virtues of a new land. But when the steamboat returned to São Paulo on 2 February 1858, the seriously ill Bates, who had begun to entertain the idea of quitting the jungles and returning home, went aboard and returned to Ega, where he began a convalescence.

Even though the fever and ague disappeared, it was clear that Bates would not be able to once again, as he put it, "turn my face westward." England and home now seemed not so dismal a prospect.

"The want of intellectual society, and of the varied excitement of European life, was also felt most acutely," he said, "and this, instead of becoming deadened by time, increased until it became almost insupportable. I was obliged, at last, to come to the conclusion that the contemplation of Nature alone is not sufficient to fill the human heart and mind." [24]

Accordingly, on 3 February 1859, five days before his thirty-fourth birthday, Bates left Ega for Belém, where he arrived on 17 March. He found the city, which he had left seven and a half years before, much changed. "It was no longer the weedy, ruinous, village-looking place" that he had found when he first came there in 1848.

Streets had been paved, and handsome houses and public buildings had replaced many of the run-down and badly constructed buildings that Bates remembered. More important, at least to Bates, the people had cast off much of the strictures of the Church and had embraced the customs of northern Europeans rather than the Portuguese. There were booksellers, a library, and four daily newspapers.

Like all transformations, however, the metamorphosis of Belém had come with a high price. Food and lodging were now exorbitantly expensive, and the lower classes were in real want, many of them reduced to actual famine. Typical was the example of oranges and bananas, both of which in the old days had basically been free. Now they were available only from street vendors at a very high price.

A much worse development, at least to the naturalist, was the desecration of the nearby forest. Roads were being hacked willy-nilly through the areas where Bates and Wallace had spent so many happy days collecting when they first arrived in the Amazon.

Little of the pristine wilderness that surrounded Belém in 1848 remained in 1859, although Bates predicted that the jungle would eventually reclaim its own and the new roads would be lined with the verdure that he first experienced. Instead, of course, the destruction of the rain forest would continue for the next century and a half, and by 2009, the sleepy river town of Belém had grown into a metropolis with a million and a half people.

On 2 June 1859, Bates boarded an American ship, the *Frederick Demming*, bound from Belém for New York, from where he would go on to England. As the ship passed down the estuary the next day, he saw, for the last time, the forests of the Amazon. That night, while the ship lay at anchor in the mouth of the great river, waiting for the wind, the old ambivalence—English home and hearth or roaming the wilds of the tropics—returned. As Bates said, those were "the saddest hours I ever recollect to have spent."[25]

The following day the *Frederick Demming* entered the Atlantic Ocean. On 6 June, some four hundred miles off the mouth of the Amazon, the ship began to pass through patches of floating grass, tree trunks, and withered foliage. "Among these masses," recalled Bates, "I espied many fruits of that peculiarly Amazonian tree the Ubussu palm; this was the last I saw of the Great River."[26]

WALLACE, A YEAR AFTER HIS RETURN to England in 1852, published his *A Narrative of Travels on the Amazon and Rio Negro*, in which he laid out some arguments for the process of natural selection. But according to biographer H. Lewis McKinney, "He definitely thought evolution was the explanation but wisely refrained from further comment until 1855." [27] In that year he published a paper that made it clear that he was an evolutionist, but it was not until 1858 that he wrote the paper that many believe should have given him priority over Charles Darwin in the formation of the principle of natural selection, the basis of evolution.

Wallace, who was at the time in the Malay Archipelago doing research that further buttressed his views on natural selection and evolution, sent the paper to Darwin, who immediately recognized its astonishing similarities to what he had already written but not yet published.

Charles Lyell and Joseph Hooker, concerned that their friend Darwin might be preempted, had his allegedly earlier formulation of the principle read to the Linnean Society, followed by Wallace's paper. They also urged Darwin to expedite publication of his long-gestating *On the Origin of Species*, and the book appeared the following year.

Thus Wallace, whose observations in the Amazon and later in the Malay Archipelago led him independently of Darwin to formulate the principle of natural selection, is credited as a codiscoverer of the principle. Indeed, Darwin himself did so credit him—once referring in a letter to Wallace as its being "your own and my child."

Wallace's later attempts to reconcile theology with evolution and his embrace of spiritualism dismayed and disheartened his many admirers and put a cloud, still not dispelled, over his considerable scientific achievements.

As for Bates, who had returned to England just a few months before publication of the *Origin*, any doubts he harbored about the process of natural selection and the theory of evolution had been laid to rest. Indeed, his own work in the Amazon added another important stone to the foundation of the edifice of evolution.

While in the rain forest, Bates observed what became known as Batesian mimicry. Bates documented the phenomenon of two different species that resemble each other very closely except that only one has natural protective defenses, such as stingers or a bad taste or perhaps even poison. The species lacking these defenses is nevertheless protected from predators because the predator is conditioned by a previous encounter with the real thing.

Only natural selection could account for mimicry, and Bates's research was used to buttress Darwin's argument. Indeed, the master himself pronounced Bates's 1862 paper on the subject "one of the most remarkable papers I have ever read in my life." [28]

Bates's account of his Amazon journeys, *The Naturalist on the River Amazons*, was published in 1863 and was justly praised as one of the great scientific travel books of the century. Not so incidentally it was also a source of much-needed income for the always financially precarious author. But the experience of writing the book was not a happy one. Indeed, he observed that he would rather spend eleven years in the Amazon than write another book, and he wrote no others. Instead Bates concentrated on his duties as assistant secretary of the Royal Geographical Society.

LONG AFTER WALLACE AND BATES had left the Amazon, the third member of the trio of naturalists, Richard Spruce, continued his own solitary botanizing and exploring in the Amazon Basin and beyond the Andes. He did not return to England until 1864.

Wallace and Bates's voyages up the Río Negro, the Uaupés, and the Solimões were estimable personable achievements to be sure, and each made lasting contributions to science, most notably in providing solid evidence for natural selection and the theory of evolution. But the larger goal—ascending the Amazon to its northern headwaters in the Andes and perhaps even crossing to the other side of that formidable mountain barrier—eluded them. This their unassuming colleague Richard Spruce accomplished.

Spruce, after three months botanizing in the regions around Belém, finally left that city on 10 October 1849, aboard the *Tres de Junho*, an eighty-ton trading brig bound for Santarém. Sailing upstream on a river might at first seem unusual, but the vast width of the Amazon—in many areas the shoreline is barely discernible from midstream—and its relatively slow-moving current enabled the experienced mariner to tack as necessary and make headway, albeit at times very slowly, upriver. Indeed, the total elapsed time for this particular voyage from Belém to Santarém, approximately five hundred miles, was less than seventeen days, a respectable thirty miles a day.

Spruce's preparations for his journey into the interior and a stay of indeterminate length at Santarém, where he planned to set up his headquarters, are instructive. Among his provisions were quantities of something described as "hard toasted bread," farina, and pirarucu, which Spruce said comprised "large strong-smelling slabs of salted fish from the Amazon, which only necessity and much practice can bring any one to relish." [29]

He also carried eggs, coffee, sugar, and in something called a *patuab-alaio*, which he said was indispensable for any traveler, there was stored in special compartments Bates's plates and flatware. This handy carry-all also had special places for two-quart bottles of molasses, whiskey, vinegar, and other liquid necessities. He may have been going into the jungles, but he would eat off plates with proper knives, forks, and spoons.

In addition, Spruce carried letters of credit to a merchant in Santarém and also that indispensable item that all foreigners were obliged to have in those regions—a large quantity of copper coins, the preferred medium of exchange. Spruce's bag of such coins weighed nearly a hundred pounds.

Spruce and his assistant King landed in Santarém around noon on 27 October 1849, and that very day they set up housekeeping in a rental arranged for them by Captain Hislop, the owner of the *Tres de Junho* and a resident of the town, and who had been on and about the Amazon for forty-five years.

Although as we have seen, Bates had not tarried at Santarém, Wallace was still there when Spruce arrived, and the two botanized together and met for convivial meals until 19 November, when Spruce and King departed by trading canoe for Óbidos, the next way station for mid-nineteenth-century naturalists on the journey up the Amazon. Wallace left a week later, but as previously noted, because of the wind and current the three men arrived very nearly at the same time at Óbidos.

While at Óbidos, Spruce and King made a short excursion, at least in distance, up the nearby Trombetas and into a tributary, the Aripecurú, to see the rapids and cataracts of that river. They celebrated Christmas Day on the beach by the rushing stream by toasting their less adventurous colleagues back in England.

This idyll almost ended in disaster three days later when King became separated from Spruce and their Indian guide. No sooner was he found than both Spruce and King foolishly dispatched the Indian back to the camp to prepare their dinner and proceeded on their own through the forest.

In short order they realized that they had no idea in which direction lay their camp and that they were alone in an area that abounded in jaguars, alligators, and poisonous vipers. Sleep was out of the question in such a hostile environment, so they pressed on, stopping only to rest until the moon had risen enough to help light their way as they staggered through the encircling vines, rotting stumps, and marshland, or waded through the shallow ponds along their path.

At last, in the middle of the night, they miraculously arrived at their camp, "sadly maltreated and wayworn," as Spruce wrote in his journal. He continued at some length about the episode so, he said, "to give some idea of what it is to be lost or benighted in an Amazonian forest. . . . Let the reader try to picture to himself the vast extent of the forest-clad Amazon valley; how few and far between are the habitations of man therein; and how the vegetation is so dense that, especially where the ground is level, it is rarely possible to see more than a few paces ahead; so that the lost traveller may be very near to help, or close to some known track or landmark, without knowing it." [30]

Spruce's cautionary tale is as relevant to the trekker or hiker in the twenty-first century as it was in 1849. A few steps off the designated track or trail and one can quickly find oneself completely alone in the rampant vegetation of the tropical rain forest. Even though companions might be just a few feet away, they have become invisible. Coupled with a violent rainstorm or darkness, the situation can quickly become dangerous, even life-threatening.

In spite of the scare that he and King had been given—indeed Spruce admitted that it took them a full week to recover—they stayed in the area of the cataracts for four days before heading back down the Aripecurú to the Tapajós and then down the Amazon to Santarém, where they arrived on Three Kings Day, 6 January 1850. Here they settled in until October.

Spruce's long stay in Santarém in 1850 coincided with some of the highest water levels in the Amazon Basin in anyone's memory. In 1849, the high-water mark was reached on 12 June, but in 1850, this level had been exceeded by 15 April. However, the water did begin to subside, as usual, in mid-June.

All life on the Amazon is attuned to the rise and fall of the water. As the water begins to rise in the autumn, people along the river's banks are obliged to move farther back—often relocating entire villages—where they await the fall of the water and then begin to plant beans, rice, and other staples in the rich soil deposited along the natural levees or terraces that form as the water slowly recedes. Two or even three crops are possible until the waters of the Amazon begin the annual, inexorable rise to cover the narrow strips of cultivated land along its banks. The indigenous peoples have taken advantage of this cycle for millennia.

The unusually high water and widespread flooding in 1850 had a more deadly side effect, however. In April, word reached Santarém of the outbreak of yellow fever at Belém. Santarém was spared, but the pandemic lingered on in Belém until 1851, when it carried off Edward Wallace and sickened Henry Walter Bates.

Many prophylactic measures were taken by the citizens of Santarém, who were convinced that one or perhaps the combination of all of them had forestalled an epidemic. Spruce the scientist was having none of it. He dismissed them all.

He characterized the firing of field pieces in the streets to clear the atmosphere and prevent the fever from entering Santarém as "an amusing process." He was also contemptuous of the burning of brands of white pitch raised on poles throughout the city, although he admitted that the "perfume" from the fires was rather pleasant.

But it was his skepticism about "the most efficacious precaution of all"—the kissing by the devout of the small wooden statue of St. Sebastian in the cathedral—that caused talk. The faithful, who were convinced that their show of piety had moved the saint to intervene and save their city, condemned the impious *estrangeiro*'s failure to kiss the statue. But, as Spruce wryly observed, since the apostate "contributed his mite towards the expenses of the feast, his crime was considered venial." [31]

The high waters prevented Spruce from his usual rounds of botanizing and exploring, but he was satisfied with the respectable number of plants he was able to collect. However, by October he had become restless and anxious to roam farther afield. Accordingly, Spruce "fixed on the mouth of the Río Negro for my next centre of operations." [32]

Now began Richard Spruce's real exploration and study of the Amazon and its headwaters and tributaries. Could he have known when he set foot in a small sailing canoe in Santarém on 8 October 1850 that he would never return to the lower reaches of the great river? Or that he would return to England not from Belém but from a port across the Andes on the Peruvian coast? Or that his return to his native land would not be for fourteen years? A more important question might be, Would he have cared? Probably not.

By his own account Spruce was happiest botanizing alone and far from the demands of society. "My delicate health and retiring disposition have combined with my love of botanical pursuits to render me fond of solitary study," he wrote, "and I must confess that I feel a sort of shrinking at the idea of engaging in the turmoil of active life. . . ."

For now, Spruce's chief concern was reaching the Río Negro, which he entered aboard his small craft on the morning of 10 December 1850. That evening, after sixty-three days on the water, he and the faithful King disembarked at Manaus.

Their long voyage upriver—a stronger than usual current and sparse winds combined with the heavy weight of the canoe and only two paddlers—was very trying for Spruce. He and King spent most of the time lying under the *tolda*, the thatched roof shelter, dozing or reading books and old newspapers. As Spruce said, "We were indeed heartily sick of the protracted voyage, and glad to do anything in our power to accelerate it." [33]

Spruce did admit that the voyage was memorable for the staggering numbers of alligators seen along the banks of the Amazon above Óbidos. This phenomenon had also been remarked upon forty years earlier by Humboldt and by Spruce's contemporaries Bates and Wallace. All of them had good reason to be wary of these noble but dangerous creatures, but on at least two occasions, impatient with not being able to go about his work, Spruce slipped over the side of the canoe and swam ashore to have a look around.

Since those halcyon times, when sightings of the crocodile, the alligator, the caiman, and the jaguar were ordinary occurrences, their wanton slaughter to satisfy demands for their hides drove them almost to extinction throughout the vast swaths of South American jungle and river basin that was their former range.

The situation has improved somewhat of late. The amphibians have made a comeback of sorts, but no one writes today of sighting "vast numbers of alligators," as did Spruce in 1850. Indeed, this author saw only two small caiman on a journey of almost nine hundred miles on the Amazon and the Ucayali and various black-water tributaries and lakes in July 2009. And the sighting of the jaguar is a rare occurrence, indeed, although my own naturalist guides had seen one swimming across a black-water creek just a week before my arrival.

Spruce remained in Manaus until 14 November 1851, during which time he managed to put together at least two sizable shipments of plant species for George Bentham back in London, in which he said in a covering letter to his patron, "You will find absolutely nothing common."[34]

The first of the shipments was taken downriver to Belém in April 1851 by Spruce's companion King, who was to take the collection on to London. It is not recorded why Robert King decided to return home, and his absence is referred to only obliquely by Bruce and then in a rather complaining way. "I am now alone," he said to Bentham in the same letter referred to above, "and have to do the whole of the drying as well as the collecting. . . ."[35]

But solitude was ever the friend of Richard Spruce, and when he left Manaus for the upper Río Negro, he was indeed alone, except for a crew of six Indians, traveling in a canoe that he had bought and outfitted himself. This was a great advantage, said Spruce. "I was also master of my own movements; could stop where and when I liked, save that it was necessary to keep the Indians in good humour."[36]

Spruce was entering territory that had already been covered by Wallace and Humboldt, but neither of those worthy predecessors had done so with his thoroughness or single-mindedness.

By 28 December, Spruce, who was encamped below the falls of São Gabriel, was writing to the curator at Kew Gardens that he had dried and was preparing for shipment an astonishing three thousand specimens. But he lamented in the same letter that he had had to perform a form of botanical triage, concentrating on only those plants that seemed more exotic and ignoring hundreds of others. Clearly, he said, he would have to revisit the Río Negro to set this right.

In this long letter Spruce mentions that he has heard of the death of Edward Wallace of yellow fever but equally alarming was that he had received news that Alfred Wallace was reported near death from fever at São Joaquim, a settlement at the mouth of the Uaupés.

Although São Joaquim is just a few miles upstream from where Spruce was camped, there lay between the two friends that formidable natural barrier, the great cataracts of São Gabriel. After much hauling and portaging, Spruce's Indian crew finally deposited him and his equipment in the little town of São Gabriel on 15 January 1852. During the ordeal of surmounting the cataracts, Spruce almost gave in to despair.

As he wrote in a letter to his friend John Teasdale the following summer, "It may be true, as Humboldt says, that 'perils elevate the poetry of life,' but I can bear witness that they have a woeful tendency to depress its prose." And, he added, most of the voyage up the Río Negro provided him with "much to show and little to tell." [37]

After Santa Isabel, however, there was little to show but much to tell, almost all of it about the tribulations of river travel. But his gloom passed as he settled in for the summer in a small house at São Gabriel and once again could botanize.

São Gabriel was not without problems, certainly. There was the continuing shortage of foodstuffs, but a greater problem was that the town was infested with vampire bats, if one can call it a problem since that creature's fearsome reputation is largely unearned.

Spruce, by the simple expedient of covering himself completely while he slept, escaped being bitten, even though his house was overrun with the creatures. He also provided a small glimpse into his psyche in his descriptions of the habits of this universally feared and despised little flying mammal.

His neighbors in São Gabriel had a cat that stationed itself next to the bed of their sleeping children and kept the bats at bay. A cat lover himself, Spruce applauded the industry of the watch-cat. His love of cats, he opined, had probably been the reason that "sagacious dames have at divers times foretold of me that . . . I should die a bachelor, which, if I live not to get married, is likely enough to come true." [38]

Wallace, who had recovered from his bout of fever on the Uaupés and was on his way home to England, turned up at São Gabriel, and he and Spruce were reunited.

To their great amusement, the two friends found that their years of solitary wandering had made it difficult to converse intelligibly without lapsing into Portuguese about a third of the time. After Wallace returned to England, Spruce teasingly wrote to him, asking "what progress you are making in the English tongue, and whether you can by this time make yourself understood by the natives."[39]

Spruce set out for Wallace's old stomping grounds on the Uaupés at the end of August 1852 and explored there until March 1853, when he descended that river back to the Río Negro, where he once again headed upstream, reaching San Carlos on 11 April.

Here he was more or less stranded for the next six months, beset by lack of food, the relentless barrages of mosquitoes, and also at least one life-threatening situation. Spruce and the only other Europeans in the town, two Portuguese, became alarmed at rumors of a planned massacre by the Indian inhabitants during the upcoming Feast of San Juan.

For several anxious days, the well-armed whites and their families remained barricaded inside a house while the increasingly restive and very drunk Indians roamed the streets outside, firing off their weapons.

Eventually, the situation stabilized itself. Spruce wasn't sure if the show of force by the whites had cowed the Indians or if it was that their supply of the local spirits had run out as had their supplies of powder and shot during their exuberant displays. In any event, Spruce and the Portuguese continued to keep their arms close by and a wary eye on their Indian neighbors.

Finally, on 27 November 1853, Spruce began what was for him a true pilgrimage, traversing the Casiquiare in the footsteps of the venerated Alexander von Humboldt. Indeed, on the morning of 29 November, Spruce reached Solano, where he met the aged Silvestre Caya Meno, who not only remembered the Jesuits but doubtless had seen Humboldt himself when he passed through Solano on 10 May 1800.

On 21 December 1853, Spruce entered the Orinoco, which, he admitted, was an emotional moment for him when he thought of the "illustrious voyagers" who had preceded him there.

Four days later, on Christmas Eve, he disembarked at Esmeralda still euphoric at having navigated the Casiquiare as Humboldt had done a half century before. He was equally impressed by his first sight of Esmeralda, which Spruce said occupied the most beautiful natural site he had seen in South America. The wide river lay on one side, and to the west rose the lofty Cerro Duida.

But he was quickly disabused of any notions that Esmeralda was a paradise. On the contrary, Spruce wrote, it was an inferno. The town comprised a handful of miserable huts, the straw doors of which seemed sealed. Nothing moved in the small square. The town appeared deserted. "I thought the scene inexpressibly mournful. . . . But the utter absence of living things was only apparent, not real. If I passed my hand across my face I brought it away covered with blood and with crushed bodies of gorged mosquitoes. In this you have a key to explain the unearthly silence."[40]

Spruce nevertheless stayed on in Esmeralda, awaiting the arrival of the provincial commissioner who had invited him to accompany him on the search for the sources of the Orinoco. However, after waiting around for four days—Spruce later learned that the commissioner had lost his job and could not join him—he left Esmeralda to explore the Cunucunuma, a black-water river fed from the slopes of Mt. Duida. But by 7 January, he was back on the Casiquiare.

His journey back down the Casiquiare was a leisurely one punctuated by explorations of several of the tributaries of that stream, and he did not arrive back in San Carlos until 28 February 1854; this would be his headquarters off and on for almost two years.

The next few weeks were spent botanizing around San Carlos and preparing the specimens he had acquired on the Casiquiare and the Orinoco for shipment to Belém and then on to London.

When all was in order, Spruce was ready to set out again. The plan was to ascend the Río Negro to Pimichín and then take the road to Yavita, as Wallace had done in 1851, and from there go by boat to San Fernando de Atabapo. Spruce was, of course, also following, albeit in reverse, the route of his hero Humboldt.

From San Fernando, which he left on 18 June 1854, it was an easy trip to the confluence of the Atabapo and the Orinoco and then on to Maypures, where he arrived on 19 June. At Maypures, Spruce collected over a hundred different plant species in just four days and also supervised the slaughter and preparation of an ox, his main task being picking maggots out of the quickly spoiling meat.

By the end of the month he was back in San Fernando and dangerously ill from fever, exacerbated by the exigencies of travel and hard work. During his illness, he was many times near death, no doubt aided and abetted by an Indian woman who had been hired to care for him.

"This woman—Carmen Reja by name—I shall not easily forget," said Spruce. "She was a Zamba—that race by which nine-tenths of the most heinous crimes are said to be committed in Venezuela. . . ."[41]

For over a month Spruce suffered the tortures inflicted on him by his putative nurse, but finally he was rescued on 13 August by a Portuguese trader who carried him back to the Río Negro, from where he made his way back to San Carlos, where he arrived on 28 August.

Finally, on 23 November 1854, Richard Spruce left San Carlos and returned to Manaus, where he arrived on 22 December. His three-year journey exploring and botanizing along the Río Negro and the Orinoco was marked by great successes and the discovery of thousands of new species; but, as ever, Spruce was humbled by nature and his own perceived shortcomings. As he wrote so tellingly to Sir William Hooker from San Carlos on 19 March 1854,

> In returning from one of my long expeditions, I always feel a sense of humiliation at the little I have been able to effect for other sciences besides botany, and especially when the country traversed is perhaps more interesting to the geographer than to the botanist; nor does it console me to reflect that one person cannot do everything. . . . But there are persons who would have done much more, and someone will come after me, possessing more health and strength, aided by industrious hands, and with resources of every kind at his disposal, who will complete whatever I have left imperfect.[42]

This self-effacing and rather winning letter was written at not even the halfway point in Spruce's remarkable South American sojourn. Indeed, perhaps his most important work still lay ahead of him.

After three months in Manaus, Spruce left again for another expedition, which like all previous ones was marked only by a rather nebulous itinerary and no fixed schedule. But compared to his earlier adventures, when Spruce left Manaus on 14 March 1855—accompanied by a new assistant named Charlie, a sailor he hired in Manaus—it was in the relative luxury of the *Monarca*, another of the three steamboats that had begun service on the Amazon in 1853.

The trip to Manaquiri, which in 1851 had taken a week in a canoe, now was accomplished in just ten hours, and in short order the *Monarca* passed also Tabatinga and Loreto, two small places that nevertheless loom large in the story of the Amazon, and by 1 April they were in Iquitos, which Spruce described as "a considerable village." The next day the *Monarca* reached the proper beginning of the Amazon—the junction of the Ucayali and the Marañón rivers.

In spite of the rapidity of the new mode of travel, Spruce, like many travelers before and after him, still grew impatient. As he said, the trip of some fifteen hundred miles could have been done in one week instead of two except for the inordinate amount of time taken up with loading the wood for the fires that drove the boilers.

Delays aside, if one can call refueling stops such, on 2 April, they reached the village of Nauta, a few miles up the Marañon and the terminus for the little steamer. Spruce was now obliged to revert to the old and familiar means of travel in the hinterland—a canoe rowed by Indians.

As had happened before, this was no easy task, and it was not until 16 April that arrangements were made for two such craft and Spruce and Charlie were able to leave Nauta.

The old jungle hand easily made the transition to the less commodious and decidedly slower mode of travel. The mosquitoes were the usual misery, but Spruce could take refuge ashore beneath a newly acquired mosquito tent. However, when he reached Yurimaguas on the Río Huallaga, a major tributary of the Marañon, he became seriously ill with diarrhea and influenza.

Charlie, the amanuensis acquired from the docks and saloons of

Manaus, proved not so adaptable. In Yurimaguas, one of his many unsavory traits, which had started to surface on the voyage up the river—a propensity to mistreat the Indians—blossomed forth with a vengeance.

Not being able to speak any language except English, Charlie imagined every conversation in Portuguese or Spanish to be full of slights directed at himself, and he would fly into a murderous rage directed toward the author of the perceived slights.

A few days after their arrival in Yurimaguas, Charlie attacked without provocation the old Indian sacristan, injuring him badly. Later that day, during dinner at the village priest's house, he turned on a Portuguese traveler and threatened to kill him with a pickaxe. Only Spruce's immediate intervention saved the poor man's life.

Spruce himself came to realize that Charlie's probable motive for coming on the voyage upriver was to murder him and make off with his small cache of money. He thus took to sleeping with a revolver under his pillow until he could rid himself of this obvious psychopath.

Finally, he was able to hire two Indians, at great cost, to transport the criminal back downriver to Manaus. He later learned that the two Indians murdered Charlie and dumped his body in the Amazon just below the mouth of the Ucayali.

What could have possessed the mild-mannered and cultivated botanist to pick up such an unsavory and obviously dangerous character on the docks of Manaus? Spruce's rather lame explanation might be of interest to the armchair psychologist.

While in Manaus, he wrote, he met several adventurers who had come to the Amazon Basin to prospect for gold. "Many of these had passed through Barra [Manaus] before I arrived there," he said, "but I still met several, and amongst them an English sailor who seemed a very quiet fellow, and whom I engaged to accompany me to Peru, thinking that a stout companion like him would be invaluable to me . . ."[43]

Whatever the reasons for engaging Charlie may have been, Spruce was now rid of him, but now uncharacteristically he began to have serious doubts about the enterprise itself. As he wrote to George Bentham, "I am inclined to repent having come on this expedition. . . ."[44]

Whatever, the cause of this malaise or depression—illness, the unfortunate affair of the ne'er-do-well sailor, the unexpected expenses, or the days, even weeks, of not being able to botanize—by the time he left Yurimaguas, the scene of such despair, and headed farther up the Huallaga, Spruce had begun to recover his old ebullience and enthusiasm.

Much of the recovery was also due to his now being close to one of his major goals—the Andes. He had first glimpsed the mountains on 2 May, while still two days' journey from Yurimaguas, and he had an epiphany not unlike that when he first entered the Orinoco. As he exclaimed in a letter to his friend Teasdale in London, "I enjoyed my first view of the Andes!" His excitement is almost palpable since the sentence was underlined in the letter.

At the tiny settlement of Juan Guerra, Spruce transferred to a very different sort of transport. As he engagingly described it to Teasdale, "When you consider the amphibious life I had led for six years . . . you will understand that I found the transition from a canoe to a horse rather abrupt. I am, however, too old a traveller to be taken aback by anything. . . ."[45]

His mount was not a horse but a mule, "a large white macho," sent by a Don Ignacio, a native of Mallorca now resident at Tarapoto, who had promised to aid Spruce in his scientific work. Debarking from the canoe, Spruce mounted up and set out cross-country to Tarapoto, which, even in 1855, was a town of some twelve thousand people. The town, which lies at about fifteen hundred feet, is surrounded by the foothills of the Andean Cordillera, and the temperate climate and abundant rainfall ensured that it would be richer in botanical specimens than any area Spruce explored in his long stay in South America. Thus it would be his headquarters from 22 June 1855 until 23 March 1857.

At Tarapoto, Spruce also acquired another assistant, a young man named Charles Nelson, who, happily, turned out to be more reliable and trustworthy than the scoundrel Charlie. Nelson would remain with him until he left Tarapoto. Spruce's letters during this period provide colorful and sometimes alarming accounts of his encounters with the various snakes, insects, and other creatures that can cause misery or even death to the unwary in these regions.

Spruce was bitten by scorpions and tarantulas, stung hundreds of times by wasps, and always there were the mosquitoes. He also barely managed to escape injury or death from the many encounters and strikes by the snakes he encountered.

But his account of the near-death experience of one of his servants from snake bite is informative. The man was bitten on the hand by a particularly dangerous reptile, a *urrito-machácui*, or parrot snake, while crawling on the ground in pursuit of a turkey for Spruce's dinner.

Spruce and Nelson spent the next three days ministering to the unfortunate Indian. They lanced the wound, attempted to suck the venom out, and applied poultices to the arm, which swelled to alarming proportions. All the while the poor man moaned in agony and his relatives wailed outside the hut.

On the third day, Spruce and Nelson's ministrations began to take effect, and the Indian began to recover. Spruce later learned that if the man had died, his own life would have been forfeit since he had sent the Indian on the almost fatal errand. Such was the law of the region.

Spruce's second year at Tarapoto was an unnecessary extension since, as he said, he had exhausted the collecting possibilities. A certain sameness had set in. But he was obliged to stay on longer because of the high waters, and another perilous situation had arisen, this one man-made.

An antigovernment uprising created turmoil in Tarapoto and the surrounding countryside, but it was more opéra bouffe than serious revolution—at least for Spruce, who nevertheless went about armed just in case.

For some of the townspeople, however, the uprising was very serious, indeed. A young friend of Spruce's who was sympathetic to the revolutionaries was executed when government troops swept through the region.

Finally, on 23 March 1857, Spruce began his long and long-delayed journey into Andean Ecuador. His route, ironically, was almost the exact reverse of that of La Condamine in 1743.

Spruce's own journey, a distance of five hundred miles, took him from Tarapota, back down the Huallaga, up the Marañon to the Pastaza and the Bobonaza to Canelos, and then across the mountains to Baños and hence to Riobamba. He was then out of the Amazon Basin and its multitudinous headwaters and tributaries.

At Baños, Spruce seems to have departed, albeit briefly, from his rigid scientific approach to life and nature. But even the most dedicated scientist can nod off. (See, for example, Alfred Russel Wallace's embrace of spiritualism.) Spruce himself fell under the sway of that chimera called the "hidden treasure of the Incas," which was said to be stashed away somewhere in the mountains of northern Ecuador.

The legend, as most such are, was replete with the mysterious disappearances of treasure seekers, and there was the obligatory treasure map, a copy of which surfaced and which Spruce was allowed to see, as well as a detailed guide. Spruce made a copy of the map and translated the guide. He included both in a paper that he sent to the Royal Geographical Society, along with the suggestion that perhaps a person with the time and sufficient means might pursue the matter further.

Spruce himself, after this flirtation with legends of hidden Incan treasure, continued his botanizing, working independently on the western slopes of the cordillera, until 1859. Early that year he was deputized by the India Office to collect seeds and young plants of the cinchona—the bark of which is the source of quinine, then the only effective treatment for malaria—and transport them out of the country for the establishment of plantations in the Far East.

By the 1850s quinine was being used in large quantities in the treatment of malaria, and a dependable source of quinine was essential to the ever-expanding British Empire, which was delayed and even halted in many areas of Asia and Africa—the so-called "white man's grave"—where malaria was a scourge. The disease still affects some five hundred million people worldwide and there are a million deaths a year. For many of these sufferers quinine is still the only available drug.

Quinine—the name derives from a Quechua word for the cinchona tree, *quina*—had been known and used by the Indians of South America for centuries. It was brought to Europe, where it was used to treat malaria in Rome as early as 1631, by Agostino Salumbrino, a Jesuit missionary in Peru. Indeed, it was popularly known as Jesuit's bark.

There is a further tale—apocryphal but, like all such, no less interesting—attached to the cinchona tree and its miraculous properties. The Countess Chinchón, wife of the viceroy of Peru, supposedly became ill with malaria in 1630, but recovered after being treated with a concoction made from the quina tree. Allegedly, when she later returned to Spain, she brought back some of the miracle cure, and word of it began to spread throughout Europe.

As attractive as the story of the Countess Chinchón is, it was laid to rest in 1941 by A. W. Haggis in an article in the *Bulletin of the History of Medicine*. It seems the countess never had malaria, or if she did she didn't recover from it. She died at Cartagena en route home to Spain.

No matter, a century later Carl Linnaeus, expanding on the work of La Condamine, who reported on cinchona and brought back samples from his own sojourn in Peru in the 1730s, honored the Countess Chinchón and La Condamine by attaching both their names to the tree, although that great namer of all things botanical took some liberties with the spelling of the countess' name. The tree is called *cinchona*.

Spruce readily agreed to the cinchona scheme, recognizing that establishing plantations in the Far East would ensure the survival of the various species, which were in real danger of being wiped out by the indiscriminate, even reckless destruction of the trees by the *cascarilleros*, the bark gatherers, who had the mistaken idea, prevalent throughout Ecuador, that the bark was used not for medicine but to make a dye.

Spruce set out for the cinchona forests on 11 June 1860 and once again found himself looking down into the headwaters of the Amazon, into the valley of the Pastaza, from the eastern flanks of Chimborazo. Skirting the great volcano and after much difficulty he arrived at the cinchona forests on the western flank of the mountain, at an altitude ranging from two thousand to five thousand feet.

There now enters another of those Englishmen who seem to pop up every generation or so and change the course of empire. This particular gentleman was Clements Markham, who had come back to Peru—this was his third visit—on a mission, to collect cinchona seeds and seedlings and transport them out of the country for possible cultivation in the Far East. Markham also was operating under the aegis of the India Office, but his commission had come directly from the secretary of state for India.

Markham was well aware that Spruce was already fulfilling his mandate, but he felt that Spruce needed a confederate so had engaged a young Scotsman, Robert Cross, as an assistant. Cross now was dispatched across the mountains to join up with Spruce in the cinchona forests.

Other than their nationality and their enthusiasm for botany, Spruce and Markham were exact opposites in every way. The gentle and self-effacing Spruce, whose original specialty was mosses, would doubtless be appalled that his scientific fame and reputation are irrevocably tied to this man, who was anything but of a "retiring disposition."

Markham was a young, handsome, flamboyant, self-serving former navy officer who did not hesitate to use his social connections—his mother was the daughter of a baronet and an aunt was a countess—to advance both his career and his scientific agenda, which coincided perfectly with the Victorian ideal of ensuring British hegemony in war, the arts, and the sciences.

Although never enchanted with navy life, Markham served from 1844 until 1851, when he resigned his commission. Rumors have persisted that there might very well have been a more shadowy reason for the termination of his naval career. Markham was a homosexual. He married and fathered a daughter, but his vocal and unstinting support for a succession of younger protégés fed the rumors about his true sexuality— as indeed was true of Humboldt, Spruce, and others who were attracted to the Amazon Basin.

Markham had become enthralled with South America as a young naval cadet aboard a ship that had called at Rio de Janeiro, Valparaiso, and Callao, the port of Lima, during a four-year cruise, and he was anxious to return there. Thus, after resigning his commission, the twenty-two-year-old, aided by a munificent gift from his indulgent father, set out for South America on 20 August 1852, arriving back in Callao on 16 October. After a slow journey through the interior, he arrived at Cuzco, the ancient capital of the Incas, on 20 March 1853.

Although untrained in the sciences, Markham made up in enthusiasm what he lacked in formal scientific study, and he threw himself into observing the geography, flora, and fauna of the area adjacent to the headwaters of the Amazon in Peru. He also worked at perfecting his Spanish and becoming fluent in Quechua, the better to study the history of the Inca Empire, another abiding passion.

Clements Markham's second stay in Peru was cut short by the death of his father, and he returned to England in September 1853 to see to the estate. But during the succeeding years his thoughts returned again and again to one of the many botanical specimens that he had encountered in Peru—the cinchona tree.

After his arrival in Peru in 1860, it was no difficult task for the worldly and ambitious Markham to take charge of the cinchona operation and later take the lion's share of the credit for its ultimate success. While Spruce and Cross did the drudge work of gathering the cinchona seeds and coaxing some of them to sprout, Markham was plotting how to smuggle seeds and seedlings out of the country. Peru, not surprisingly, was anxious to maintain a monopoly on quinine and forbade the export of the cinchona seeds.

Spruce and Cross did their work well and with dispatch—no easy task since the country was going through yet another of its periodic political and military upheavals. The cinchona seeds, some 100,000 of them, and the seedlings, several hundred, were dispatched in two separate consignments, but everything was en route by November 1860.

Sad to relate, the smuggled seeds did not, as hoped, lead immediately to thriving cinchona plantations in India and Ceylon. But by 1880, the plantations were up and running, and in one year over a million pounds of cinchona bark sold on the London market.

The Dutch, meanwhile, were pursuing the same goal and were more successful. Also using smuggled seeds, but from a more powerful form of cinchona, which may or may not have helped in successful generation, they established plantations on the island of Java, which came to overwhelmingly dominate the world market. By the 1930s, Java was producing 97 percent of the world's supply of quinine and would remain the primary source until the island was overrun by the Japanese in World War II.

The Japanese occupation of Southeast Asia led to quinine being synthesized in 1944 although the exact chemical composition of quinine was confirmed by French scientists as early as 1817. However, the cost of producing the synthetic version, compared to production from the bark of the cinchona tree, still gives the natural substance a decided edge. Then, too, the natural drug still remains the treatment of choice for severe cases of malaria.

A steady and reliable supply of quinine ensured that vast areas of Asia and Africa, which had hitherto been off-limits to anyone but the most hardy, or foolish, of Europeans, could be exploited.

However, gratitude for the ready availability of quinine is not limited just to potential or actual sufferers of malaria. Others have reason to be grateful for the work of those enterprising Englishmen and Dutchmen as well. Generations of drinkers of gin and tonic have toasted their initiative.

Richard Spruce stayed on in South America until 1 May 1864, when he embarked at Payta aboard a mail steamer for Panama, where he crossed the Isthmus to the Atlantic, sailing for England on 7 May. He arrived in Southampton on 28 May 1864—"after an absence from England of 15 years all but 10 days," as he recorded in his journal.[46]

He was now forty-seven years old and had spent nearly a third of his life traversing the rivers, jungles, deserts, and high mountains of Brazil, Peru, and Ecuador. During this long sojourn he sent back specimens of more than seven thousand species, almost all of them new to science.

Richard Spruce had the universal respect of the botanical community. He was made an honorary fellow of the Royal Geographical Society in 1866 and an associate of the Linnean Society in 1893. But no other honors were bestowed on him for his great services to science. It is unlikely that he either noticed or was bothered by this neglect.

In spite of the various infirmities either caused by or exacerbated by his many years in the jungle, Spruce lived to be seventy-six years old. He seemed happy living alone in his modest cottage in Yorkshire, albeit in relative poverty. He spent the last thirty years of his life there corresponding with and receiving many distinguished colleagues and working on his vast collections of plants.

Clements Markham, in contrast, came to be recognized as the preeminent geographer of the Victorian age. Indeed, his detractors' protestations to the contrary—the criticisms were and are that his many books, articles, and translations are marked more by enthusiasm than by scholarly rigor or any original scientific insights—he reaped many honors in his lifetime.

His greatest strengths were as a proselytizer, organizer, and promoter—not least of himself. Thus he was rewarded with the presidencies of both the Hakluyt Society and the Royal Geographical Society and, of course, a knighthood.

# The Great Rubber Boom

ONE OF THE RECURRING MYTHS THAT BEGUILED THE CONQUISTA-
dors and their successors was the fabled land of El Dorado, where, it was
said, even the streets were paved with gold. Another was the existence of
an emerald the size of a hen's egg, which was worshipped by the Indian
tribes and kept in a specially consecrated temple until the white man
came. The fabled jewel had then been spirited away and hidden in the
farthest reaches of the high Andes or the rain forest.

The true riches of the Amazon, of course, did lie hidden in the forests
that bordered the river and its hundreds of tributaries, but this would not
be evident until the seventeenth century, with the discovery that quinine

was effective against malaria. But it was not until the nineteenth century that the Amazon finally came into its own, through exploitation of another natural product—rubber—without which the industrial world would not have been possible.

The basis for the world's rubber industry is a tree native to the Amazon rain forest, *Hevea brasiliensis*. And the giant industry that grew from the exploitation of this tree was based on a gathering system that was simplicity itself and has been little improved upon since the first Amazonian Indian slashed the bark of the Hevea and discovered it exuded a milky white fluid, latex.

Using a procedure not unlike the tapping of sugar maples by their cousins, the Native Americans of New England, the Indians of the rain forest learned to systematically slash the tree, which they called "the weeping tree," and collect the sap, which they called caoutchouc, in cups or gourds attached to the trunk.

The latex was then flattened between banana leaves and fashioned into a sort of waterproof cloth. For centuries latex had been used by the Indians to make waterproof footwear and capes, crude bottles for liquids, and the balls for their games.

The early European explorers had been made aware of this substance, but it was left for Charles-Marie de La Condamine, as he traveled downstream on the Amazon in 1743, to observe the various uses of caoutchouc by the Indians he encountered in the settlements along the river.

Earlier, in Peru, La Condamine had similarly studied the bark of the cinchona tree, and his observations and paper on the subject helped popularize the use of the alkaloid quinine, derived from the bark of the tree, in the treatment of malaria. Since cinchona was extracted from the bark of the tree, which had to be stripped from the trunk, the exploitation of the drug would in just over a hundred years after La Condamine's journey lead to the almost complete destruction of the cinchona tree in its natural habitat.

After his Amazon trek, La Condamine passed some months at Cayenne in French Guiana, where he worked closely with another Frenchman,

François Fresneau, who had done considerable research on the gathering of latex and the fashioning of various objects out of rubber by the natives.

La Condamine sent some samples of the substance to Europe, and after he returned to France, he published a paper on Fresnau's research on the gathering of latex and its many uses. This paper—"Mémoire sur une résine élastique, nouvellement découverte à Cayenne par M. Fresneau: et sur l'usage de divers sucs laiteux d'arbres de la Guiane ou France équinoctiale"—was widely read, and the use of the new product spread throughout Europe.

Almost immediately it was discovered that latex was useful for rubbing away or erasing lead pencil marks. Hence the word *rubber*. The India rubber eraser soon became ubiquitous in homes and offices around the world.

Latex continued to be used to make rather mundane objects such as erasers and rubber shoes until the middle of the nineteenth century. Some half-million pairs of the shoes were exported annually to the United States from Brazil.

However, latex, besides being rather homely, was also unstable, and the rubber industry remained small until the process of vulcanization was devised by Charles Goodyear in the 1830s.

Goodyear's process not only guaranteed a longer life for rubber products, it gave birth to a giant new industry. Footwear, washers, packings, conveyer belts, and insulation for the new electrical wires were just some of the uses for the new product, which contributed mightily to the rise of the modern industrial state. But it was not until the growth of another industry, the manufacture of bicycles, that the rubber industry began truly to flourish.

The first tires for bicycles, which were solid, added only marginally to the comfort of the rider. The pneumatic tire, patented in 1889, created a boom that coincided with the bicycle craze in Europe and America. Within eight years some three million bicycles were being turned out annually.

The bicycle fad, which lasted not even a decade, was replaced by not just a fad but a whole new way of life. The world had now begun to take to the roads on a new mode of transportation, the automobile.

The automobile, which has been called the fourth necessity—after food, clothing, and shelter—has since its introduction fueled a great percentage of the economic growth of every major industrial power. And the rubber industry benefited mightily. Few industries have been so symbiotic as the rubber industry and automotive industry. All cars, after all, need four tires and a spare, and in 1916 alone the United States automobile industry produced 1,525,578 new cars. Other industrialized countries were soon following suit. Automobiles were soon coming off assembly lines in the millions of units.

The automobile created a demand for tires that increased exponentially each year. But the automobile industry also created demand for other rubber products, such as hoses and belts. The rubber industry entered a period of phenomenal growth, doubling its output every two years.

Most of the world's rubber still came from South America, and the sophisticated trade and manufacture of rubber products remained firmly tied to a system as old as work itself—the back-breaking labor of the *seringueiros*, the rubber collectors of the rain forest.

As their Indian and slave ancestors had done for centuries, the seringueiros, who themselves were little more than serfs or slaves, made the incisions in the trees and collected the sap by hand. Walking the well-trod paths in the steaming jungles, these tappers went from tree to tree gathering the sticky sap from the Hevea. The yield of two men, working in tandem, seldom exceeded three gallons a day from 100 to 120 trees.

What the latex represented and what was to be done with it seldom, if ever, crossed their minds as they made their rounds. The buckets of sap might help alleviate their debts at the company store or to the *patrão*, or patron, who completely controlled their lives—an endless round of gathering the latex to pay off the traders and exploiters to whom the seringueiros had mortgaged themselves for the gewgaws and worthless trinkets fobbed off on them.

In the course of a year, one tree might yield three or four pounds of rubber. Therefore, these "plantations" in the rain forest necessarily comprised many square miles and many thousands of trees, with the concomitant vast force of seringueiros to gather the latex.

At the beginning of the commercial exploitation of the rubber trees, the work was somewhat easier since the seringueiros were able to work close to the river banks. But as the demand for their product increased, the more accessible trees were overtapped and began to die. Consequently the seringueiros were obliged to go farther and farther into the forests. By the early 1850s the forests near the mouth of the Amazon were essentially exhausted, and the industry moved upriver, deep into the forests of Amazonas.

Rules were promulgated to prevent overtapping the latex, and inspectors did their best to see that they were enforced. But the reforms were introduced too late. Brazil maintained its tight control over the harvesting and its lead in production of latex, but the decline had begun.

Clements Markham, of cinchona fame, was one of the first to recognize that the seringueiros were killing their arboreal golden goose. As early as 1853, he remarked on the devastation being wrought by the overtapping of the rubber trees, and as with the cinchona, he presciently noted that it would be necessary in the future to guarantee more reliable sources of rubber since Brazil was destroying the natural supply in the Amazon Rain Forest.

Markham had, by 1870, through great ambition and also through the success of the cinchona experiment, risen to a position in the scientific and business establishments to promote yet another audacious undertaking, one that would have perhaps even more far-reaching effects than ensuring the supply of quinine.

Markham was certain, as he had been with cinchona, that seeds of Hevea brasiliensis, the rubber tree, could be collected in the Amazon and sent to India or Ceylon in order to establish plantations, which would ensure a stable and dependable supply of rubber.

Brazil forbade the exportation of seeds of the rubber tree in order to maintain its monopoly, but Markham was able to obtain a few seeds, and the first experiments were begun. They ended in disaster. How could it have been otherwise? The climate in the area of India where the trees were planted in no regard matched that of the equatorial rain forest where the plant was native.

The failure of this first experiment was by no means a deterrence, quite the contrary. Indeed Markham did not acknowledge failure. Instead he began to think on a larger scale, reasoning that the acquisition of many thousands of seeds would broaden the enterprise enough to ensure success.

Enter now a resident of the Amazon, one of those extraordinary types, whom for centuries England has produced so prodigally, especially in Victorian times. Or perhaps these types were what produced the Victorian era. In any event, Markham, with the timely intervention of Sir Joseph Hooker, the director of the Royal Botanic Gardens at Kew, found his man in Amazonia, an enterprising, or at least adventurous, thirty-year-old Englishman who could have been the prototype for a character of Joseph Conrad.

Henry Alexander Wickham had knocked about the rain forests of South America since the age of twenty and in 1876 was living a precarious existence with his wife on a small plantation near Santarém. There, with the aid of a few Indians and some whites—rebel holdouts from the American Civil War, who had fled to South America rather than surrender and swear allegiance to the Union—Wickham was grubbing a living out of the jungles by gathering and exporting latex.

At Markham's behest, Wickham organized an expedition, which traveled by canoe up the Tapajós and then overland on foot into a wild and unknown region of Amazonia, to gather seeds from the Hevea for shipment to England.

The seeds he and his crew gathered, some seventy thousand of them, were wrapped in banana leaves and then transported back down the Tapajós to the Amazon, where they were loaded onto a chartered cargo vessel, the *Amazonas*, near Santarém. The ship then proceeded downriver.

To allay suspicions, and avoid almost certain confiscation of the illicit cargo, Wickham called on the governor at Belém and spent a social evening at the governor's mansion regaling him and his guests with tales of the area upriver from Belém.

As for his cargo, Wickham assured the governor that it was fragile botanical specimens for the gardens at Kew and therefore any delay could be fatal to the plants.

Meanwhile the *Amazonas*, on Wickham's orders, had kept up a full head of steam to ensure a hasty departure as soon as Wickham obtained the necessary permissions to get under way.

Wickham's disingenuous appeals—he was aided in the fraud by the British consul in Belém—had their effect on the gullible Portuguese. He thanked them for their hospitality, said his good-byes, and quickly made his way to the harbor, where he boarded a dinghy and was rowed out to the *Amazonas*. In a short time, the ship was in the broad estuary of the Amazon, bound for the open sea and England.

History is full of ironies and coincidences, and one of the more resonant of the latter is that while Wickham was smuggling the Hevea seeds out of Brazil, in Germany an inventor named Nikolaus August Otto was testing the first four-stroke internal-combustion engine. A true symbiosis—rubber and automobiles—which for good or ill would transform the world thus began in 1876.

Wickham disembarked the *Amazonas* at Le Havre and sped across the Channel, where he arranged for Hooker to dispatch a train to meet the ship and collect the cargo when it docked at Liverpool.

Markham, Hooker, and the staff at Kew were overjoyed at Wickham's successful knavery and at once the botanists at Kew set about the planting of the Hevea seeds. Within a few short weeks several thousand seedlings were thriving in the greenhouses of Kew.

The seedlings grown from the purloined seeds were shipped to Ceylon, where the first true rubber plantations were established. Others followed throughout Southeast Asia, particularly in Thailand, Indonesia, and Malaysia.

These first trees took many years to mature, and there was much confusion on the part of the tappers as to how to get the Hevea milk, the latex, out of the tree without destroying the tree itself. This had never been much of a problem in the Amazon, where the seringueiros cared not a whit about the tree as they slashed into it with their knives and machetes. There were thousands more trees awaiting the harvest.

A carefully laid out plantation was a different matter altogether. The trees must be kept alive and harvested regularly. Eventually, it was learned that although a Hevea might look full grown, it must be about ten years old to produce latex. As for harvesting, again through trial and error, the tappers in the growers in the Far East learned how to properly extract the latex. A first cut was made and allowed to heal, which took only a day. Then the tapper would return and shave off a thin layer, and the latex flowed readily.

By 1910 it was clear that the great experiment was a success. The wild Hevea brasiliensis of the Amazon jungles was now domesticated and growing in orderly rows and producing on plantations all over Southeast Asia.

As for the larcenous Wickham, he never repeated his success of 1876, and until a few years before he died in 1928 at the age of eighty-two he lived always under the cloud of insolvency. Toward the end of his long life he received an annuity from the Rubber Growers Association of London and various cash grants, which somewhat eased his financial predicament. And a knighthood by George V in 1920 no doubt made his relative penury easier to bear.

The domestication of Hevea was a botanically unique occurrence. All cultivated plants were once wildings, but no other plant made the transition from feral to domestic in such short order. In just thirty years the transformation of Hevea was complete.

But the domestication of Hevea also brought about a concomitant wildness in the rubber industry. Everyone seemed to want to get into the rubber business. Companies were formed, shares were sold, and the promise of great fortunes to be made beguiled the unwary. Cabdrivers and society matrons, ditch diggers and tycoons, it made no difference. Anyone who could rustle up a dollar, or a shilling, or an inheritance put the money into rubber shares.

Prices of the raw product soared to a high of $3.06 per pound in 1910, but by 1913 had declined to $.82 per pound. The fortunes that were made overnight by speculating in rubber shares were lost just as quickly as the stocks declined precipitously. And the price of rubber continued to decline, reaching a low of $.35 in 1920.

Everything, especially the product itself, turned out to be on paper. The plantations in Southeast Asia were producing very little rubber, it seems. Wild rubber, particularly from Brazil, still was the leader and would remain so until 1914, when the plantations finally began to come into their own. In that year domestic rubber amounted to 60.4 percent of world production. In two years the ratio was three to one. And by 1919 plantation rubber constituted 87 percent of world production—348,574 tons of cultivated to 50,424 tons of wild.

Not even the ongoing debate as to which product was superior—purists held out for wild rubber, even though it was far more expensive—dampened the enthusiasm for the domesticated product. By the beginning of the twenty-first century the Asian market share had grown to more than 90 percent of the world's natural rubber.

The shareholders may have lost their shirts, but the plantation owners and producers in the Far East were making vast profits in spite of the bust since it cost only $.25 to produce a pound of rubber.

The day of reckoning was soon at hand in the Amazon, however. The great expansion of the industry in Brazil had largely been financed on credit, from the brokerage houses and banks in the financial centers of America and Europe to the supply and shipping houses in Belém, Manaus, and Iquitos, to the patrãos on the plantations and estates, and down to the seringueiros themselves toiling in the forests of Amazonas.

The belief was rock solid that the gold that grew on trees would continue to finance a way of life that under the best of circumstances was precarious and unsustainable. Even allowing for the miserable and often nonexistent wages paid to the seringueiros of the rain forest, the Brazilian producers could not hope to match the per pound production costs of rubber from the Far East. The slide into economic ruin began.

Rubber production continued, to be sure, in the Amazon basin, and there was an upsurge during the war years beginning in 1914. But the boom years were over. By the 1930s, production of natural rubber in Brazil was what it had been in the 1870s.

The collapse of the rubber market led to a period of extreme social dislocation as well. Unemployed seringueiros and others of the dispossessed who never could hope to pay off their debts to the patrãos turned on them and the overseers and went on a rampage, burning and pillaging. Many of them left the forests altogether and settled in the already rapidly declining cities along the river and its tributaries, further fueling unrest and exacerbating problems that would remain unresolved well into the next century.

To be sure, efforts were made to counter the competition of the Eastern plantations by introducing the more orderly plantation system into South America. A leader in this movement was the Ford Motor Company. But the trees that easily survived in the wild struggled to survive the diseases and insect pests that flourished in the neat rows of a plantation environment. In 1945, in less than twenty years, the vast Ford enterprise, called Fordlandia, had been abandoned, destroyed by a fungus, *Microcyclus ulei.*

But the idea planted by Henry Ford in Brazil did not completely die with the rows of Hevea brasiliensis planted at Fordlandia. Others would take up the cause of plantation-grown latex in Brazil, but every hoped-for revival of the Brazilian rubber industry was aborted by Microcyclus ulei.

However, plant science has made tremendous gains since Henry Ford's debacle in the Amazon, and there is hope that selective breeding of different varieties of wild trees that are resistant to the virus can lead to a resurgence of the rubber industry in Brazil.

The effort has been led by the French tire company Michelin, which saw its early hopes of reestablishing viable rubber plantations also threatened if not ended by the virus. Machinery brought into the area from the Amazon by Firestone, the previous owner of the property where Michelin is working, was contaminated by Microcyclus ulei.

Now, however, French and Brazilian scientists appear to have made a breakthrough in developing a fungus-resistant rubber tree. Field trials of the new varieties offer hope that Brazil could once again become a world leader in natural rubber production.

Wild rubber has all along continued to be gathered in the rain forests of Brazil, and it continues to play a role, but a small one. Since wild Hevea latex is, if anything, even more expensive to gather today. Thus Brazil now produces just 3.4 percent of the world's natural rubber, not enough latex to supply even domestic needs.

Therefore until the hoped-for revival of a large, viable domestic natural rubber industry, which is still only a dream, Brazilian industry must continue to import rubber from those competitors in the Far East that destroyed its native rubber industry. But the vast rubber plantations in Asia are not immune to Microcyclus ulei, and through some accidental or purposeful introduction of the virus there, the rubber industry and the world could be thrown into chaos.

The one product that posed a serious threat to natural rubber, whether from the wild or from plantations, was, of course, synthetic rubber. The chemical composition of rubber had been known since the early 1900s, but the substance was not manufactured in appreciable quantities until World War II, when supplies of natural rubber were cut off by the Japanese invasion of Southeast Asia.

By the early 1960s, the production of synthetic rubber had far outpaced the production of natural rubber. But recent production figures from the International Rubber Study Group show a decline in the yearly growth in production of synthetic rubber while the production of natural rubber has grown.

And, of course, natural rubber is universally acknowledged to be superior to the synthetic variety. Indeed the natural product constitutes a significant percentage of the composition of a passenger car tire, 15 to

30 percent, and an even greater percentage of a commercial truck tire, 30 to 40 percent.

Another economic reality would seem to portend a shift back to greater use of natural rubber—the ever increasing price and ever decreasing supply of petroleum, the basis of synthetic rubber. It takes seven gallons of petroleum to produce one automobile tire.

WHEN THE RUBBER ERA IN BRAZIL ended, it was the collapse of not just an industry but a way of life, which was comparable in many ways to the reign of King Cotton in the American South in the years before the Civil War.

Like their counterparts in the antebellum South, the Brazilian plantation elite built their empires on the backs of the desperate and the oppressed, many of whom were native workers, who though nominally free were as firmly tied to their masters as any serf in czarist Russia or any slave in the cotton states of the Old South. Indeed, hundreds of thousands of the workers had been slaves. That institution was not abolished in Brazil until 1888.

But official emancipation did not by any means end the enslavement and the exploitation of the Brazilian rubber tappers, many of whom were indigenous people. The most egregious treatment, or at least the best documented, was that of the Putumayo Indians of Peru by the Peruvian Amazon Rubber Company, which was basically a British company run by one of the most ruthless of the rubber barons, Julio César Arana.

A series of articles in a British magazine first brought attention to the abuse of the Indians in 1909, and a year later Roger Casement, consul general in Rio de Janeiro, was sent to investigate. Casement was particularly well suited to the task since it was his 1904 report that had exposed the crimes against the natives in the Belgian Congo by the minions of King Leopold II.

Casement's report on his two extensive trips to the Putumayo region, in 1910 and 1911, shocked the conscience of the world. In chilling detail Casement listed the abuses against the Indian slaves of the rubber industry.

No punishment was beyond the pale. Men and women and children were routinely confined in stocks for as long as several months if they were accused of shirking work or if they had attempted to escape their bondage. Flogging, amputation of limbs, even burning people alive were commonplace occurrences.

The British public was understandably outraged, and questions were asked in Parliament. One exchange in the House of Commons was particularly telling as regards the tension between the entrenched interests and the reformers. J. G. Swift MacNeill, member of Parliament for South Donegal, was outraged that the British vice-consul in Iquitos was also an agent for the Peruvian Amazon Rubber Company, the very firm targeted in the report as one of the chief malefactors.

In high dudgeon, Swift MacNeill, who not so incidentally had been the prime mover in abolishing flogging in the Royal Navy, questioned why Francis Dyke Acland, the under secretary of state for foreign affairs, who was submitting to questions, could not see that the vice-consul was "in an antagonistic position as agent of the rubber company."[1]

"I cannot admit that a British subject is unable to fulfil his duties perfectly honestly even although he may be an agent of a rubber company," rather huffily replied the under secretary in a startling but not surprising display of upper-class solidarity.[2]

Casement's exposé did result in somewhat better treatment of the Indians, and some of the worst offenders were actually charged. However, the collapse of the rubber industry did more than official action to alleviate the sufferings of the Putumayo and the other indigenous peoples of the Amazon.

In 1911, Casement was honored for his work in South America with a knighthood. The following year he resigned from the foreign service and settled in Ireland, his birthplace, where he took up the cause of Irish independence. Thus it is not his humanitarian work that ensured his posterity but his efforts as an Irish patriot, nationalist, and revolutionary—efforts that led to his downfall.

Convinced that German intervention in Ireland might speed Irish independence, during the Great War, Casement traveled to Germany, where he hoped to persuade the Germans to mount a military expedition, made up of Irish prisoners of war, to Ireland.

The Germans rebuffed the idea of such an Irish brigade, but they did agree to provide weapons to the Irish rebels. Casement returned to Ireland separately on a German submarine and was immediately arrested when he came ashore. The Easter Rising began the following Monday, 24 April 1916, but Roger Casement was by then in a cell in the Tower of London. Like many of his famous predecessors in the Tower, he was charged and convicted of treason and sentenced to death.

Many well-known figures came to Casement's defense, but any thoughts of clemency were undermined by the circulation of selections from the notorious "Black Diaries," in which Casement allegedly laid out in explicit detail his homosexual assignations, affairs, and conquests in the years 1903, 1910, and 1911, which included his travels in the Amazon.

Whether the diaries were actually written by Casement or were forgeries concocted to discredit him has been argued since they were made public. Now the majority viewpoint is that Casement was homosexual and that the diaries are indeed in his hand, a view that was considerably reinforced with the publication of the complete diaries in 2002, which set off another round of controversy.

One commentator, Cóilín Owens, writing in the *Irish Literary Supplement*, while admiring of Casement's noble efforts on behalf of the abused workers in the rubber industry in the Congo and the Amazon, conflates that abuse with the psychological abuse that Casement visited on the defenseless lower-class men and boys on whom he sexually preyed while doing his humanitarian work.

By implication, Owens equates Casement's behavior with that of the behavior of the rubber barons in that, like them, he took "advantage of his position in these remote colonies, by virtue of his legal and financial independence, and his status as a mobile European to prey on men—pilots, porters, policemen, delivery boys—who regarded him with deference." [3]

Granted, Casement's sexual predations did not rise, or sink, to the level of the abusive, even murderous, behavior of the rubber barons. But did they not, as well, take advantage of their own legal and financial independence to exploit and abuse the workers of the forests in the Congo and the Amazon?

Owens is not content to condemn Casement's alleged sadomasochism and pederasty. He credits him with an even worse failing, even a crime. "In the not too distant future when the history of sex tourism comes to be written," he says, "the evidence from Casement's sorry document [the Black Diaries] must put him among its pioneers." [4]

Casement, however, had many illustrious sex tourist predecessors. Sir Richard Burton, James Boswell, Gustave Flaubert, and Lord Byron, among others, had forged ahead of him in trying to escape the more straitlaced climes of northern Europe for more exotic locales in pursuit of illicit if not illegal pleasures. However, only a few seem to have made the Amazon a stopping point on the sexual tourism circuit.

Treason and sexual deviancy—the notorious case of Oscar Wilde was still fresh in the minds of a prudish British public—sealed Roger Casement's fate. On 3 August 1916, less than four months after his arrest, he was hanged at Pentonville Prison in London.

Whatever the feelings in Ireland were concerning Casement's sexuality, he is considered a hero in his homeland, but as his biographer B.L. Reid wrote, he was a "singularly ineffectual one." Whatever the assessment, Casement's remains were returned to Dublin in 1965, and he was given a state funeral with full military honors.

While the Casement drama was playing out in England, the rubber boom was dying out in Brazil. During its heyday, the extraction of rubber from the rain forest created wealth on a scale that surpassed any conquistador's dreams of El Dorado.

Like their North American Gilded Age counterparts, the newly rich rubber barons created a society and an aristocracy as rigid and hierarchical as any in feudal Europe. Sleepy river towns, which had begun life in the seventeenth and eighteenth centuries as mission outposts, grew into sophisticated cities, or what passed as such considering that just a few miles outside their boundaries there lay an impenetrable and dangerous jungle.

Manaus boasted an opera house, which legend has it was built to attract Enrico Caruso himself. If indeed the great tenor was approached, he resisted the blandishments of the rubber barons to travel a thousand miles up the Amazon. However, many other great artists made the journey, including the soprano Adelina Patti and the ballerina Anna Pavlova.

Farther upriver, in Peru, 2,000 miles from the Atlantic, Iquitos, just below the junction of the Marañon and the Ucayali rivers, which forms the Amazon proper, developed into a major port. The population has grown to almost 400,000, even though it remains reachable only by boat or airplane.

Iquitos has its own eccentric monument to the rubber boom, the Casa de Fierro, the Iron House. Designed by Gustave Eiffel for the International Exposition of Paris in 1889, the Iron House was bought by the rubber baron Anselmo del Aguila, who had it disassembled and the pieces transported to Iquitos, where it was reassembled on the Plaza de Armas.

But the civilized veneer of the Amazonian plantation aristocracy was just that, a thin coating, which as we have seen did not extend to questions of conscience in regard to the rubber tappers on whose backs their rickety civilization rested.

Were not the seringueiros, whether mestizo, Indian, or black, no matter the conditions under which they labored, better off than tribes that still dwelled in the deep recesses of the Amazonian jungles? the plantation aristocracy reasoned. And, of equal importance, the souls of the workers were assured of salvation through the intervention of the Church and its emissaries.

With the collapse of the rubber trade, the seringueiros, who had been able to supplement their always precarious existence with the few dollars earned by tapping the trees, were reduced to even more desperate poverty.

As for the impoverished rubber barons, a few retreated to their plantations. There, they moved from gilded room to gilded room as the jungle inexorably invaded their disintegrating and moldering mansions. Attended by an ever decreasing number of servants, they waited there in vain for a revival of an industry that had made them virtual royalty in the Amazon.

Others were quick to embrace new opportunities. The rubber boom might have ended, but there were other resources to be exploited—timber, minerals, and vast tracts of land for agriculture and cattle ranching. The world's attention would soon begin to focus on these other riches of the Amazon Basin, the production of which by century's end would dwarf many times over the wealth based on the product of one species of tree.

# Exploitation, Despoliation, or Conservation

*The River Sea in the New Millennium*

IN THE TWENTY-FIRST CENTURY, FEW DEBATES STIR SUCH PASSION as the tension between the advocates of untrammeled and unregulated economic growth and those who advocate strict oversight and the limiting of such growth. The former say the attendant benefits of minimum or limited oversight outweigh any environmental costs, particularly if the result is the increase in the living standard of the developed world and the raising of the living standards of the third world. Opponents of this view see only despoliation of nature and the destruction of the planet for the benefit of the rapacious and the venal.

Often lost in the give and take between these opposing forces are the voices of those who search, almost in vain, for any viable middle ground. Indeed, neither side is much willing to grant that there might be a middle ground.

At the nexus of the war between the "despoilers" and the "environmentalists" is the Amazon Rain Forest. The prodevelopment forces argue that the development of the region not only offers them business opportunities and the chance to reap immense profits but that their actions also benefit the people of what are still third world countries.

Environmentalists argue, with almost religious zeal, that the preservation of the vast unspoiled, green expanse of the rain forest is crucial to the survival of the planet. They have dubbed the Amazon Basin "the lungs of the earth," which while useful as a slogan in gaining adherents for their cause has been questioned by no less an authority than the compilers of *The Smithsonian Atlas of the Amazon.*

These scientists have pointed out that the earth's oxygen supply has been built up over the eons because the rate of photosynthesis, which produces oxygen, is greater than the rate of organic decomposition, which uses up oxygen. In the Amazon the two processes are in balance—the rate of photosynthesis equals the rate of decomposition—so the Amazon rain forest adds very little to the oxygen side of the ledger.

Indeed, marine phytoplankton play a larger role in the production of oxygen. [1] But these lowly organisms, which are essential to the health of the planet, are not as dramatic or attention-grabbing as the dramatic, towering trees of the tropical rain forest.

While certainly sympathetic to the cause of "saving" the rain forest, the authors of the *Atlas* take the side of the environmental scientists who argue that the debate should focus on biodiversity, not the oxygen supply. The rain forests are the richest ecosystems ever to exist in the evolution of the planet. And, of these, the most important and by far the largest is the Amazon Basin.

More than twenty-five thousand known species of flowering plants and five thousand vertebrates have been catalogued in the Amazon, and there are probably countless more to be discovered. Some three thousand species of fish have been identified in the Amazon, 10 percent of the world's total. As for invertebrates, their number is many times over that of the plants and the vertebrates.

The ongoing debate between the adversaries over the proper course of intervention or nonintervention in the rain forest has grown even more intense now that the issue of global warming has been added to the mix. Meanwhile each day thousands of acres of the rain forest fall victim to the chainsaw, the axe, the earth mover, and fire.

Like all social movements and disruptions, the rain forest debate has produced its share of zealots, activists, and martyrs. This latter group comprises Sister Dorothy Stang, Wilson Pinheiro, Brother Vicente Cañas, and of course, Francisco Alves "Chico" Mendes, whose story is perhaps the best-known and the most resonant of all.

Chico Mendes was born in 1944 into a family of Brazilian rubber tappers in Acre State. While still a small child he became a tapper himself but watched helplessly as the market for wild rubber collapsed and the workers not only lost their livelihood but began to be displaced as ranchers and loggers bought up the forest land.

In his early twenties, Mendes began to become active in a protest movement of rubber tappers, which was organized to halt the deforestation and the spread of cattle ranches. The tappers' chief weapon was moral suasion, although they were not above chaining themselves to trees, blocking roads, and commandeering logging equipment.

At the beginning of the movement, Mendes had some success in persuading the workers on the ranches to ally themselves with the tappers. But the ranchers were determined to pursue their own goals and to wipe out what was clearly becoming an insurgency of the poor and the dispossessed.

In July 1980, in an ominous portent of what lay ahead for the movement, the organizer and activist Wilson Pinheiro, who also had worked as a tapper and was a mentor of Mendes, was gunned down in the offices of the Brasiléia Rural Workers Union.

While Pinheiro's murder was not the first in the campaign of fear and intimidation by the landowners, it did signal an escalation of their efforts to put down what they saw as a direct threat to a system of peonage that had been in effect since the early sixteenth century in Brazil. In the next decade, over a thousand so-called militants would die at the hands of loggers and ranchers or their hired gunmen.

Mendes, who was a natural politician and charismatic leader, used Pinheiro's murder-martyrdom to advance the cause of land reform. He became a member of the left-wing Partido dos Trabalhadores, the Workers Party, and was elected to the local council in Xapuri. He was also the founder and president of the Xapuri Rural Workers' Union.

His rather utopian goal, at least it was seen to be so by his powerful detractors, was the creation of forest preserves in which local people would continue their traditional tapping of the rubber trees and the gathering of Brazil nuts for export.

Soon, however, Mendes raised his sights even higher and called for all the rubber tappers of Brazil to organize into a unified bloc, the National Council of Rubber Tappers.

The huge gathering of the tappers in Brasilia in 1985 garnered international press and the attention of environmentalists and labor sympathizers around the world. Mendes was now a famous man, with all of the attendant advantages and disadvantages that such celebrity can bring. He came to the attention of the Environmental Defense Fund and the National Wildlife Federation and was flown to Washington, where he lobbied to halt or redesign a road project in Brazil before the Inter-American Development Bank.

His efforts were successful, and Mendes, who had by now abandoned his militant Marxism for environmentalism, which he saw as a more effective way of achieving his goals, launched a new campaign to save the endangered forests.

Meanwhile in Mato Grosso State, Brother Cañas was working to protect the ancestral lands of the Enawene Nawe Indians from similar incursions by the cattle-ranching interests. The Jesuit, who had lived among the Enawene Nawe since 1974, successfully petitioned the national government to guarantee that the Indians' rights in the land would be guaranteed.

It was an act that, in the volatile situation that was fast spiraling out of control, almost guaranteed retribution by the ranchers. And their response was not long in coming. The meddlesome priest must be got rid of if they were to pursue their plans for expanding their domains, and on 6 April 1987 a group of ranchers or their accomplices invaded the priest's home in the Indian village where he lived and stabbed him to death.

Brother Cañas's murder was a clear warning to Mendes that his own life was in danger. Indeed, his enemies were even more implacable and even more dangerous. One, in particular, Darly Alves da Silva, had not only been stopped by Mendes from a planned deforestation project but had also been accused of murder by Mendes.

On 22 December 1988, Chico Mendes was gunned down either by da Silva and his half brother, Oloci, or their hired gunmen. In 1990 the brothers were tried and sentenced to prison for shooting into a crowd of rubber tappers, and there then followed another trial in which they were convicted of the murder of Chico Mendes. For Mendes's murder they received even longer sentences. But as was not unusual in Brazil, the brothers, either through bribery, or collusion, or both, managed to escape and disappear into the jungles.

Their crime, rather than bringing environmental activism to a halt, shone a bright light on the despoliation of the rain forest and the plight of the rubber tappers. The issue became of worldwide interest and led to a series of sweeping reforms—at least by the standards of a country that hitherto had few if any environmental controls.

The Brazilian government responded to the worldwide revulsion at Mendes's murder by halting the policy of tax subsidies for ranching in the Amazon and establishing forest preserves for the rubber tappers.

These modest reforms helped to mute somewhat the outcry over

Mendes's death, but they were nowhere extensive or broad-ranging enough to halt the expansion of ranching and the ongoing deforestation—and, of course, the increasing impoverishment and exploitation of the indigenous population.

In 2007, nearly 60 percent of the most productive and useful farmland was still owned by just 3.5 percent of Brazil's landowners. Only 1 percent of such land was in the hands of the poorest 40 percent of the poorest farmers. And, of course, adverse international opinion did not halt the intimidation and murder of the land reformers by the hired thugs of the ranchers.

On 12 February 2005 there occurred an even more shocking crime than the killing of Chico Mendes and Brother Cañas—the murder in the village of Anapú, in Pará State, of Sister Dorothy Stang, a seventy-three-year-old member of the order of the Sisters of Notre Dame de Namur.

Like Brother Cañas, Sister Dorothy was much influenced by the so-called liberation theology, which stressed justice for the poor and political activism, and which became popular among the more left-leaning Roman Catholic priests and nuns. She had come to Brazil in the early 1970s and immediately took up the cause of the Indians and peasants of the forest settlements.

Lest anyone mischaracterize his sister as a retiring, pious, contemplative nun , David Stang, her brother, was quoted in *The New York Times* as saying she was tough, smart, and very political. "None of this ooey-gooey little nun bit," he said. "She was like a Mack truck." [2]

Sister Dorothy stayed on in the country, becoming a naturalized citizen and working tirelessly for land reform and the introduction of environmentally sound practices. Her beliefs were summed up on a T-shirt emblazoned with the slogan A MORTE DA FLORESTA É O FIM DA NOSSA VIDA ("The death of the forest is the end of our life").

Her zealous and fearless advocacy of the rights of the poor and dispossessed would inevitably collide with the vested interests of the ranchers and loggers and lead to disaster.

Early on the morning of 12 February 2005, Sister Dorothy left her house in Anapú to walk to a meeting. A few yards along the trail, she was stopped by Rayfran das Neves Sales and Clodoaldo Carlos Batista, two local farmhands. Sales was carrying a pistol.

The peasant who was to accompany her to the meeting came upon the scene but hid himself in the bushes by the side of the path.

In response to Sales and Batista's question if she was armed, Sister Dorothy replied that she had only a Bible, which she then opened and began to read from the Beatitudes, all the while proceeding on her way: "Blessed are the poor in spirit: for theirs is the kingdom of heaven. Blessed are they that mourn; for they shall be comforted. Blessed are the meek: for they shall inherit the earth."

She got no farther. Sales opened fire, hitting her in the abdomen. He then shot her in the back. As she lay in the path, she was shot four more times in the head.

The brutal killing of an elderly nun so horrified the civilized world that the Brazilian government could not ignore the outrage. Troops were dispatched to Pará to keep order, and several government ministers flew in by helicopter to attend Dorothy Stang's funeral.

In addition, in a departure from the usual system of justice in the Amazon region of Brazil, the two assailants were quickly arrested, as was Amair Feijoli da Cunha, who hired them on behalf of two landowners, Regivaldo Pereira Galvão and Vitalmiro Bastos de Moura, who allegedly wanted the activist nun murdered in order to put a stop to her agitating on behalf of the peasantry. Sales and da Cunha were each sentenced to twenty-eight years in prison. Batista received seventeen years.

Galvão, one of the alleged masterminds, was released after his attorneys successfully argued that he had no interests in the lands that Dorothy Stang was trying to protect and thus had no motive for ordering her murder.

The case against Moura was stronger—he had supplied the defendants with the murder weapon, which was later found in his house—and in

May 2007 the wealthy landowner was convicted of ordering the murder of Sister Dorothy and sentenced to thirty years in prison, the maximum allowable.

Anyone sentenced to more than twenty years in a Brazilian prison is automatically guaranteed a retrial, and at Moura's new trial, in Belém in May 2008, when Sales, who had testified against Moura, recanted, the jury decided in Moura's favor. He was a free man.

The acquittal of Moura caused outrage in Brazil and around the world. Could the poor ever be assured of protection and equality before the law? asked human rights advocates, the Church, and the leftist national government.

Attention now shifted back to Galvão, who in an act of extreme, but unsurprising, arrogance, in November 2008 produced documents showing that he not only had a direct interest in the lands that Dorothy Stang had tried to have set aside for the native population—an action that led directly to her death—but that he had deeds proving ownership of the disputed lands.

The federal prosecutor immediately charged that not only were the documents that Galvão submitted to the land commission forgeries but that they directly contradicted Galvão's sworn testimony in 2005 that he had no interests in the property and thus would have had no reason for wanting Sister Dorothy dead. Galvão was thus, according to the prosecutor, not only a forger but a murderer. He was rearrested and charged in December 2008 and was to be put on trial for forgery and for the murder of Sister Dorothy Stang.

In April 2009 a three-judge panel ordered the rearrest and a retrial of Vitalmiro Bastos de Moura and also a new trial of Rayfran das Neves Sales, the man who had confessed and then recanted firing the bullets into Dorothy Stang.

Although justice had been delayed, it was not denied. The triggerman Sales's sentence was later confirmed and both Galvão and Moura came to trial again in April 2010. Juries found the two men guilty of planning the killing of Doroth Stang and paying her killer, and Galvão and Moura were each sentenced to thirty years in prison.

The assassinations of Sister Dorothy Stang, Wilson Pinheiro, Brother Vicente Cañas, and Chico Mendes were not just violent aberrations in an isolated and lawless region of Brazil. Hundreds of others have been killed in the struggle to secure land for the landless and to stop the rampant destruction of the rain forest.

The violence and the ensuing worldwide attention had already led the populist government of President Luiz Inácio Lula da Silva to act. Lula da Silva was himself a founder of the Partido dos Trabalhadores, the Workers Party, of which Chico Mendes was an early member.

Indeed, in February 2005 the Lula da Silva government set aside millions of acres of rain forest in Pará State for a preserve and a national park. Whether this action further inflamed the opposition, the ranchers and loggers, enough for them to order the murder of Dorothy Stang, which occurred just a few days later, it certainly added further fuel to an already combustible atmosphere.

In December 2006, another vast swath of rain forest, almost sixty thousand square miles, was set aside as a preserve in Amapá State, in the Guyana Shield region in the north—with over a third of the land limited to scientific research and the general public barred. This national park is now the largest in the world.

Environmentalists were quick to praise the actions of Lula da Silva's regime, which has now set aside 43 percent of the Amazon Rain Forest for conservation. But activists point out that nearly 20 percent of the rain forest has already been destroyed, most of it in the south—the area of greatest concern to the opponents of deforestation. And perhaps of even greater concern to environmentalists is the fact that more than a third, nearly 38 percent, of the Brazilian rain forest remains unprotected.

Nevertheless, preservationists were hopeful that the steps taken by the Brazilian government would do much to end the grip of the powerful ranching and logging interests that have historically dominated the politics and economy of the region. Their optimism might be just that, however, considering the forces allied against them.

Further complicating the issues of global warming, deforestation, and the role of the rain forest in climate change is the fact that reputable scientists have called into question some of the findings of their more environmentally active and outspoken colleagues who have come down firmly on the side of the conservationists and preservationists.

Joe Wright, a research biologist at the Smithsonian Tropical Research Institute in Panama, has pointed out that most of the tropical rain forest in existence today is not primary growth but secondary growth. And further, he maintains, as farmers abandon the land and move to the cities, new vegetation soon takes over. "On the whole," he says, "the amount of land covered by vegetation is stable." Not only does the vegetation come back, says Wright, but "many animals adapt to the environment, and 80 percent of biodiversity is preserved."

Predictably, many, if not most, of Wright's colleagues disagree with his optimistic assessments. Indeed, Bill Laurance, a colleague at the institute in Panama but who has concentrated on the Amazon, questions Wright's extrapolation of his research from a small area in Panama to the vastly greater area of the Brazilian rain forest. "Joe," says Laurance, "is naïve."[3]

But a more eminent scientist than Joe Wright has also questioned the effect of global warming. The physicist Freeman Dyson, from his exalted perch at the Institute for Advanced Study at Princeton, appeared at first to embrace the views of the environmentalists, denying that he had said that global warming wasn't a problem because it was obvious that it was. It was also obvious, he said, that we should be studying it and trying to understand it.

That said, indulging in a typical Dysonian contrarianism that maddens even his admirers, who are legion, and infuriates his opponents, whose numbers are equally large, he delivered himself of the opinion that the problems of global warming are "grossly exaggerated"—most particularly by former vice president Al Gore and James Hansen, the head of the NASA Goddard Institute for Space Studies.

Dyson called Gore climate change's "chief propagandist" and said that both he and Hansen were guilty of "lousy science." Worse, their flogging of a doomsday scenario was distracting the public from "more serious and immediate dangers to the planet," nuclear proliferation being at the top of his list.

As further proof of his contrarian bona fides—"I am proud to be a heretic. The world always needs heretics to challenge the prevailing orthodoxies," he proudly told one interviewer—is his suggestion that carbon dioxide might actually be good for the planet. Carbon dioxide is essential for plant growth, he notes, and if there is more of it perhaps there might be more greenery in the world, not less.

Alas, said Dyson, in the debate, "The biologists have been pushed aside. Al Gore's just an opportunist. The person who is really responsible for this overestimate of global warming is Jim Hansen. He consistently exaggerates all the dangers."

But what if the computer models that Hansen relies on for his projections and that Dyson so derides turn out to be not just prophetic but scientifically correct and carbon dioxide is the culprit?

Dyson had an answer for that as well. In a paper entitled "Can We Control the Carbon Dioxide in the Atmosphere?" which by his own admission he would like to be judged by, he advocates a vast carbon bank of fast-growing trees—as many as a trillion—which would remove the excess $CO_2$ from the atmosphere. [4]

Dyson did not let his imagination rest with his carbon bank. He also proffered the idea of genetically altered trees that would consume vastly more carbon dioxide than ordinary, garden variety trees.

Naturally such a world-famous physicist would come under fire from the environmental community—"pompous twit," "a cesspool of misinformation," "mad scientist" were typical responses—but he also became something of a hero to the naysayers. His "lousy science" epithet directed at Hansen and Gore would evolve into the "junk science" mantra among the well-organized and well-financed opposition to government action on global warming.

Thus Freeman Dyson is perhaps not unlike the great naturalist Alfred Russel Wallace, the cofounder of the theory of natural selection, who dismayed his fellow scientists by embracing spiritualism in his old age. Or perhaps Dyson's contrarianism is just the innate skepticism of the true scientist. As his friend and admirer the Nobelist Steven Weinberg said, "I have the sense that when consensus is forming like ice hardening on a lake, Dyson will do his best to chip at the ice."[5]

Whatever the merits of the views of each side in the debate on global warming, environmental scientists have rather clearly embraced the view of *The Smithsonian Atlas* that the Amazon Basin and Rain Forest are neither the lungs of the earth nor the earth's air conditioner. That is a distraction from the larger issue.

Of more importance is the effect that the destruction of the rain forest will have on rainfall, which is directly linked to the amount of moisture given off by the forests of the earth, of which more later.

The increased attention of the environmental and scientific community on the health of the rain forest of Brazil and the pressure of nongovernmental organizations such as Greenpeace and The Nature Conservancy have led to that country's becoming a recognized world leader in environmental law. But laws, as progressive and well meaning as they may be, are only as effective as their enforcement procedures, and in that regard Brazil is woefully deficient.

Brazil has never set up an adequate system to ensure that violators of its environmental laws are charged and prosecuted. According to The Nature Conservancy, 80 to 90 percent of the very farmers whom the environmental statutes were designed to protect ignore the laws altogether.

While the murders of the Brazilian environmental activists engaged the attention of the print and broadcast media around the world— nothing concentrates the mind as well as murder—another cause célèbre, one with potentially far more impact, was developing in Ecuador.

In 1993, the indigenous people in the extreme northwestern part of the rain forest, two thousand miles from Pará State, brought suit for more than $27 billion against the American oil giant Texaco for allegedly causing not only irreparable harm to the environment but also 1,401 deaths from cancers caused by the release of billions of gallons of oil-polluted wastewater and mud, by-products of the drilling and extraction of crude oil by that company from 1972 to 1990. Texaco, said the plaintiffs, had stored the effluent in unlined ponds or piped it directly into streams throughout the region.

The suit was complicated not only by its transnational aspect—during the period in question Texaco was a partner of the Ecuadorean national oil company, Petroecuador—but by the fact that many of the principals were affiliated with people at the highest levels of the Ecuadorean and American governments.

The leftist president of Ecuador, Rafael Correa, fond of baiting Uncle Sam and a close ally of Hugo Chavez of Venezuela, is a partisan of the plaintiffs in the suit. Thus Chevron (which had bought Texaco in 2001), convinced that it is impossible to get a fair trial in Ecuador, employed lobbyists to push for trade sanctions against that country if the trial proceeds. Among these lobbyists is former U.S. Senate majority leader Trent Lott. And former secretary of state Condoleezza Rice once served on the board of directors of the Chevron Corporation.

The plaintiffs in the suit are not without their own big guns. Chief among these is the lead attorney, Steven Donziger, an old Harvard Law School friend of President Barack Obama. Donziger thoroughly familiarized then-senator Obama with the case, and the president is known to look favorably on the Indian plaintiffs having their day in court.

The real issue was the culpability of the Chevron Corporation, whose purchase of Texaco made it the third-largest corporation in America and thus a very large influence in geopolitics. With its massive investment, Chevron assumed, perhaps unwittingly—the heads of the company did not apprise stockholders of the severity of the situation for several years—responsibility for arguably the largest American corporate headache in history, not even discounting the troubled automobile or financial services industries.

When the suit was filed in 1993, Texaco responded to the charges by saying that the company had acted in good faith and had strictly abided by Ecuadorean environmental law. The hundreds of sites had been left in good condition when Texaco ceased operations in Ecuador, Texaco asserted. When Chevron succeeded Texaco as the defendant in the lawsuit, the corporation naturally pursued the same argument.

The case has not only legal and financial ramifications. It also concerns the fiduciary versus the moral obligations of a corporation, i.e., the tension between the demands of the stockholders and those of the larger society. And if a company has been found to be negligent, indeed willfully so, should there be limits to compensation for the injured plaintiffs? Such a large settlement could conceivably destroy a corporation even as large as Chevron.

The case took a startling turn in August 2009 when two businessmen, Wayne Hansen and Diego Borja, wearing bugging devices, made video and audio recordings that purportedly showed that highly placed officials and prominent Ecuadorean citizens—the judge overseeing the case and the sister of President Correa were cited—were possible parties to a bribery scheme that would have netted $3 million in cleanup contracts in the event of a ruling against the company.

As *The New York Times* reported, Chevron denied any involvement in the bugging and maintained that the company had no connection to Hansen, whom they portrayed as nothing more than a whistle-blower who was "offended by unethical behavior." The company did admit that Borja had once been an employee and that out of concern for his safety and that of his family the company had paid for them to move to the United States. It was later revealed that the company was also paying his and his family's living expenses.

Chevron's demand that the judge in the case, Juan Núñez, should be removed—he allegedly said in one of the clandestine recordings that he planned to rule against the company—was met. Núñez, who denied any wrongdoing, nevertheless did recuse himself from the case.

The plaintiffs in the suit, however, set off their own bombshell in late October when they revealed that one of the men who had made the recordings, Wayne Hansen, was a convicted felon. In 1986, he had conspired to transport 275,000 pounds of marijuana from Colombia to the United States. To further undermine Hansen's credibility as a witness, the lawyers for the Peruvians revealed that he had more recently, in 2005, lost a lawsuit brought against him by a woman who charged that he had unleashed his pit bulls on her and her dog. [6]

But the environmental issues raised by the Chevron–Texaco–Peruvian peasant imbroglio might be even more profound and certainly longer lasting than any questions of culpability or compensation. The affected area at the center of the lawsuit is laced by streams that feed into the Río Napo, a major tributary of the Amazon. Any pollution directed into the watershed of the Upper Amazon Basin, particularly toxic petroleum wastes—it matters little whether it is by design or by carelessness—has ominous implications for the vast area downstream.

PETROLEUM PRODUCTS or their derivatives are not the only pollutants threatening the Amazon and its basin. The Río Huatanay, which flows hard by Cuzco, is seriously polluted by runoff—raw sewage and any number of other effluents that are the by-products of a modern city. The problem is exacerbated downstream when the Huatanay enters the Urubamba.

That stream is exponentially polluted by agricultural runoff and raw sewage from towns and villages as it wends its way through the iconic Sacred Valley of the Incas, a place firmly embedded in the psyche of not just the nation but much of the world. Both Machu Picchu and Cuzco, situated at opposite ends of the valley, are designated UNESCO World Heritage sites, and their chief connection is the dangerously polluted Río Urubamba. However, the vast floodplain, wetlands, and forests of the lower Amazon face the most serious ecological problems—none of them caused by rapacious oil companies or municipal polluters.

Much of the literature on the Amazon Basin uses the terms white water, black water, and clear water to describe the main river and its tributaries. The latter two terms are essentially used correctly. The first, which is used to describe the Amazon, is totally misleading.

The staggering amounts of sediment from the Andes give the Amazon its distinctive year-round color, a muddy brown, which in spite of the immense amounts of water added by less silt-laden black-water and clear-water tributaries is barely diluted on its flow to the Atlantic. It is by no means a white-water stream anywhere along its length.

At the city of Óbidos, the narrowest point of the downstream Amazon—the river is barely a mile wide at that point—the amount of sediment passing annually has been measured at approximately 1.2 billion tons.

Only some 25 percent of this sediment is deposited in the lower reaches of the Amazon, not enough to create a delta, a defining characteristic of many other river systems. And the strong Amazon tidal bore, the *pororoca*, also plays a large part in dismantling any buildup of sediment at the mouth of the river. These walls of water that rush up the river can be more than six feet high. They are strongest during the spring tides and can be dangerous to fisherman. River surfers, however, have been quick to take them on in great numbers.

The vast flow of the Amazon carries the remaining 75 percent of the sediment into the Atlantic, where a third of it is carried by the Southern Equatorial Current up the northeastern coast of South America and deposited along the shore from French Guiana to Venezuela, where it mixes with sediments from another large river system, the Orinoco.

The sediment from the Amazon has a more important function in the scheme of things than beach replenishment in French Guiana, Suriname, Guyana, and Venezuela, however. The muddy outflow of the Amazon is rich in nutrients that contribute significantly to the growth of phytoplankton in the Atlantic.

The microscopic phytoplankton—they are visible only when they form the vast colonies that lend a greenish cast to the water—are essential to life on earth. They are not only the bottom-most link in the oceanic food chain—without them there would be no food for krill, which is the primary food source for baleen whales—their vast colonies produce much of the oxygen in the earth's atmosphere. It is estimated that 50 percent of the oxygen produced by all plant life on earth is the result of photosynthesis in phytoplankton.

Sediment carried by the Amazon is the chief source of nutrients for the forests, wetlands, grasslands, and floating meadows of the Amazon floodplain. These natural areas, which are a vital link in the food chain and also contribute to the oxygen supply of the earth, are themselves under the ever-increasing attack of loggers, cattle ranchers, and industrial-scale agriculture.

The loggers came first, with the first settlers in the Amazon, who felled trees to build shelter for themselves and for firewood and charcoal. But it wasn't long before demand was created for an exotic new wood that had little or nothing to do with shelter or cooking—mahogany. Cabinetmakers in Europe and North America, as well as in the Spanish viceroyalties, recognized at once that here was a wood that was unique in its beauty, and their almost insatiable demand for it has nearly caused the disappearance of the tree.

Centuries of overharvesting have created a scarcity that has led to an astronomical increase in the value of mahogany. No rain forest product—rubber, quinine, cacao, charcoal, firewood, building materials, or fuel for steamboats—has the pound for pound value of mahogany. With the exception of coca, no product increases in value so rapidly from the forest to finished product. And like the growing of coca, the cutting of a mahogany tree is a crime in Brazil.

The decimation of the remaining mahogany trees of the rain forest—as terrible as their loss is—is perhaps the smallest part of the problem. Equally serious is the infrastructure, as rudimentary as it is, that is necessary to reach the trees and then bring them out of the jungle.

Roads must be cut to enable logging vehicles to reach the site of the tree or trees. And roads necessarily open hitherto inaccessible areas for settlement and farming, further degrading the rain forest. Often the trees are simply dragged out of the forest to an assembly yard or to the river bank for transport. Either way the landscape is irrevocably scarred and much collateral damage done to the forest. Greenpeace has estimated that thousands of kilometers of illegal roads have been built in Pará State, the epicenter of mahogany logging and export in Brazil.

As mahogany logging proceeded apace, it was inevitable as the supply began to run out that the rapacious lumbermen would begin to move onto the off-limits Indian lands, which hold the largest surviving stands of mahogany in the Amazon region. In some cases, the Indians are complicit in the illegal logging in order to supplement their meager earnings and their subsistence way of life.

The pitifully few dollars paid to an Indian or a Brazilian peasant—as little as $30 per tree—is the beginning of an ever increasing rise in the value of a single large tree as it's passed from hand to hand in the shadowy export lumber market. Ultimately this one tree, when it is sawed and processed, will be used to make furniture products worth upwards of $300,000, when the tables, chairs, wardrobes, and other pieces of furniture are put on sale at such retailers as Harrods in London or Bloomingdale's in New York.

Even though the amount that the peasant or Indian of the rain forest receives is minuscule compared to the final value of the mahogany tree on the world market, it looms large in a country where the per capita income is less than $200 a month—and only a fraction of that in the rural areas and the Indian lands. Little wonder that the Indian, the peasant, the logger, and the middleman risk fines or imprisonment or even death to bring the "green gold" out of the forest.

As forests were sacrificed for firewood and charcoal to supply the day-to-day needs of towns and cities along the river, the growth of cities such as Belém, Santarém, Manaus, and Iquitos, and even farther afield in Brazil, there was further destruction of the forests to supply lumber for the building booms in the urban areas. Between 1950 and 1980 the population of Manaus grew from 139,000 to 611,000, and Belém's population increased from 233,000 to 992,000.

As always any progress, particularly in a historically backward and isolated area such as the rain forest, often comes with a high price. It has ever been thus. In the 1850s, when steamboats began service on the Amazon and its tributaries, many miles of forest were leveled to supply the vast amounts of firewood required for their boilers.

Another seemingly benign product of the rain forest—chocolate—one that no amount of bad publicity can ever dissuade addicts from abusing, has also caused deforestation, but cacao cultivation has not been as deleterious as other practices.

Chocolate had become something of a craze in Spain by the mid-sixteenth century and spread from there throughout Europe. Brazil became the leading exporter of cacao in the seventeenth century, and today the country is still the fifth-largest producer of cacao in the world.

Cacao, the beans of which are turned into everything from truffles to hot fudge sauce, however, grows best in the shade of a forest canopy, and thus many of the taller trees have been left standing.

By the 1930s jute had replaced cacao as the leading cash crop, and much of the remaining forest in the floodplain was now cleared to make room for jute farming. This natural fiber, which is second only to cotton in its many uses and applications, was an obvious candidate for cultivation, and it soon assumed great economic importance in Brazil and the Amazon.

Jute farming, however, suffered the same fate as the cultivation of rubber and quinine. As with those products, it was soon discovered that it was cheaper and easier to produce jute in Asia, and by 2008, India was producing 66 percent and Bangladesh 25 percent of the world's jute. Brazil's share had shrunk to eight-tenths of 1 percent of the total.

Whatever the causes for the destruction of the rain forest—supplying fuel for steamboats, cultivation of cacao, jute, or soya, or lumbering, either legal or illegal—by 1980 the primary or secondary forests of the Amazon floodplain had been disastrously reduced, which hastened the growth of a much more damaging threat to the region—the cattle industry.

Cattle have been raised in the Amazon since colonial times, but as clear-cutting and burning created vast acreage suitable for cattle, the cattle industry burgeoned into a giant business and an equally giant threat to the environment.

According to Greenpeace, arguably the world's leading environmental group and most visible gadfly, the greatest annual average deforestation in the world is in the Brazilian Amazon, and cattle ranching is responsible for 80 percent of the damage. As Greenpeace also pointed out in a July 2009 report entitled "Slaughtering the Amazon," 90 percent of the on-going deforestation in the Amazon is illegal.

To accommodate their vast herds, the cattlemen have cleared and burned millions of acres of forest, a practice that gains momentum with every rise in the price of beef. In 2000, there were an estimated forty-seven million cattle in the Amazon region, but by 2009 the number had grown to eighty million, the largest herd in the world. But the problem is even greater than these figures reveal. The Amazon herd, which by any measure is enormous, represents only a third of the total number of cattle in all of Brazil.

Not only does pasturage for the cattle replace the rain forest, the cattle themselves present a threat to the viability of the habitat. They destroy the native plants and grasses and the wetlands and the famous floating meadows, which provide shelter for thousands of species of native fish. And in one of the supreme ironies of nutrition science, the beef that the cattle provide is costlier and lower in protein than the fish that the cattle are replacing as a prime food source for the local population.

The Greenpeace report did spur action on the part of four of the largest meat producers in the world, which met with the environmental group on 5 October 2009 at a conference in São Paulo. The companies agreed to cease purchasing beef produced in newly deforested areas of the Amazon rain forest.

Purchasers of tanned leather announced similar intentions. As *The New York Times* reported on 7 October 2009, however, the government of Luiz Inácio Lula da Silva was "conspicuously missing" from the conference.

The Brazilian government's nonparticipation in the conference is not surprising since in July 2008 it had inaugurated the Agricultural and Livestock Plan, which made $41 billion available in credit lines to boost agricultural and livestock production. Thus President Lula da Silva's regime is a direct stakeholder in the very industry it seeks to monitor. According to Greenpeace, the Brazilian government has $2.65 billion in shares in global beef and leather processors.

The government's role in oversight is further complicated, according to *Times* reporter Alexei Barrionuevo, because it is "struggling to reconcile its social and development goals in the Amazon with its desire to be a major player in global climate change talks."

This desire was manifest by the president of Brazil convening a conference in Manaus in November 2009 to discuss deforestation in the Amazon. Representatives of the nine countries in the Amazon region were invited, but only two high-ranking officials actually showed up— Lula da Silva and President Nicolas Sarkozy of France, which still controls French Guiana.

The other nations in the region sent lower level delegates to the conference, which was designed to forge a united front before the climate talks involving most of the world's leaders, scheduled for Copenhagen in December 2009.

Officials stressed that the absence of other leaders of the nine-nation Amazon region in Manaus had to do with political wrangling rather than with those nations' views on deforestation and climate change. However, the failure of the conference pointed up the difficulty of forging a united front in addressing the issue of deforestation in the Amazon. Lula da Silva didn't help matters much when he said if "gringos" were so concerned with the issue then they should pay for it.

However well-meaning or enlightened the government of Brazil may be, the fact that the country is the world's leading exporter of beef and the second leading exporter of tanned leather is central to any negotiations. The influence of the cattle industry can never be underestimated.

On the environmental threat scale, another, perhaps even more damaging agricultural product—soybeans—was introduced in the 1960s by the conglomerates and agribusinesses that have thrived in the permissive atmosphere that is Brazil. Indeed, as *The New York Times* reported on 22 August 2009, one farmer has a permit to clear 12,500 acres of rain forest to make way for soybean production.

An environmental group has offered to pay $12 an acre, per year, not to clear the land, which is conservatively estimated to be worth $1,300 an acre if it is cleared. The farmer, who purports to be concerned about the environment, is understandably torn by the struggle between the ecological forces and those governed by the marketplace.

In the four decades since soybeans began to emerge as a major crop in the Mato Grosso—an ecologically ironic term since it means "thick forests"—cultivation of that ubiquitous legume (soy appears in everything from baby food to vodka) is now widespread in the Amazon proper. Brazil is now the world's second-largest exporter of soybeans.

In 1984 Brazil was producing 672 million bushels of soybeans. In 2007, the output totaled over 2.2 billion bushels. Thus soybean production, with the attendant deforestation, is now considered by many ecologists to be a greater threat to the rain forest than cattle, logging, road-building, or mining.

The land that supports these two giant agribusinesses was once covered by dense forests that had to be clear-cut and then burned to make way for pasture and cropland. And a resonant example of the unintended consequences that can result from environmental regulations is the disparity between the price of cleared land and that of forested land. It is cheaper to buy forested land and clear-cut and burn it than it is to buy already developed land.

Thus deforestation continues apace, with clouds of smoke blotting out the sun over hundreds of square miles as the felled trees are reduced to ash. Brazil is now one of the leading air polluters in the world. The country ranks fourth in the world in greenhouse gas emissions, a leading cause of global warming.

Brazil maintains that it is making progress, however. In November

2009 at the time of the abortive deforestation conference in Manaus, it was announced that the country would reduce greenhouse gas emissions between 36.1 and 38.9 percent by 2020. Further deforestation was at its lowest level in twenty-one years.

The social ramifications of the burgeoning agribusinesses in the Amazon are just as troubling. According to Greenpeace, various human rights groups, and Brazil's own government, thousands of farm and ranch workers are held in a form of debt bondage and peonage that are nothing less than slavery. Indeed, casting euphemisms aside, the UN Commission on Human Rights identified it as such.

Responding to the criticism, on 11 March 2003, President Lula da Silva announced a National Plan for the Eradication of Slavery and set up a National Commission for the Eradication of Slave Labour by 2006. The problem turned out to be not so susceptible to government pressure.

Farmers and cattlemen continued to recruit impoverished and ignorant peasants in the villages of the backcountry and ship them off to isolated farms and ranches, where they were forced to work off the costs of their food and shelter, which in the event amounted always to more than they were theoretically earning. There was no way for them to escape the ever escalating debt they incurred, and armed gangs were employed to ensure that they did not escape.

As a measure of how widespread the practice continued to be after the government announced its antislavery program, in 2008, two years after the deadline set for eliminating slavery in Brazil, the antislavery taskforce freed 4,634 workers from bondage. It can only be assumed that many more went undetected.

Meanwhile, a continent away, in the Andes, a more troubling and potentially even more catastrophic ecological scenario has begun to play out. Global warming, which is directly tied to the destruction of the rain forest, is causing the rapid melting and retreat of the glaciers in the high mountains.

The glaciers and snow melt of the Andes are the chief sources of water in the many months in which there is no rainfall. Indeed, for all practical purposes they are the only sources of water in the coastal areas of Peru, where 60 percent of the population lives. Lima, the capital and home to some nine million people, has an average annual rainfall of just 7 millimeters or .27 inches. Thus the city must, perforce, rely on the water from the glaciers and snowpack of the high Andes.

Farther south along the coast, the situation is perhaps even more dire. There in the desert regions, which are completely dependent on the rivers flowing from the Andes, the local people are exacerbating the problem by destroying the last vestiges of the *huarango* forests. The huarango flourished along the streams flowing down the valleys from the Andes and for millennia in addition to providing food and timber was a major factor in combating soil erosion and increasing soil fertility, providing refuge for birds and small animals, and, most important, helping to conserve scarce water.

Today only 1 percent of the original huarango forests remains, and in spite of prohibitions by local authorities and protective measures promoted by environmental groups, the carnage continues. The huarango continues to be ruthlessly exploited by woodcutters for firewood and charcoal.

Some 70 percent of the glaciers of the tropical regions of the world are in the mountains of Peru. Among them is the Qori Kalis Glacier, which drains the largest ice cap in the tropics, the Quelccaya. The ice cap is receding at a rate of almost seven hundred feet per year, and the glacier is retreating at a proportionally alarming rate as well.

The water from the Qori Kalis feeds into the Vilcanota and thence into the Urubamba River, one of the major tributaries of the Amazon. It takes no great leap of the imagination to conjure up what the loss of this water would mean to the ecology of the Amazon and to the world's oceans. Fifteen to twenty percent of all the fresh water entering the world's oceans enters via the Amazon estuary, and any threat to that source would have global repercussions.

The disappearance of the glaciers and the ice pack is not, of course, limited to the High Andes. The phenomenon is occurring as well on the

Tibetan Plateau, in the European Alps, in Africa—the legendary Mt. Kilimanjaro will, by even the most conservative estimates, be ice-free by mid-century—and along the West Coast of the United States.

The Tibetan Plateau contains the largest mass of ice on earth after the Arctic and Antarctica, and this melting ice feeds most of the major river systems of Asia. During the dry seasons, all the water for these river systems comes from the glaciers and ice fields of the plateau, and they are rapidly disappearing.

Illustrative and typical is the 1.7-mile-long Baishui Glacier No. 1, in southwest China, which has receded 830 feet in the last twenty years. Writing in *The New York Times*, 26 September 2009, Orville Schell, quoting the Chinese glaciologist Yao Tandong, says that this glacier and two-thirds of the other eighteen thousand glaciers in the region could well disappear in the next forty years.

Predictably, these figures have been challenged, and even Dr. Yao has said that no one can predict with certainty how soon or how much the glaciers will retreat. But he is certain that retreat they will—indeed, they have done so already at an alarming rate—and the ensuing disaster will be incalculable for a vast segment of the earth's population.

Closer to home, California, with a population of thirty-seven million people, relies on water from the snowpack of the Coast Ranges, the Southern California mountains, and the Sierra Nevada, all of which are threatened. The state thus faces, in the not too distant future, two equally bleak prospects.

As the temperatures rise, there will be less snow added to the annual snowpack, and the snowpack itself will melt. Thus there will be less water available from the snowpack during the drier months.

Instead of the snowfalls that replenish the snowpack, there will instead be massive rainfalls. These vast amounts of water dumped on the western slopes of the mountains will cause widespread flooding and mud slides. And since existing storage facilities will be overwhelmed by the flow, the water must be allowed to flow wastefully into the sea.

Thus in the twenty-first century, water, that most common of substances, bids fair to become the earth's most precious commodity, outpacing even oil. The pursuit and the conservation of water will be a defining issue, affecting every citizen of the world, whether he or she be a resident of an advanced society such as California, a struggling farmer in China or India, or a villager eking out a meager subsistence far up a black-water tributary in the Amazon Basin.

MEANWHILE THE AMAZON, which begins life as a trickle of water from a glacier high in the Andes and ends thousands of miles away in a vast estuary, still flows as it has for millennia, undammed and unbridged.

That is true, of course, only of the Amazon itself. Several of the tributaries have been dammed, and plans for other hydroelectric projects have energized the environmentalists who decry the almost certain ecological damage from the proposed dams.

The proponents of new hydroelectric projects in the Amazon Basin—there are currently seventy under consideration—saw their case substantially strengthened by a massive blackout in Brazil in 2001 and an even greater one on 10 November 2009, which affected eight hundred cities, including Brazil's two largest, Rio de Janeiro and São Paulo, and left sixty million people in the dark. They argue, not without some merit, that if Brazil is to take its rightful place among the economic superpowers, it must have an adequate and reliable supply of electricity.

Itaipú, the hydroelectric facility at the center of the controversy over the massive power outage in 2009, is on the Río Paraná, the border between Brazil and Paraguay, many miles from the Amazon. But the repercussions extended to the Madeira, the largest of the Amazon's tributaries, where two massive hydroelectric dams are planned at Santo Antonio and Jirau.

The dams on the Madeira, according to opponents, would inundate an estimated 204 square miles, displace an already threatened indigenous tribe, wipe out untold numbers of fish species, and add to global warming. Further, with its vast infrastructure the dam projects would bring in more loggers, miners, and, worst of all, more soybean farms. One group estimated that increased soya production might eventually cover some twenty-seven thousand square miles.

There are other tributary dams already producing electricity in the Brazilian Amazon, and each of them has generated as much controversy as electricity. The lake formed by the dam for the Balbina plant near Manaus, on the Uatumã, inundated fifteen hundred square miles. The plant, which supplies only 30 percent of the electricity needed by Manaus, is generally judged a financial and environmental disaster.

Meanwhile Brazil is pressing ahead with other such projects. The proposed Belo Monte dam and hydroelectric plant on the Xingua is projected to provide eleven thousand megawatts, three thousand fewer than Itaipú, but still a massive amount of power. Predictably, Belo Monte has run into fierce opposition from conservationists and ecologists, as well as defenders of the rights and lands of indigenous peoples. Lawsuits, legal briefs, appeals to various courts, and petitions to government ministries have pushed backed the earliest possible completion date to 2015, which even then is admittedly optimistic.

But as the exigencies of industrialized society increasingly intrude on the rain forest—with the attendant insatiable demand for agricultural products, timber, oil, minerals, and hydroelectric power—can this ancient world survive?

Brazil's annual electric power needs to increase by three thousand megawatts annually, and 85 percent of the country's power now comes from hydroelectric facilities. Inevitably any important new facilities must perforce be built along the tributaries in the Amazon Basin, which is recognized as having the greatest hydroelectric potential in the world. Fortunately, the main river itself is too silt-laden to be seriously considered as a candidate for hydroelectric projects.

Greed, altruism, rapacity, generosity, preservation, exploitation, religious fervor, even genocide have been colliding in the Amazon for centuries. But until relatively recently the tensions and struggles between the forces of action and reaction were confined to the region.

The realization of the interconnectedness of all environmental issues has had the salutary effect of bringing the problems facing the Amazon Basin to the attention of the world. Failure to address and resolve the very real problems in the Amazon—be they deforestation, greenhouse gas emissions, or water pollution—will surely have global consequences.

Can it be possible—indeed, is it not more than likely—that the fate of the planet depends upon what transpires in the mountains, valleys, jungles, and floodplain of the River Sea?

ALL MEANINGFUL JOURNEYS are personal excursions, but a journey on the River Sea involves not just geography and sightseeing but immersion in a thousand years or more of history. Therefore, choices must be made and, however unwillingly, a form of triage instituted. First of all, one must choose which areas of the river to experience firsthand. As for writing about it, there is the equally difficult decision as to which historic personages to treat at length and which of the many pressing contemporary issues facing the rain forest to address.

In addition, as with any legendary place, the traveler inevitably will run up against the old hand who assures him that the place is nowhere close to what it was in the days before it was ruined. Implicit in this, of course, is that your very presence is contributing to the decline and may, in fact, be hastening it. Even Herodotus, in the fifth century BC, no doubt had to listen to accounts of the "real" Thebes from both the Egyptians and the expatriates from Greece and Rome.

It was ever thus, but the visitor to the Amazon has an easier time of it. In the Amazon it is not difficult to transport yourself back to the black-water creeks and forests that La Condamine, Humboldt, Bates, Spruce, and their contemporaries traversed in the eighteenth and nineteenth centuries.

One has but to go up on the deck of a boat, in the middle of the night, and listen to the waters of the great river lapping against the sides of the vessel, which is moored to a tree on the riverbank. Or watch a solitary fisherman glide silently by in his dugout canoe or a man in a small boat heading downstream with a load of bananas to sell in one of the small river towns—towns all but invisible from the river since they are set far back on higher ground to escape the rising waters during the flood stage.

And there can be no more thrilling sound or beautiful sight than a flock of scarlet macaws as they make their noisy way overhead from their feeding ground to their roosting place, the sunlight glancing off their brilliant plumage.

And where else does a naturalist plunge his hand into the black water on a pitch-dark night and hand you a small caiman to stroke or make a sudden grab into palm fronds and withdraw an immense tarantula and place it into your outstretched and trembling hand? All the while giant bats wheel and turn overhead.

As your skiff makes its way up a creek, pink river dolphins splash alongside, a half-dozen varieties of monkeys swing in the trees, and sloths do what sloths do, which is, of course, nothing.

Lest one is lulled into complacence, for shore excursions the guides and naturalists outfit you in heavy leather gaiters that reach to your knees. This is not an idle precaution. The fer-de-lance, a pit viper that causes more human fatalities than any snake in the Americas, is ubiquitous in the Amazon Basin. Between 1990 and 1993, the Brazilian Ministry of Health reported that there were sixty-five thousand recorded snake bites in that country. Deaths, while numerous, were only a fraction of that number, but a bite by this deadly snake would be a very serious thing indeed hundreds of miles upriver from the nearest hospital.

In the Amazon one can walk just a few feet beyond where a path through a village ends and find oneself startlingly, even disturbingly alone. I had a chilling experience in one such village. The footpath ended at impenetrable undergrowth just a few yards from the last of a row of thatched-roofed huts, and as I stood there I heard sounds of an animal clearly in distress. But I could go no further without a machete to hack my way through.

The drama being played out in the undergrowth beyond soon became clear when I heard other noises close by. I looked down to see a litter of puppies, their eyes not yet open, lying by the path. I quickly realized that the gruesome noises from the jungle were being made by the mother dog, which had no doubt been attacked and dragged away by some beast of prey. I immediately thought of Humboldt's faithful companion, which had suffered the same fate. And my own guides had seen a jaguar just the week before.

In a gesture as pathetic as it was useless, I moved the puppies into the shade and brought them water. The villagers regarded this futile exercise with a mixture of curiosity and resignation as I walked by them to return to the boat that had brought me. Eking out a subsistence living left them no time for such niceties as animal rescue.

Domestic animals might not be a high priority among the majority of the indigenous peoples of the Amazon, but many of them have signed on to the preservation of wild creatures. The giant nature preserves in the Amazon Basin ensure that generations will continue to enjoy the tree sloths, the many varieties of monkeys, the pink river dolphins, and perhaps one of Alfred Russel Wallace's "lords of the soil"—the mighty jaguar.

Preserving animal species is not just good science. It is also good business. Nature travel is a significant part of the economies of the countries of the Amazon Basin, providing jobs for the local people and attracting large amounts of foreign currency.

The modern counterparts of the friars and monks who came to South America in the colonial era to save souls are the far more politically active religious whose primary task today is a more equitable distribution of the region's vast wealth and lands. They are now aided and abetted by many other nongovernmental organizations, one of the most notable being the Médecins Sans Frontières. Among the more moving sights along the river is the organization's riverboat clinic, manned by these "doctors without borders," secular saints who bring modern medicine to the poor and dispossessed of the Amazon.

The future of the villages and small towns of the Amazon Basin, however, mirrors that of the rural areas of more advanced societies. Each year many thousands flee the hardships of river and village life for Lima, Manaus, Belém, Iquitos, and other burgeoning cities, which have seen their populations explode with the influx of millions of campesinos. Lima, for example, is now home to fully one-third of the population of Peru.

In one of the ironies of demographics, the exodus of the population from the rain forest might be its salvation. As the cities of Peru, Ecuador, and Brazil struggle to absorb the mass influx from the hinterlands and remain viable, much of the rain forest might well revert to the vast, sparsely populated region of enduring mystery, enchantment, and myth.

As for the cities, Lima was founded by Pizarro and is thus a completely colonial construct, resplendent with baroque invention. Even though it is across the Andes from the Amazon and sustained by water from the west of the cordillera, it is there, in the museums and churches, which are often the same, that one best understands the affinity between, and the melding of, Indian and Spanish, the mestizo culture.

No artifact illustrates this better than a seventeenth-century painting, *The Last Supper*, attributed to Diego de la Puente, in the Monastery of San Francisco. Jesus is, of course, at the head of the table, but to his right is a woman, in mestizo society a combination of Mary, the mother of Christ, and the Pachamama, the Earth Mother venerated by the ancients.

At the table are the disciples, but also in the room are various onlookers, some of them clearly indigenous peoples, small children, and some dogs. The food being served includes *cuy* (known to gringos as guinea pig), a staple of the Peruvian diet, and, of course, potatoes.

At the National Museum of Archaeology, Anthropology, and History, one gains a quick understanding of the many layers of Peruvian history, particularly that the Incas were just the latest, last, and briefest—albeit the most famous—of the civilizations that arose in Peru.

Cuzco, the capital of the Empire of the Sun, which lies in the headwaters of the Amazon, both exhilarates and depresses. Only the foundations, which now serve as platforms for the many churches, monasteries, and the great cathedral, survive of the Qorikancha, the Temple of the Sun, and the palaces of the Inca and his court. But the red-tiled-roof city instantly seduces, and it is, of course, the gateway to the Sacred Valley of the Incas and the most famous archaeological site in South America, if not the world, Machu Picchu.

The legendary lost city of the Incas, on a peak often shrouded in mist—

in a rare conjunction of science and poetry, the area is called a cloud forest—overlooks the Río Urubamba, a thousand feet below.

The Urubamba, which itself is part of that sliver of water from a glacier in the high Andes south of Cuzco, is only a few yards wide here in a gorge flanked by nearly vertical peaks. But it will grow ever larger as it is joined by countless other streams as it makes its way across the continent until at last it becomes the River Sea.

# ACKNOWLEDGMENTS

Every writer is indebted to a host of individuals and institutions that have eased the path and made a book possible. In my own case, the first of these is my agent, Peter Matson, of Sterling Lord Literistic, who kept the faith. Second, of course, is my publisher, Jack Shoemaker, and his colleagues at Counterpoint Press.

Of equal importance are the guides and naturalists from International Expeditions, who introduced me to the mysteries of the River Sea; the grandeur of the Andes; the glories of Lima, Cuzco, and the Sacred Valley of the Incas; and that nonpareil of archaeological sites, Machu Picchu. Only the most jaded of travelers could fail to be swept along by the enthusiasm of Hernando Vellenas, Robinson Rodriguez, George Davila, and Fernando Baca. Their love of the natural world combined with their messianic zeal for their cultural heritage immeasurably enriched my travels and my life.

Friends, family, librarians, archivists, researchers, and colleagues too numerous to mention have supported and encouraged me and listened, sometimes raptly, to my tales. To all of them I am grateful. But one, the late Philip Earnshaw, is owed special thanks. His generosity enabled me to finish this book without undue worry, and thus I will always be grateful to that great and good friend.

Marshall De Bruhl
Asheville, NC
June 2010

Chapter 1: *The River Sea*
*From the Andes to the Atlantic*

1  "You have to have it in your genes": Smith, "*Explorers Pinpoint Source of the Amazon.*"
2  "it is absurd": Goulding, *The Smithsonian Atlas of the Amazon*, pp. 23–24.
3  "the rivers of Europe": Wolfe and Wolfe, *Rubber: A Story of Glory and Greed*, p. 35.
4  "the uninhabited banks": Humboldt, *Personal Narrative*, p. 233.
5  "It's a pretty spot": Smith, "*Explorers Pinpoint Source of the Amazon.*"
6  "Nothing I have read": *Full Circle with Michael Palin*, episode 9: Peru/Colombia.

Chapter 2: *The Incas*
*The Rise and Fall of the Empire of the Sun*

1  "The small speck": Prescott, *History*, p. 907.
2  "It was not long before Atahualpa": Ibid., p. 947.

Chapter 3: *The Search for El Dorado*
*Gold, Spices, and Blood*

1  "an idea flashed across his mind": Prescott, *History*, p. 1077.
2  "the love of adventure": Ibid., p. 1077.
3  "repugnant both to humanity and honor": Ibid., p. 1078.
4  "hoped to relieve the provinces of Peru": Simon, *The Expedition of Pedro de Ursúa & Lope de Aguirre in Search of El Dorado and Omagua in 1560–1561*, p. 3
5  "*Confessio, confessio*": Ibid., p. 42.
6  "This was the miserable end": Ibid., p. 45.
7  "had not left the evil ways": Ibid., p. 85.

8   "even the most hardened men": Ibid., p. 87.

9   "found him on his couch": Ibid., p. 92.

10  "He was scarcely twenty-six": Ibid., p. 93.

11  "I am a rebel": Ibid., pp. 190–194.

12  "Commend thyself to God": Ibid., p. 227.


Chapter 4: *Conquistadors for Christ*

*The Holy Fathers and the Indigenous Peoples*

1   "felt that he was battling": Prescott, *History*, p. 936.

2   "These laws began": Thomas, *Conquest*, p. 71.

3   "Everything that has happened": Las Casas, *A Short Account*, p. 3.

4   "a profound and impassioned soul": qtd. in Las Casas, *In Defense of the Indians*, p. xvii.


Chapter 5: *The Great Powers in the Amazon Basin*

*The Struggle for Control*

1   "who gave his name to America": Fernández-Armesto, *Amerigo*, p. ix.

2   A full discussion of the Soderini letter is in both Markham, *The Letters of Amerigo Vespucci*, Introduction, and Fernández-Armesto, *Amerigo*, pp. 126–132.

3   "The tradition was secure": Fernández-Armesto, *Amerigo*, p. 186.

4   "I told him that he had undone me": Qtd. in Trevelyan, *History of England*, p. 509.

5   "maliciously broken and infringed": Qtd. in Ibid., p. 510.

6   "take particular care": Markham, *Expeditions into the Valley of the Amazons*, p. 45.

7   "to put a bridle on": Qtd. in Ibid., p. 139.

8   "their small amount": Ibid.


Chapter 6: *Nature's Grand Laboratory*

*European Science Discovers the Amazon*

1   "the tiresomeness of a weary": Qtd. in Smith, *Explorers of the Amazon: Four Centuries of Adventure Along the World's Greatest River*, p. 179.

Chapter 7: *The Peruvian Evangeline*
*The Journey of María Isabel de Jesus Gramesón y Godin*

1   "Any one but you": "Voyage of Madame Godin," p. 311.
2   "Go your ways, Sir": Ibid., p. 328.
3   "On board this vessel": Ibid., pp. 330–331.
4   "I can even readily conceive": Ibid., p. 334.
5   "the gentle impulse of a heart": Ibid., p. 334.

Chapter 8: *"I Must Find Out About the Unity of Nature."*
*The Explorations of Alexander von Humboldt*

1   "one cannot speculate": George, "Jean Louis Antoine de Bougainville,"
    in *Dictionary of Scientific Biography*, vol. II, p. 343.
2   "A determined will": Humboldt, *Personal Narrative*, p. 7.
3   "the sight of the sea . . . visit the peninsula": Ibid., p. 17.
4   "Those who have not traveled": Ibid., p. 208.
5   "during the night": Ibid., p. 218.
6   "The morning was fresh and beautiful": Ibid., p. 233.
7   "In this interior": Ibid., p. 233.
8   "brought us a clear sky": Ibid., p. 242.
9   "Sometimes he used the sacristan's stick": Ibid., p. 251.
10  "one of the most important": A.P.M. Sanders, "Johann Baptist Von
    Spix," in *Dictionary of Scientific Biography*, vol. XII, p. 578.

Chapter 9: *Three Eminent Victorians in the "Garden of the World"*
*Wallace, Bates, and Spruce Explore the Amazon*

1   "The five years of the voyage": Sir Gavin de Beer, "Charles Darwin,"
    in *Dictionary of Scientific Biography*, vol. III, p. 566.
2   "the country of the Amazon": W.H. Edwards, *A Voyage Up the River
    Amazon*, p. iv.
3   "any dinner party conversation": Yoon, "Reviving the Lost Art," p. D4.
4   Qtd. in H. Lewis McKinney, "Henry Walter Bates," in *Dictionary of
    Scientific Biography*, vol. I, p. 501.
5   "I have a rather": Wallace, *A Narrative of Travels*.

6   "Slender, woody lianas . . . my first arrival at Pará [Belém]": Bates, *The Naturalist on the River Amazons*, p. 11.

7   "Where are the dangers": Qtd. in John Hemming, *Tree of Rivers*, p. 138.

8   "Our imagination wandered": Wallace, *A Narrative of Travels*, pp. 93–94.

9   "I rose long before sunrise": Bates, *The Naturalist on the River Amazons*, p. 69.

10  "we passed a delightful time": Ibid., p. 94.

11  "Mr. Wallace chose the Río Negro": Ibid., p. 95.

12  "I had now a dull time": Wallace, *A Narrative of Travels*, p. 119.

13  The letter is in the Wallace Collection, Natural History Museum, London.

14  "rewarded by falling in with": Wallace, *A Narrative of Travels*, pp. 165–166.

15  "On entering this house": Ibid., p. 190.

16  "the green fields, the pleasant woods": Ibid., p. 211.

17  "In the whole Amazon": Ibid., p. 232.

18  "the fever immediately": Bates letter, 13 June 1851. Wallace Collection, Natural History Museum, London.

19  "With what pleasure": Wallace, *A Narrative of Travels*, pp. 277–278.

20  "is covered with": Bates, *The Naturalist on the River Amazons*, p. 138.

21  "I sat up for two or three hours": Ibid., p. 138.

22  "Refined society": Ibid., p. 140.

23  "alligators were rather troublesome": Ibid., p. 141.

24  "The want of intellectual society": Ibid., p. 141.

25  "the saddest hours": Ibid., p. 202.

26  "Among these masses": Ibid., p. 203.

27  "He definitely thought": H. Lewis McKinney, "Alfred Russel Wallace," in *Dictionary of Scientific Biography*, vol. XIV, p. 134.

28  "one of the most remarkable papers": Qtd. in H. Lewis McKinney, "Henry Walter Bates," in *Dictionary of Scientific Biography*, vol. I, p. 501.

29  "hard toasted bread": Spruce, *Notes of a Botanist on the Amazon & Andes*, vol. 1, p. 54.

30  "sadly maltreated": Ibid., p. 95.

31  "the most efficacious precaution": Ibid., pp. 116–117.

32  "fixed on the mouth": Ibid., p. 166.

33  "We were indeed heartily sick": Ibid., p. 191.

34  "you will find nothing common": Ibid., pp. 227–228.

35  "I am now alone": Ibid., p. 231.

36  "I was also master of my own movements": Ibid., p. 290.

37  "It may be true": Ibid., p. 276.

38  "sagacious dames have at divers times": Ibid., p. 301.

39  "what progress you are making": Ibid., p. 320.

40  "I thought the scene": Ibid., p. 404.

41  "This woman": Ibid., pp. 463–466.

42  "In returning from one of my long expeditions": Ibid., pp. 442–443.

43  "Many of these had passed through Barra": Ibid., vol. 2, p. 31.

44  "I am inclined to repent": Ibid., p. 32.

45  "When you consider the amphibious life": Ibid., p. 35.

46  "after an absence from England": Ibid., p. 314.

Chapter 10: *The Great Rubber Boom*
*An Amazonian Gilded Age*

1  "in an antagonistic": Debate on the Peruvian Amazon Rubber Company.

2  "I cannot admit.": Ibid.

3  "advantage of his position": Owens, "Queer Eye From the Irish Guy."

4  "In the not too distant future": Ibid.

Chapter 11: *Exploitation, Despoliation, or Conservation*
*The River Sea in the New Millennium*

1  "Indeed, marine phytoplankton": Goulding, *Smithsonian Atlas of the*

*Amazon*, p. 19.

2   "None of this ooey-gooey . . .": *The New York Times*, 3 May 2010.

3   "On the whole . . . Joe is naïve": *Der Spiegel Online*. 13 August 2009.

4   "The physicist Freeman Dyson. . . . from the atmosphere": Dawidoff, "The Civil Heretic."

5   "I have the sense": Qtd. in Ibid.

6   "The plaintiffs in the suit . . . and her dog": Romero and Krauss, "Chevron Offers Evidence" Krauss, "Revelation Undermines Chevron Case."

"A Lady's Voyage Down the Amazon," in *Stories of Enterprise and Adventure: A Selection of Authentic Narratives*. London, 1874.

Babcock, Glenn D. *History of the United States Rubber Company: A Case Study in Corporation Management*. Bloomington, IN, 1966.

Barthel, Manfred. *The Jesuits. History and Legend of the Society of Jesus*. Trans. Mark Howson, New York, 1984.

Bates, Henry Walter. *The Naturalist on the River Amazons*. London, 1863. Gutenberg E-text ed.

Burns, E. Bradford, ed. *A Documentary History of Brazil*. New York, 1966.

Campbell, Thomas J. *The Jesuits. 1534–1921*. London, 1921.

Coates, Austin. *The Commerce in Rubber: The First 250 Years*. Oxford–New York, 1987.

Columbus, Christopher. *The Four Voyages*. Ed. & trans. J. M. Cohen. London, 1969.

Davis, Wade. *The Lost Amazon. The Photographic Journey of Richard Evans Schultes*. San Francisco, 2004.

Dawidoff.

Deloate.

*Der Spiegel.*

Descola, Jean. *The Conquistadors*. Trans. Malcolm Barnes, New York, 1957.

Díaz, Bernal. Trans. J. M. Cohen, *The Conquest of New Spain*. London, 1963.

*Dictionary*

Edwards, William H. *A Voyage up the River Amazon, Including a Residence at Pará*. London, 1847.

Elliott, J. H. *Imperial Spain, 1469–1716*. London, 1963.

Fernández-Armesto, Felipe. *Amerigo: The Man Who Gave His Name to America*. New York, 2007.

French, Michael J. *The U. S. Tire Industry: A History*. Boston, 1991.

Furneaux, Robin. *The Amazon: The Story of a Great River*. New York, 1970.

Goulding, Michael, et al. *The Smithsonian Atlas of the Amazon*. Washington–London, 2003.

Grann, David. *The Lost City of Z: A Tale of Deadly Obsession in the Amazon*. New York, 2009.

Gutiérrez, Gustavo. *Las Casas: In Search of the Poor of Jesus Christ*. Trans. Robert B. Barr, Maryknoll, NY, 1993.

Hemming, John. *Tree of Rivers: The Story of the Amazon*. New York, 2008.

Humboldt, Alexander von. *Personal Narrative of a Journey to the Equinoctial Regions of a New Continent*. Abridged and trans. Jason Wilson. Intro. by Malcolm Nicolson. London–New York, 1995.

Kamen, Henry. *Philip of Spain*. New Haven–London, 1997.

Krauss.

Las Casas, Bartolomé de. *A Short Account of the Destruction of the Indies*. Ed. & trans. Nigel Griffin, London, 1992.

_____. *In Defense of the Indians*. Ed. Stafford Poole, DeKalb, IL, 1992.

Lockhart, James. *Spanish Peru: 1532–1560*. Madison, WI, 1994.

London, Mark, and Kelly, Brian. *The Last Forest: The Amazon in the Age of Globalization*. New York, 2007.

Markham, Clements R. *The Letters of Amerigo Vespucci and Other Documents Illustrative of His Career*. London, 1894.

_____, trans & ed. *Expeditions into the Valley of the Amazons, 1539, 1540, 1639*. repr. Boston, 2005.

McCaa, Robert. "Spanish and Nahuatl Views on Smallpox and Demographic Catastrophe in the Conquest of Mexico," in *Journal of Interdisciplinary History*, vol.25, no. 3 (Winter, 1995), pp. 397–432.

McIntyre, Loren. "Claiming Amazonia," in *Americas*, vol. 51, May 1999.

Medina, José Toribio, and Lee, Bertram T. *The Discovery of the Amazon: According to the Account of Friar Gaspar De Carvajal and Other Documents*. New York, 1934.

Minta, Stephen. *Aguirre: The Recreation of a Sixteenth-Century Journey Across South America*. New York, 1994.

Moorehead, Alan. *The White Nile*. New York, 1960.

_____. *The Blue Nile*. New York, 1962.

Morison, Samuel Eliot. *The European Discovery of America: The Southern Voyages. 1492–1616*. New York, 1974.

Owens.

Palin.

Prescott, William H. *History of the Conquest of Mexico; History of the Conquest of Peru*. Modern Library, 1-vol. ed. New York, n.d.

Reynolds, Steve. "Nicolas Baudin's Expedition to the Terres Australes," in *Journal of the Marine Life Society of South Australia* 12, December 2001.

Robinson, Alex, et al. *The Amazon*. Guilford, CT, 2000.

Romero.

Sibaja, Marco. "Suspect Quizzed Over Murder of Eco-activist Dorothy Stang," in *The Observer*, 28 December 2008.

Simon, Pedro. *The Expedition of Pedro de Ursua & Lope de Aguirre in Search of El Dorado and Omagua in 1560–1*. Trans. William Bollaert, Repr. Boston, 2005.

Smith, Anthony. *Explorers of the Amazon: Four Centuries of Adventure Along the World's Greatest River*. New York, 1990. Repr. Chicago, 1994.

Smith, Donald. "Explorers Pinpoint Source of the Amazon," National Geographic News. 21 December 2000.

Spruce, Richard. *Notes of a Botanist on the Amazon & Andes*. 2 vols. London, 1908.

_____. *Report on the Expedition to Procure Seeds and Plants of the Cinchona Succirubra or Red Bark Tree*. London, 1861.

St. Clair, David. *The Mighty, Mighty Amazon*. New York, 1968.

Stone, Roger D. *Dreams of Amazonia*. New York, 1985.

Thomas, Hugh. *Conquest. Montezuma, Cortés, and the Fall of Old Mexico*. New York–London, 1993.

Trevelyan, George Macaulay. *History of England*. London, 1926.

"Voyage of Madame Godin Along the River of the Amazons in the Year 1770," in *Perils and Captivity*. Edinburgh, 1827.

Wallace, Alfred Russel. *A Narrative of Travels on the Amazon and Rio Negro, with an Account of the Native Tribes*. 5th ed. London–New York–Melbourne, 1895.

_____. *My Life. A Record of Events and Opinions*. 2 vols. New York, 1905.

Weinstein, Barbara. *The Amazon Rubber Boom: 1850–1920*. Stanford, CA, 1983.

Whitaker, Robert. *The Mapmaker's Wife*. New York, 2004.

Wolf, Howard, and Wolf, Ralph. *Rubber: A Story of Glory and Greed*. New York, 1936.

Wood, Michael. *Conquistadors*. Berkeley–Los Angeles, 2000.

Yoon.